FANTASY AND REALITY
IN HISTORY

FANTASY AND REALITY IN HISTORY

Peter Loewenberg

New York   Oxford
OXFORD UNIVERSITY PRESS
1995

Oxford University Press

Oxford   New York
Athens   Auckland   Bangkok   Bombay
Calcutta   Cape Town   Dar es Salaam   Delhi
Florence   Hong Kong   Istanbul   Karachi
Kuala Lampur   Madras   Madrid   Melbourne
Mexico City   Nairobi   Paris   Singapore
Taipei   Tokyo   Toronto
and associated companies in
Berlin   Ibadan

Chapter 2, "The Pagan Freud," originally appeared in Robert S. Wistrich, ed.,
Austrians and the Jews in the Twentieth Century:
From Franz Joseph to Waldheim, and is reprinted here
by permission of Macmillan and St. Martin's Press.

Library of Congress Cataloging-in-Publication Data
Loewenberg, Peter, 1933–
Fantasy and reality in history / Peter Loewenberg.
p.   cm.
Includes bibliographical references and index.
ISBN 0-19-506763-0
1. Psychohistory.   2. Irrationalism (Philosophy)
I. Title.
D16.16.L65   1995   901'.9—dc20   94-43804

9 8 7 6 5 4 3 2 1
Printed in the United States of America
on acid-free paper

for Josefine and Jonathan

ACKNOWLEDGMENTS

I appreciate my good colleagues in history and in psychoanalysis, and those in both, who read and responded to earlier versions of this work: Peter Baldwin, Werner and Marianne Bohleber, Robert Dallek, Samuel Eisenstein, David James Fisher, Saul Friedlander, Alfred Goldberg, Joshua Hoffs, Mardi Horowitz, Judith M. Hughes, Albert Hutter, John Kafka, Michael Kater, J. Reid Meloy, David Myers, Robert Nemiroff, Robert Pois, Robert Pynoos, Dagmar Richter, Stanford Shaw, Jerald Simon, Jonathan Steinberg, Albion Urdank, and Ernest Wolf. Discussions with my colleagues in the history of science, Norton Wise and Robert Westman, introduced me to Ludwik Fleck. Consultations and deciphering of holographic texts by Rena Freedman, Frederick Redlich, Arnold and Ora Band were indispensable. I have learned much from the stimulation and friendship of Nancy Chodorow, Peter Gay, David Horowitz, Mauricio Mazón, Robert Ross, Nellie Thompson, and my UCLA graduate research seminars on creative cultural and scientific groups and on modern nationalism.

The study of V. V. Zhirinovsky would not have been possible without the generosity and indispensable aid of Jack Sontag, head of the Russian Desk, U.S. Department of State. I am indebted to the Hon. Nüzet Kandemir, Turkish ambassador to the United States, and Sermet Atacanli, counselor to the Turkish Embassy, for Turkish government materials. I am grateful for productive discussions of Zhirinovsky with the members of the Second Annual University of California Interdisciplinary Psychoanalytic Consortium at Lake Arrowhead on 23 April 1994.

Mark Patterson and Thomas Roberts of Sigmund Freud Copyrights, Wivenhoe, Colchester, England, were helpful; James H. Hutson and Alan Teichroew of the staff of the Manuscript Division, Madison Wing, Library of Congress, Washington, D.C., facilitated my research in the Sigmund Freud Collection. Barton Bernstein provided humor and moral support in the clinches and discoveries. I would not have gained access to the C. G. Jung Collection, Archive of the Swiss Federal Institute of Technology, Zurich (ETHZ), without the aid and good offices of the archivist, Beat Glaus. Daniel Hell, director, and Thilo Hahn, Ambros Uchtenhagen, and Frau Irmay gave me indispensable aid when it mattered in the archives of the Burghölzli Hospital. Huldrych Koelbing and Heidi Seger of the Institute of the History of Medicine, University of Zurich, were helpful with their excellent resources. To B. Stadler, the archivists, and staff of the Staatsarchiv of Kanton Zürich, I am grateful for many courtesies which facilitated my research in the records of the Cantonal Sanitätsdirektion. Hans W. Walser, the late Fritz Meerwein, and Emanuel Hurwitz were gracious and offered essential orientation to a visitor from America who relied on it. Siegfried Nasko, director of the Karl Renner Museum, Gloggnitz, and Oberarchivskommissar Lorenz Mikoletzky of the Austrian Staatsarchiv, Vienna, made my research on Karl Renner pleasant and exciting. The reference librarians and interlibrary loan service of the UCLA Research Library performed with promptness and exactitude.

It is a pleasure to acknowledge three grants from the Foundation Pro Helvetia, Zurich, and the good offices of Hanne Zweifel-Wüthrich, in facilitating my research in Zurich. The kindness and tact that made me feel at home and furthered this study were provided by Kurt and Kati Spillmann in Zurich and Cortona; Ferdinand and Joanna Meyer in Zollikon, Flims, and Celerina; Thomas and Dalia Smolka in Vienna, London, New York, and Boca Raton. I thank my editor, Nancy Lane, for her persistence, reality, and vision.

My research assistants, David Lee and Sonja Fritsche, worked with initiative and fortitude. My children, Sam, Anna Sophie, and Jonathan, are my compass, and my dear wife, Josefine, is my gyroscope.

CONTENTS

FANTASY AND REALITY
IN HISTORY

INTRODUCTION:
ON PSYCHOHISTORICAL METHOD

Psychohistory is often defined as an "auxiliary science" like numismatics or statistics, which may, with profit, be "applied" to history. I propose something more radical and ambitious—a dual discipline and a dual career—that is not subordinate but integral at the point of contact between the subject (the researcher or clinician) and his or her data (documents and texts or analysands). Both disciplines, in the form of the new dual discipline, are in force and in action at the initial perception of the data, the "fact," or configuration. Each discipline has what Ludwik Fleck terms a "thought style." The thought styles and assumptions of history and psychoanalysis are quite compatible: both disciplines are historical, narrative, and hermeneutic sciences of meanings. As Fleck pointed out:

> Truth is not "relative" and certainly not "subjective" in the popular sense of the word. It is always, or almost always determined within a thought style. One can never say that the same thought is true for A and false for B. If A and B belong to the same thought collective, the thought will be either true or false for both. But if they belong to different thought collectives, it will just *not* be *the same* thought![1]

Readers, students, and colleagues often ask, "How do I *do* psychohistory? What are the tools and guideposts to method? What should I look for in a text or a cultural artifact to enrich my understanding of psychological meanings?" The psychohistorical method is an amalgam of psychoanalytical clinical technique with humanistic historical analysis. Both disciplines engage with the task of discerning the latent meanings behind a manifest communication or behavior. In the final analysis, the value of an inference is whether it is productive of new data and insights or initiates a reconstellation of the existing data in a new pattern or configuration that enhances our understanding. What follows are some concrete examples of sensing and formulating latent unconscious meanings illustrated from my researches in modern European history.

My conclusions are the product of more than three decades of integrating clinical psychodynamics with history. I refer to an integration, or better said, a blending, or merging, rather than an "interface" because I mean a true intermeshing of the fields of history and psychoanalysis, not only at the conceptual level but at the historian's initial contact with data and the psychoanalyst's clinical encounter with the analysand. Every historical datum has multiple emotional meanings and every psychological feeling state has a historic-political-social setting and context.

This book is a study of irrationality in history. Part I proposes psychohistorical theoretical and clinical perspectives on social structure and culture, including Freud's critical stance toward the morality of Judeo-Christian culture, the creative position of ethnosocial marginality, and the psychosocial specifics of group cultural creativity. Part II offers case studies from the pornographic sexual politics of the nineteenth-century British Liberal prime minister William E. Gladstone; to interpretations of the self-sacrifice of the German-Jewish foreign minister Walther Rathenau; to the opportunism of Austrian President Karl Renner; to the primitive splitting of the contemporary Russian fascist Vladimir Zhirinovsky. Part III interprets manifestations of anxiety in history, and its expressions in racism, anti-Judaism, nationalism, and some neglected reciprocal relationships between clinical and political techniques of crisis management.

Historians and social scientists are given to the pieties of "objectivity," as though they do not "know" in some corner of consciousness that much in their personal life is irrational, that we are all what in earlier times was called "passion driven." As Spinoza put it, "Men may differ in nature from one another insofar as they are agitated by . . . passions, and insofar as one and the same man is agitated by passions is he changeable and inconstant."[2] If we are honest, we are aware that every choice of topic, emplotment, strategy of emphasis and presentation that we make, as well as those irritants and discomfitures that are expunged, cut, not faced and not dealt with, is contingent on half-understood intimate considerations.

This is far from a reduction of creativity to "nothing-but" psychodynamics. Life as lived and the individual's struggles with figures and conflicts of the past and in the present are changed, adapted, and aesthetically molded to the exigencies of plot, narrative, and drama, as well as to the politico-socio-cultural "realities" and current internal and external political correctness as the creative work is shaped and marketed.

Those who are privileged to be clinicians know daily the intimate relationship between a personality and its sublimations. What makes psychoanalytic work with creative people—writers, journalists, film professionals, and yes, academics—so rewarding is to observe the interaction of the subtle fabric of fantasies, reality, and creativity.

I have changed my views of this integration in the past twenty-five years because of both clinical and historical work. I have added to my uses of the classic psychoanalytic model primarily in the areas of ego psychology—the adaptation of persons to crises and the function of anxiety at critical historical junctures; object relations—the internalization and splitting of significant developmental figures and symbols; a sensibility to issues of injured self-esteem and narcissism; and the empathic involvement of the self as a tool of perception, which was clinically termed the countertransference and now goes under the rubric intersubjectivity.

Psychoanalytic ego psychology has a natural and integral "fit" with history because, unlike drive psychology, ego psychology is time specific, it is contextual and historical. This becomes clear when we look at Freud's analysis of the actions of Rebecca West in Henrik Ibsen's *Rosmersholm*:

> How could it come about that the adventuress with the "fearless, free will", who forged her way ruthlessly to her desired goal, should *now* refuse to pluck the fruit of success when it is offered to her? She herself gives us the explanation in the fourth Act: "*This* is the terrible part of it: that *now*, when all life's happiness is within my grasp — my heart is changed and my own past cuts me off from it."[3]

Freud is here working with historical time-specific behavior. This is clinically superior to his earlier static-instinct psychology because everyone has a multiplicity of drives and instincts at all times. To interpret to a patient that a given piece of conduct is an expression of an instinctual aggressive or libidinal drive may give him or her small comfort but offers no real enlightenment or prospect of control. To illustrate with a clinical vignette:

> *A man is puzzled about why he took an impulsive trip to South America for a liaison with a lover. The tryst was ungratifying and disappointing.*
>
> A libidinal instinct interpretation would presumably have explained to him his sexual urges, but a time-specific exploration of his current reality and ego functions disclosed that the patient's current lady friend had just departed for a three-month stay in a foreign country. This placed his impulsive conduct in the configuration of a narcissistic defense that, although it was rooted in earlier life experiences, was now specific to this particular time and situation of loss, and could be interpreted as stemming from feelings of abandonment and the need to fill the inner void left by what was perceived as the desertion by his previous lover.

Such a coping mechanism for dealing with object loss is a social as well as an individual psychodynamic category of understanding predicated on the socioeconomic class, moral conventions, and cultural patterns of the time, person, and culture. Each level complements and elucidates the other. The social bears upon and conditions the person, and the individual cannot be historically or psychologically "known" without learning his or her sociocultural setting in as much nuanced richness as possible. This imperative is, or should be, a matter of course in clinical work. The more we know of our patient's environs, ethnic patterns, family, work, social subgroups, and religious and cultural life and meanings, the more we may effectively help. Yet it is not taken for granted in applied psychoanalytical "research" that an equally intense engagement with the historical and cultural frame of behavior is necessary for the explanation to bear conviction. The clumsily named "mechanisms of defense," a term more appropriate to engineering than to human feelings, are a social as well as an individual psychodynamic category of understanding. The individual carries within himself or herself the internalized mores, norms, and ideals of the culture. There is a mutual interaction between social structure and the individual psyche, with both of the variables being independent and dynamic. Neither side is inert or static. Neither the intrapsychic nor the social alone are sufficient to psychosocially explain Gladstone, Freud, Rathenau, Renner, Zhirinovsky, or us.

NOTES

1. Ludwik Fleck, *Genesis and Development of a Scientific Fact* (Chicago: University of Chicago Press, 1979), p. 100.

2. Cited in Albert O. Hirschmann, *The Passions and the Interests: Political Arguments for Capitalism before Its Triumph* (Princeton: Princeton University Press, 1977), p. 52.

3. Sigmund Freud, "Some Character-Types met with in Psycho-Analytic Work" (1916), in *Standard Edition of the Complete Psychological Works of Sigmund Freud,* translated under the general editorship of James Strachey in collaboration with Anna Freud, assisted by Alix Strachey (italics mine) and Alan Tyson, 24 vols. (London: Hogarth Press, 1953–1975), 14:325.

I

PSYCHOANALYSIS, SOCIAL STRUCTURE, AND CULTURE

1

WHY SOCIAL SCIENCE NEEDS PSYCHOANALYSIS: FROM WEBER TO FREUD

Truth is unobtainable; humanity does not deserve it.
                                            Sigmund Freud, 1936

One can foresee a revolution or a war, but it is impossible to foresee the consequences of an autumn shooting-trip for wild ducks.
                                            Leon Trotsky, 1929

If two people are repeatedly alone together, some sort of emotional bond will develop between them.
                                            Phyllis Greenacre, 1954

No choice of subject, in conversation, in psychotherapy, and certainly in the discourse of the political and social sciences, is random or accidental. Each researcher and reader is attracted by specific themes, conflicts, and achievements of their subject. Every social scientist has an implicit theory of psychology and motivation; some theories are limited to common sense and proximate causes of specific decisions, others to rational interest models of politics. The best researchers struggle for the deepest possible understanding of the inner life of their subjects interwoven with the context of the development of historical and cultural processes. The issue is whether the psychological model is conscious and explicit or unconscious and unexamined, whether it is adequate to its task, whether it is complex and rich enough to give a satisfying explanation of life.

There are notable similarities in the purposes of the psychotherapist and the social scientist. Clinicians have a therapeutic objective, they work to assuage pain, and to achieve character change and adaptation at times of critical life crises and decision making. To these ends they seek a holistic understanding of the patient's experience as a human being, and by explanation and interpretation attempt to increase insight, open new options for conduct and life choices.

Social scientists also may be interested in facilitating change in institutions or social relationships, and historians wish to alter views of the past or they would not be writing. Like clinicians, they pursue all aspects of their subject's functioning in quest of a depth understanding of thought and behavior, of critical shaping pressures, conflicts, and junctures of decision making, to build as coherent as possible a picture of life in a social historical forum of action. Both psychoanalysts and historians utilize narrative explanations. Their answers to the questions Why did things turn out as they are? and How did the current situation come to be as it is? are to provide a rich, complex web of longitudinal temporal narrative explanation—a historical explanation.[1]

Max Weber argued in his classic paper "Science as a Vocation" that all values are subjective. No natural scientist can tell us the "meaning" of life, no physician can define a worthy life for others, the jurist should not prescribe laws, the cultural historian cannot establish which cultural phenomena are "worthwhile," and the social and political scientist should not presume to impart values as "science" because "the ultimately possible attitudes toward life are irreconcilable, and hence their struggle can never be brought to a final conclusion."[2] This means that the vast realm of interrelated commitments, values, meanings, and motives, which are *always* present and active at various levels of consciousness, is left to the inner world of the researcher and to those humanistic disciplines that deal with the subjective life, such as theology, moral philosophy, and psychoanalysis. I argue that psychoanalysis has, albeit imperfectly, best charted the inner terrain of conflict and motive, integrity of identity, and self-definition in the external vocational, social, interpersonal arena, and in the inner sexual relational world.

The significance social scientists see in their material, the criteria they apply, the feeling of conviction they impart, the intellectual models they build and find congenial are functions of their personal psychodynamics. We can research and write rigorously and truthfully about the past only if we keep ourselves aware that we are always in a intersubjective transaction between researcher and data.

When we deal with political figures, the problem is the meaning of power to the subject and the motivation toward high office that, despite the trophies and perquisites, is not obvious. Most people derive their pleasures and gratifications from intimate relationships with family, lovers, children, and friends. But for some people, the politicians, those who seek public office, positions on stage in the limelight, the essential need is for external confirmation and the rewards of exercising power.

Psychoanalysts have long recognized that the first political institution to which we are socialized is the family. In the relations between parents and children power is unequal, asymmetrical, but always present and exercised, sometimes brutally, other times subtly. Force, coercion, intimidation, negotiation, and manipulation in all their varied forms, how to get the essential supplies of attention, resources, love, and nurture, are learned in the home, and the metaphors of politics—who has power and who obeys—are instrumentalized in the family.

In the realm of erotism, the late Robert Stoller conceptualized sexual excitement as

> an attempt, repeated over and over, to undo childhood traumas and frustrations that threatened the development of one's masculinity or femininity. . . . [T]he exact details of the script underlying the excitement are meant to reproduce and repair the precise traumas and frustrations—debasements—of childhood; and so we can expect to find hidden in the script the history of a person's life.[3]

If this is so for erotic life, how much more is it so for political life? The avid quest for power and its accoutrements is compensatory for the traumas caused to the child by a familial political situation that relentlessly drove home his or her lack of power, impotence, and vulnerability due to smallness and weakness.

II

The social scientists' most reliable initial clue to the understanding of their research is their experience of relationship to the subject. Our research *does* things to us. It may elate and thrill us, frustrate us and drive us to anger, enrage and fill us with hatred, and even, as we shall see, stymie and block our understanding and creativity. As Weber said, passion and enthusiasm are the sine qua non of scholarship:

> Whoever lacks the capacity to . . . come up to the idea that the fate of his soul depends on whether he makes the correct conjuncture at this passage of this manuscript may as well stay away from science. Without this strange intoxication, . . . without this passion, . . . you have *no* calling for science and you should do something else. For nothing is worthy of man as man unless he can pursue it with passionate devotion.[4]

The clinical term for this is *countertransference*. Research requires an immersion, always a personal dialogue with the subject, sometimes a public ventilation of these feelings, as Erikson delivered to Gandhi and as Yerushalmi recently carried on with Freud.[5]

In Sigmund Freud's corpus there are but five references to the subject of countertransference, and these are in the sense of a problem that interferes with the analysis and, if not resolved, constitutes an indication for the analyst himself or herself to resume personal psychoanalysis. In 1910 Freud wrote: "We have become aware of the 'counter-transference' which arises in [the analyst] as a result of the patient's influence on his unconscious feelings, and we are almost inclined to insist that he shall recognize this counter-transference in himself and overcome it."[6] Freud regarded the analyst as needing "a useful warning against any tendency to a counter-transference which may be present in his own mind."[7] This is no longer the current clinical view.

Today's clinicians of virtually every school of psychodynamic psychotherapy utilize their countertransference—the researcher's own subjective response to the material—as an important datum meriting close scrutiny and interpretation as a delicate and important instrument of listening to the patient's communications. The acceptance and utilization of countertransference as a tool of insight in clinical practice and research is the most important post-Freudian development in the theory of technique in the past half century. Whereas countertransference was formerly viewed as an intrusion in the analysis to be guarded against and overcome, it is now welcomed, listened to, analyzed, and utilized in treatment and research. Today the countertransference is an appropriate and essential part of any case report.

Frieda Fromm-Reichmann was among the first to champion the use of countertransference as a guide to therapy:

> The psychiatrist who is trained in the observation and inner realization of his reaction to patient's manifestations can frequently utilize these reactions as a helpful instrument in understanding otherwise hidden implications in patient's communications. Thus the therapists' share in the reciprocal transference reactions of doctor and patient in the wider sense of the term may furnish an important guide in conducting the psychotherapeutic process.[8]

More recently, psychoanalyst Leo Stone drew attention to the growing appreciation of the counter-transference as an affirmative instrument facilitating perception, whereby a sensitive awareness of one's incipient reactions to the patient . . . leads to a richer and more subtle understanding of the patient's transference striving." Stone holds that "a view of the relationship which gives great weight to the counter-transference is productively important."[9] The contemporary psychoanalyst Harold Searles, in contrast to Freud, has three columns of references to countertransference in the index to his *Collected Papers*, as well as another book of papers on the subject. Searles defines *countertransference* as "all feeling-states in the therapist." He uses those feeling-states in himself as a cardinal principle of cognition in his clinical work and research.[10]

Older models of social science would purge or work around subjective sensations and build rigid barriers to the admission of feeling in the name of an ephemeral "objectivity"; today's social scientists must realize that their feelings, sensations, and responses both to the data and to its manner of presentation are themselves a preciously significant datum of cognition. As Weber caustically commented, "'To let the facts speak for themselves' is the most unfair way of putting over a political position to the student."[11] The psychoanalytic anthropologist George Devereux stressed that

> the scientific study of man . . . must use the subjectivity inherent in all observation as the royal road to an authentic, rather than fictitious, objectivity. . . . When treated as basic and characteristic data of behavioral

science [this subjectivity is] more valid and more productive than any other type of datum."[12]

III

Social scientists tend to overlook that Max Weber's great thesis, *The Protestant Ethic and the Spirit of Capitalism* (1904–1905), was in essence propelled by the psychological dynamic of anxiety and guilt. Weber saw and delineated among Calvinists an "ideal type," a characteristic pattern of social and economic behavior of restless activity, continuous work, and an acquisitive manner of life combined with a personally ascetic tendency. As Weber noted of the Puritan: "He gets nothing out of his wealth for himself, except the irrational sense of having done his job well."[13] This restless economic activity is driven by theological anxiety— by the anxious search for signs of election. Weber draws attention to

> the tremendous internal pressure under which the sect member in his conduct was constantly held. . . . His whole social existence in the here and now depended upon his "proving" himself. . . . The capitalist success of a sect brother, if legally attained, was proof of his worth and of his state of grace.[14]

Weber delineated the phenomenology of guilt and anxiety to make entrepreneurial capitalism fused with inner worldly asceticism one driving force of Western history. But he did not understand their etiology, dynamics, and functioning in the inner world of people. For that, social scientists must turn to the work of Sigmund Freud.

In the same *fin de siècle* years of Weber's great work, Freud was developing psychoanalysis, which presumed to study and explain many things that are relevant to the social sciences; among others, the making of character, the meaning of anxiety, the dynamics of adaptation, and responses to stress.

IV

Heinz Kohut gave us the valuable concept of narcissistic rage and a differential diagnosis to distinguish this from other forms of rage. The specific distinction of narcissistic rage is "the need for revenge, for righting a wrong, for undoing a hurt by whatever means, and a deeply anchored, unrelenting compulsion in the pursuit of these aims, which gives no rest to those who have suffered a narcissistic injury."[15] I believe this Kohutian formulation has an application to politics and society that is as relevant as its individual clinical use.

In narcissistic ways the overpowering legacy and idealization of the *Imperium Romanum* was a political curse for modern Italy. The symbols of past grandeur and rule over the whole known civilized world was a crushing pressure on a small, underdeveloped land poor in resources, though rich in culture and aesthetics. The slogan of *mare nostrum* was inappropriate and a political disaster for twentieth-century Italy.

Less than fifty years after the defeat of France in 1870 and the triumphant creation of the Second Reich as the dominant military power in Europe, Germany experienced what was perceived as the shameful humiliation of defeat, dismemberment, guilt, and ostracism from the community of nations, and the imposition of reparations payments for what was then the bloodiest war in history. The emotional program of National Socialism was narcissistic revenge on the Allies, who had humbled Germany and imposed the "War Guilt" clause, Article 231 of the Versailles Treaty of 1919. The perceived injustice of the internationalization of Danzig, the Polish corridor, the loss of the Saarland, and the payment of reparations were to be righted by remilitarization, threats, power, and, if necessary, coercion.

D. W. Winnicott defined the transitional object as the symbol of the mother's presence and security for the infant and small child and the space between mother and child as the arena of first symbolization and creativity.[16] The symbolic codes of politics constitute transitional objects that give security against anxiety in a world of chaos where the multiple traumas of immigration, crowding, urban crime, ecological disasters, nationalist fanaticism and brutal civil wars, economic recession, and inflation mean uncertainty, instability, moral ambiguity, and lack of continuity with a fantasied secure past.

Politics creates and lives by symbols. This is equally true of times of stability and of crisis politics. Many elections, including the recent U.S. presidential contests, were determined by whom the majority of voters felt safest with. The slogan of Chancellor Helmut Kohl and the CDU in a German federal electoral campaign was "Wir schützen Deutschlands Zukunft!" (We protect Germany's future!).[17] The affect was of security sought and safety promised.

All adults were once small and powerless. The quest for security is lifelong. It is often displaced to money and property which, of course, is inevitably in vain. In the end the ultimate insecurity, the final defeat will claim us all.

NOTES

1. Donald P. Spence, *Narrative Truth and Historical Truth: Meaning and Interpretation in Psychoanalysis* (New York: Norton, 1982); and *The Freudian Metaphor: Toward Paradigm Change in Psychoanalysis* (New York: Norton, 1987).

2. Max Weber, "*Wissenschaft als Beruf,*" "Science as a Vocation" (1919), in *From Max Weber: Essays in Sociology,* ed. and trans. H. H. Gerth and C. Wright Mills (New York: Oxford University Press, 1958), pp. 129–56; quotation, p. 152.

3. Robert J. Stoller, *Sexual Excitement: Dynamics of Erotic Life* (New York: Pantheon Books, 1979), pp. 6, 13.

4. Weber, "Science as a Vocation," p. 135.

5. Erik H. Erikson, "A Personal Word," in *Gandhi's Truth: On the Origins of Militant Nonviolence* (New York: Norton, 1969), pp. 229–54; Yosef H. Yerushalmi, "Monologue with Freud," in *Freud's Moses: Judaism Terminable and Interminable* (New Haven: Yale University Press, 1991), pp. 81–100.

6. Freud, "The Future Prospects of Psycho-Analytic Therapy" (1910), in *Standard Edition of the Complete Psychological Works of Sigmund Freud*, translated under the general directorship of James Strachey in collaboration with Anna Freud, assisted by Alix Strachey and Alan Tyson, 24 vols. (London: Hogarth Press, 1953–74), 11:144–45 (hereafter cited as *S.E.*)

7. Freud, "Observations on Transference-Love (Further Recommendations on the Technique of Psycho-Analysis III)" (1915), *S.E.*, 12:160.

8. Frieda Fromm-Reichmann, *Principles of Intensive Psychotherapy* (Chicago: University of Chicago Press, 1950), pp. 5–6.

9. Leo Stone, *The Psychoanalytic Situation* (New York: International Universities Press, 1961), pp. 79, 81.

10. Harold F. Searles, *Counter-transference and Related Subjects* (New York: International Universities Press, 1979); *Collected Papers on Schizophrenia and Related Subjects* (New York: International Universities Press, 1965), definition, p. 771 n.

11. Weber, "Science as a Vocation," p. 146.

12. George Devereux, *From Anxiety to Method in the Behavioral Sciences* (The Hague: Mouton, 1967), p. xvii. See also Paul Diesing, *Patterns of Discovery in the Social Sciences* (Chicago: Aldine, 1971); and Michael Polanyi, *Personal Knowledge: Towards a Post-Critical Philosophy* (Chicago: University of Chicago Press, 1958).

13. Max Weber, *The Protestant Ethic and the Spirit of Capitalism*, trans. Talcott Parsons (New York: Scribner's, 1958), p. 71.

14. Weber, "The Protestant Sects and the Spirit of Capitalism," in Gerth and Mills, *From Max Weber*, pp. 320–22 passim.

15. Heinz Kohut, "Thoughts on Narcissism and Narcissistic Rage," in *The Search for the Self: Selected Writings, 1950–1978*, ed. Paul H. Ornstein, 4 vols. (New York: International Universities Press, 1978), 2:637–38.

16. D. W. Winnicott, "Transitional Objects and Transitional Phenomena," "Playing: A Theoretical Statement," "Playing: Creative Activity and the Search for the Self," "Creativity and Its Origins," and "The Location of Cultural Experience," in *Playing and Reality* (London: Tavistock, 1971).

17. *Los Angeles Times*, 14 September 1993.

2

THE PAGAN FREUD

Just see how mortal men always put the blame on us gods! We are the source of evil, so they say—when they have only their own madness to thank if their miseries are worse than they ought to be.

Homer, Odyessy

—He had a sudden death, poor fellow, he said.
—The best death, Mr. Bloom said. Their wide open eyes looked at him.
—No suffering, he said. A moment and all is over. Like dying in sleep. No one spoke.

James Joyce, Ulysses

Freud had a Jewish identity and was a cultural Hellene. Of course, both sides of the statement are true. Although there is a voluminous secondary literature on Freud's Jewish identity, there is little on his paganism.[1] It is the Hellenic-Roman aspect of Freud's person and legacy that this chapter explores. I wish to engage the culturally non-Hebraic, and indeed theologically specifically anti-Mosaic, portion of Freud's interest, commitment, and aesthetic emotional investment. Freud worshiped the culture of antiquity and shared its anti–Judeo-Christian values.

Freud was a pagan in the etymological sense that the term *paganus* was applied by the early Christian Church to those who followed Greek, Roman, and other faiths and refused to accept the only true God. As the eleventh edition of the *Encyclopaedia Britannica* (1911) put it:

> A special significance attaches to the word when applied to one who adopts that attitude of cultured indifference to, or negation of, the various theistic systems of religion which was taken by so many of the educated and aristocratic classes in the ancient Hellenic and Roman world.[2]

Freud was a Hellenic pagan in four main dimensions of his personality: (1) most importantly in his oedipal triumph over his poor Jewish merchant father; (2) in his admiration and identification with the aesthetics of what he viewed as a superior culture, and the geography of

Mediterranean antiquity; (3) in his enlightened plea for a tolerant non-judgmental sexual morality; and (4) in his personal philosophy of stoicism and in the manner in which he faced his death.

Not one of the artifacts in the sumptuous 1989 publication of Freud's personal collection of antiquities was Judaic.[3] Peter Gay in the introduction to the volume writes of Freud: "His antiquities, many of them from countries he had never visited and many of them originating in the region from which his remote ancestors had come, spoke to him of his Jewishness."[4] I would argue precisely the converse: that the substantial collection of classical antiquities Freud assembled was, at the least, non-Judaic, explicitly antibiblical, tributes to paganism. The observance of the Mosaic interdiction against graven images insured that with the exception of ritual Torah decorations, candelabra, and kiddush cups, religious artifacts that approximated human or animal figures did not exist in post-Mosaic Judaism. Where Jewish artifacts or figures, such as lions, did appear, it was not for cultic purposes. The figures Freud collected were pagan cultic and totemic figures. As Ellen Handler Spitz correctly points out: "In emphasizing that Freud elected for himself an intellectual heritage different from that of his ancestors, it seems hardly necessary to point out that none of his cherished ancient objects is in any sense Jewish and that Jewish rituals and observance were anathema to him."[5]

I suggest that the antiquities, Hellenic, Roman, and Egyptian, that Freud collected were manifest symbols of his tribute to paganism. He, of course, did not worship them, but tribute he did bring. He undertook pilgrimages to the sites of ancient glory in Athens and Rome. He wrote to Stefan Zweig in 1931: "Despite my much vaunted frugality I have sacrificed a great deal for my collection of Greek, Roman and Egyptian antiquities, have actually read more archaeology than psychology, and . . . before the war and once after its end I felt compelled to spend every year at least several days or weeks in Rome."[6]

Occasionally Freud brought further sacrifice by unconsciously destroying a beloved cult figure from his collection in order to expiate a hostile act or a fantasied aggression, or to elicit a desired gift. Freud prided himself not only on his collection of antiquities but also on his facility in not breaking them. Although he denied any special dexterity, he was proud of his skill in moving among his clutter of objects. He had no doubt that each of the rare breakages fulfilled an unconscious purpose. Each case of an "accident" with his antiquities was cherished and fondled as a relic from an archeological excavation. It was a symptomatic act to be treasured, interpreted, and worked through. He tells us in *The Psychopathology of Everyday Life* (1901):

> It is very rare for me to break anything. I am not particularly dexterous but a result of the anatomical integrity of my nerve-muscle apparatus is that there are clearly no grounds for my making clumsy movements of this kind, with their unwelcome consequences. I cannot therefore recall any object in my house that I have ever broken. Shortage of space in my study

has often forced me to handle a number of pottery and stone antiquities (of which I have a small collection) in the most uncomfortable positions, so that onlookers have expressed anxiety that I should knock something down and break it. That however has never happened. Why then did I once dash the marble cover of my plain inkpot to the ground so that it broke?

My inkstand is made out of a flat piece of Untersberg marble which is hollowed out to receive the glass inkpot; and the inkpot has a cover with a knob made of the same stone. Behind this inkstand there is a ring of bronze statuettes and terra cotta figures. I sat down at the desk to write, and then moved the hand that was holding the pen-holder forward in a re-markably clumsy way, sweeping on to the floor the inkpot cover which was lying on the desk at the time.

The explanation was not hard to find. Some hours before, my sister had been in the room to inspect some new acquisitions. She admired them very much, and then remarked: "Your writing table looks really attractive now; only the inkstand doesn't match. You must get a nicer one." I went out with my sister and did not return for some hours. But when I did I carried out, so it seems, the execution of the condemned inkstand. Did I perhaps conclude from my sister's remark that she intended to make me a present of a nicer inkstand on the next festive occasion, and did I smash the unlovely one so as to force her to carry out the intention she had hinted at? If that is so, my sweeping movement was only apparently clumsy; in re-ality it was exceedingly adroit and well-directed, and understood how to avoid damaging any of the more precious objects that stood around.[7]

This breaking was unconsciously instrumental, even manipulative, in its purpose.

The example Freud gives of breaking "a beautiful little marble Venus" as a propitiation to appease the gods and render them favorable belongs to the category of magical thinking:

One morning, for example, when I was passing through a room in my dressing gown with straw slippers on my feet, I yielded to a sudden im-pulse and hurled one of my slippers from my foot at the wall, causing a beautiful little marble Venus to fall down from its bracket. As it broke into pieces, I quoted quite unmoved these lines from Busch:

> 'Ach! die Venus ist perdu"—
> Klickeradoms!—von Medici!'
> [Oh! the Venus! Lost is she!—
> Klickeradoms!—of Medici!]

This wild conduct and my calm acceptance of the damage are to be ex-plained in terms of the situation at the time. One of my family was gravely ill, and secretly I had already given up hope of her recovery. That morning I had learned that there had been a great improvement, and I know I had said to myself: "So she's going to live after all." My attack of destructive fury served therefore to express a feeling of gratitude to fate and allowed me to perform a *"sacrifical act"*—rather as if I had made a vow to sacrifice something or other as a thank-offering if she recovered her health! The choice of the Venus of Medici for this sacrifice was clearly only a gallant act of homage towards the convalescent; but even now it is a mystery to me how I made up my mind so quickly, aimed so accurately and avoided hitting anything else among the objects so close to it.[8]

The final example Freud gives us is one of expiation for aggression:

> I had once seen fit to reproach a loyal and deserving friend on no other grounds than the interpretation I placed on certain indications coming from his unconscious. He was offended and wrote me a letter asking me not to treat my friends psycho-analytically. I had to admit he was in the right, and wrote him a reply to pacify him. While I was writing this letter I had in front of me my latest acquisition, a handsome glazed Egyptian figure. I broke it in the way I have described, and then immediately realized that I had caused this mischief in order to avert a greater one. Luckily it was possible to cement both of them together—the friendship as well as the figure—so that the break would not be noticed.[9]

Freud describes this as "a propitiatory sacrifice to avert evil." He broke his beloved Egyptian idol because of his hostility and tactlessness in offering an unsolicited interpretation to a friend.[10] The sacrifice of his newest antiquity was in expiation for inappropriate and unfair aggression.

II

Freud's symbolic codes for the conceptualization of unconscious structures and conflicts were derived from Greek mythology: Narcissus, Oedipus, Laius, Jocasta, Kronos, Zeus, Juno, Alecto, Iphigenia, the Three Fates, Medusa, Aeneas, and Ulysses. All his life he was indebted to his classical gymnasium education for opening to him the world of antiquity.

In Freud's essay for the Festschrift of the gymnasium he attended between the ages of nine and seventeen (1865–1873), he pays homage to the schoolmasters who imparted to him the humanistic spirit, the classical languages, and Greek and Roman history, which were "my first glimpses of an extinct civilization which in my case was to bring me as much consolation as anything else in the struggles of life."[11] Clearly Freud is here referring to the Greco-Roman world of pagan antiquity, not to his father's extinct civilization of the Old Testament. As if to reaffirm the rejection of his father and his Hebraic world in the new adherence to Hellenic antiquity, Freud goes on in the same essay to explicate the oedipal dynamics of a son who rejects, criticizes, and excels over his father:

> In the second half of childhood a change sets in the boy's relation to his father—a change whose importance cannot be exaggerated. From his nursery the boy begins to cast his eyes upon the world outside. And he cannot fail now to make discoveries which undermine his original high opinion of his father and which expedite his detachment from his first ideal. He finds that his father is no longer the mightiest, wisest and richest of beings; he grows dissatisfied with him, he learns to criticize him and to estimate his place in society; and then, as a rule, he makes him pay heavily for the disappointment that has been caused by him.[12]

This motif came to its fullest expression more than two decades later, toward the end of his life, when Freud returned to the twin themes of the glory of ancient Attica, as he had learned it in the humanistic gymnasium, and how this represents a triumph over his impoverished wool-merchant father who did not have the benefit of a classical education. This further piece of oedipal self-analysis, written in Freud's eighty-first year, is in the form of a letter of congratulations to Romain Rolland on his seventieth birthday. The analytic task is to understand a depression he and his brother felt in 1904 in Trieste upon learning that a long-cherished dream of at last visiting Athens and viewing the Acropolis would be realized, and to analyze the sensation of derealization that Freud experienced standing on the Acropolis, the thought: "So all this really *does* exist, just as we learnt at school!" He had a "momentary feeling: *'What I see here is not real.'*" These two phenomena—the depression in Trieste and the derealization on the Acropolis—were intimately related. The emotional connection is surpassing his father, excelling over him, traveling further than he did, and cherishing sights and evocations of antiquity for which his father would have had no appreciation. Freud's analysis:

> A sense of guilt was attached to the satisfaction in having gone such a long way: there was something about it that was wrong, that from earliest times had been forbidden. It was something to do with a child's criticism of his father, with the undervaluation which took the place of the overvaluation of earlier childhood. It seems as though the essence of success was to have got further than one's father, and as though to excel one's father was still something forbidden. . . . The very theme of Athens and the Acropolis in itself contained evidence of the son's superiority. Our father had been in business, he had had no secondary education, and Athens could not have meant much to him. Thus what interfered with our enjoyment of the journey to Athens was a feeling of *filial piety.*[13]

The eighty-year-old Freud was still working through his oedipal struggle with his father, who had died forty years earlier.[14]

III

Freud's dreams and associations bear direct testimony to his piety to classical Greece and Rome. Freud offered us what he called "a series of dreams which are based upon a longing to visit Rome." His first example:

> I was looking out of a railway-carriage window at the Tiber and the Ponte Sant' Angelo. The train began to move off, and it occurred to me that I had not so much as set foot in the city. The view that I had seen in my dream was taken from a well-known engraving which I had fleetingly noticed the day before in the sitting-room of one of my patients. Another time someone led me to the top of a hill and showed me Rome half-shrouded in mist; it was so far away that I was surprised at my view of it being so clear. There was more in the content of this dream than I feel

Bridge and Castle of Sant'Angelo.

prepared to detail; but the theme of "the promised land [*das gelobte Land*] seen from afar" was obvious in it.[15]

Freud often spoke of the work of psychoanalysis in the metaphor of archeological excavation: "It is as if Schliemann had dug up another Troy."[16] His *opus magnus, The Interpretation of Dreams,* was also in his life-time a living, multilayered text, requiring careful exfoliation of Freud's accretions and emendations to the various editions. To the Castel Sant' Angelo dream we find added in 1909: "I discovered long since that it only needs a little courage to fulfil wishes which till then have been re-garded as unattainable," and in 1925 the further association: "and [I] thereafter became a fervent pilgrim to Rome."[17]

The manifest content of this dream includes specific Christian, Clas-sical, Jewish, and secular scientific associations as well as day residue with an oedipal meaning. The day residue was an engraving he viewed in the salon of a patient the previous day. Freud specifically places the social locus of this Roman cultural artifact in the genteel environment of the home of his patient, who is a member of the *Bildungsburgertum,* the educated Viennese upper-middle class. Freud did not see this engraving in his childhood home. By contrast, when Goethe traveled to Rome, he thought of the pictures in his father's entrance hall.

> Now I see in life all the dreams of my youth. The first engravings I recall—my father hung the views of Rome in an ante-chamber—I now see in reality. And everything which I have known for a long time in paintings

and drawings, engravings and woodcuts, in plaster and cork, now stands assembled before me; wherever I go I find an acquaintance in a new world.[18]

Freud's self-description *Rompilger* is a specifically Roman Catholic usage, acknowledging the Christian Rome. The Castel Sant' Angelo was the fortress of the popes that was connected to the Vatican by a tunnel.[19] Here the popes took refuge from enemies, as when Rome was sacked by the armies of Charles V in 1527.

Behind the Christian Rome stands the pagan classical Rome. The Ponte Sant' Angelo (*Engelsbrücke*) was built by Hadrian in A.D. 135 and adorned with statues by Bernini in the seventeenth century. The castle was originally built by Hadrian as his mausoleum. The Emperor Hadrian was cursed by the Jews for the Hadrianic persecutions, which included forbidding the observance of the Sabbath and the rite of circumcision, and banning the teaching of the Torah and the maintenance of religious organization. Hadrian made Jerusalem a pagan city with the figure of a boar over its gate. No Jew was allowed to set foot in the city.

Freud recalls and associates to the concluding pages of the book of Deuteronomy, when God spoke to Moses on Mount Nebo overlooking the land of Canaan:

> You may view the land from a distance, but you shall not enter it. (Deuteronomy 33:52)

> And the Lord said to him; this is the land of which I swore to Abraham, Isaac, and Jacob, "I will give it to your offspring." I have let you see it with your own eyes, but you shall not cross there. (Deuteronomy 34:4)

These final passages of the Torah are known to all observant Jews, not only because they include God's covenant with Moses granting the children of Israel the promised land but also because these verses are read on the last day of the Jewish year. When this reading is finished, religious Jews immediately commence reading the first lines of the book of Genesis, to sustain the continuity of the learning of the Holy Writ.

When Freud wrote, "The motif of 'the Holy Land seen from afar' is easy to recognize in it." [*Das Motiv, "das gelobte Land von ferne sehen," ist darin leicht zu erkennen*], he was placing himself toward Rome as Moses was toward Israel, he was permitted to view the promised land only from afar. He dreamed of looking at but of being unable to reach the tomb of a Roman emperor, which had become a symbol of the papacy.

It is important that Freud dreamed of the bridge rather than the castle, although the two are contiguous. His view in the dream is across the bridge (*Brücke*), evoking the name of his admired Prussian professor of neurophysiology in whose laboratory he worked for six years of critical growth, who represented Freud's scientific ideal of the rigorous, positivist, precise nineteenth-century scientist. Ernst Brücke was his adored mentor who proposed and supported him for the study fellowship to Paris. Freud named his third son, Ernst (b. 1892), after his beloved teacher. Freud's associations to Brücke are analyzed in the "Non Vixit" dream in the *Interpretation of Dreams*. The emotional setting was an infraction and a reprimand:

> At the time I have in mind I had been a demonstrator at the Physiological Institute and was due to start work early in the morning. It came back to Brücke's ears that I sometimes reached the students' laboratory late. One morning he turned up punctually at the hour of opening and awaited my arrival. His words were spare and to the point. But it was not the words that mattered. What overwhelmed me were the terrifying blue eyes with which he looked at me and before which I shrank. . . . Any one who can remember the great master's eyes, which retained their wonderful beauty even in his old age, and who has ever seen him in anger, will find it easy to identify with the young sinner's emotions.[20]

Freud dreamed of the Ponte Sant' Angelo before having visited Rome. When he did eventually reach Rome in 1901, he was "overwhelmed" at what he described to Fliess as "the fulfillment of a long cherished wish," which was "a high point of my life." He contrasted the pagan Rome, toward which he felt reverence, with the Christian Rome with its false promise of eternal salvation:

> I could have worshiped [*anbeten*] the abased and mutilated remnant of the Temple of Minerva near the forum of Nerva, I found I could not freely enjoy the second [the medieval, Christian] Rome; the atmosphere troubled me. I found it difficult to tolerate the lie concerning man's redemption, which raises its head to high heaven—for I could not cast off the thought of my own misery and all the other misery I know about.
>
> I found the third, the Italian, Rome full of promise and likable.
>
> I was frugal in my pleasures, though, and did not try to see everything in twelve days. I not only bribed the Trevi [fountain], as everyone does, I also—and I invented this myself—dipped my hand in the Bocca della Verità at Santa Maria Cosmedin and vowed to return.[21]

Freud was captivated by the serene beauty of the sites of classic antiquity. He found peace and healing there and he prescribed a visit to the glories of *Magna Graecia* as a "cure" for a conversion symptom. The patient was the young Viennese conductor Bruno Walter in 1906. The symptom was a cramping paralysis with "rheumatic-neuralgic pain"

> so violent that I could no longer use my right arm for conducting or piano playing. I went from one prominent doctor to another. Each one confirmed the presence of psychogenic elements in my malady. I submitted to any number of treatments, from mudbaths to magnetism, and finally decided to call on Professor Sigmund Freud, resigned to submit to months of soul searching. The consultation took a course I had not foreseen. Instead of questioning me about sexual aberrations in infancy, as my layman's ignorance had led me to expect, Freud examined my arm briefly. I told him my story, feeling certain that he would be professionally interested in a possible connection between my actual physical affliction and a wrong I had suffered more than a year before. Instead, he asked me if I had ever been to Sicily.

When I replied that I had not, he said that it was very beautiful and interesting and more Greek than Greece itself. In short, I was to leave that very evening, forget all about my arm and the Opera, and do nothing for a few weeks but use my eyes. I did as I was told. Fortified with all the available literature about Sicily, I took an evening train for Genoa. . . . Milan and Venice were the only Italian beauty spots thus far known to me. I had purposely chosen the sea route, because I would have considered it unbearable, if not sinful, to rush in a train through cities like Florence and Rome just to get to Sicily quickly enough and be able to use for the intended purpose what little time my finances permitted me. . . . I was anxious to get to Sicily, and I took the regular steamer to Palermo the following evening. The boat was small, the seas were high, and I was disgracefully seasick, but I felt richly compensated by the splendid entrance into the port of Palermo and the sight of Monte Pellegrino in the morning air.

Mindful of Freud's instructions, I endeavored not to think of my affliction. In this I was aided by the powerful and exciting effect of my first meeting with Hellenism, which burst upon my eye and soul from every side. I was deeply impressed by the Greek theater in Taormina, the boatride on the Anapo beneath the papyrus shrubs, and the temples of Girgenti. But all these individual sights were outshone by the magnificent landscape with its grandiosely shaped mountains, the sublime solitude surrounding Syracuse, the rivers, the fields, and the nobly shaped bays. This, indeed, seemed an ideal scenery for Goethe's *Walpurgisnacht*. Thoughts of a tempestuous past, of the monuments commemorating it, and of nature that seemed to bear its imprint agitated me for weeks and made me forget the present and my troubles. In the end, my soul and mind were greatly benefited by the additional knowledge I had gained of Hellenism, but not my arm.[22]

Although Freud cherished his collection of pagan artifacts, he had no tolerance for holy places or sacred sites in the contemporary practice of religion. An unpublished letter written sixty years ago regarding the holy places in Jerusalem expresses Freud's ambivalence toward Zionism and the worship of sacred sites. In 1929 Arab riots in Palestine opposed the Zionist settlement and particularly Jewish right of access to the Wailing Wall, the remnant of the foundation of the Second Temple considered holy by Orthodox Jews. The Palestine Foundation Fund (Keren Hajessod) solicited letters around the world from prominent Jews, including Sigmund Freud, seeking support of the right of Jews to access to the Wall. Freud's answer to Keren Hajessod, Vienna:

I cannot do what you wish. I am unable to overcome my aversion to burdening the public with my name and even the present critical time does not seem to me to warrant it. Whoever wants to influence the masses must give them something rousing and inflammatory and my sober judgement of Zionism does not permit this. I certainly sympathize with its goals, am proud of our University in Jerusalem and am delighted with our settlements' prosperity. But, on the other hand, I do not think that Palestine could ever become a Jewish state, nor that the Christian and Islamic worlds would ever be prepared to have their holy places under Jewish control. It would have seemed more sensible to me to establish a Jewish homeland on a less historically burdened land. But I know that such a rational viewpoint would never have gained the enthusiasm of the masses and the financial support of the wealthy. I concede with sorrow that the unrealistic fanaticism of our people is in part to be blamed for the awakening of Arab distrust. I have no sympathy at all for the misdirected piety which transforms a piece of Herod's wall into a national relic thereby challenging the feelings of the natives.

Now judge for yourself whether I, with such a critical position, am the right person to stand forth to comfort a people deluded by unjustified hope.[23]

The cover letter from Vienna to Jerusalem was equally interesting and explains why this letter of Freud's and its glosses remained unpublished for over four decades. It is from Dr. Chaim Koffler of the Keren Hajessod, Vienna, to Dr. Abraham Schwadron, a right-wing Zionist who had a famous autograph collection in the Jewish National and University Library, Jerusalem. It reads:

The letter of Freud, with all its genuineness and warmth for us, is not propitious. And since there are no secrets in Palestine, the letter will certainly find its way out of the autograph collection of the University Library into the public eye. If I cannot be of service to the Keren Hajessod, I at least feel myself bound not to do damage. Should you wish to personally see the handwriting, then to return it to me, I will send the handwriting to you via a tourist, Dr. Manka Spiegel, who is travelling to Palestine, and who will later return the letter to me.

This letter bears a fascinating handwritten Hebrew postscript in which Schwadron responds to Koffler:

It is true that in Palestine there are no secrets . . . but I have not become naturalized. . . . The collection is without help as it was . . . it is in splendid isolation [in English transliterated into Hebrew characters] . . . it has no contact with the public, except for special things . . . it contains many manuscripts and pictures from all points of view: not to be shown and not to be handed over to anyone and as for me . . . a non-Zionist, that is to say precise and exact . . . a sense of responsibility . . . I "order you like the celestial messengers" [Daniel 4:14] to hurry . . . I promise you . . . in the name of the library that "no human eye shall see it" [Job 7:8].

With full responsibility . . .[24]

Following this biblical command, Freud's letter was sent to Jerusalem and the promise of nonpublication was kept. Although Freud was wrong about his prediction—the Jewish state does exist—as he was often wrong about other political assessments, such as that the Austro-Fascists would restrain the Nazis, sadly his interpretation about the conflict over the holy sites has as much resonance today as it did over sixty years ago. Freud was not a political Zionist and he did not believe in sanctifying stones.

IV

Freud's non–Judeo-Christian, indeed anti–Old and New Testament, position on sexual morality is most eloquently avowed when he invokes the

Greeks as a superior and more tolerant sexual and cultural ideal. For example, in the "Dora" case, Freud admonishes:

> We must learn to speak without indignation of what we call the sexual perversions—instances in which the sexual function has extended its limits in respect either to the part of the body concerned or to the sexual object chosen. The uncertainty in regard to the boundaries of what is to be called normal sexual life, when we take different races and different epochs into account, should in itself be enough to cool the zealot's ardour. We surely ought not to forget that the perversion which is the most repellent to us, the sensual love of a man for a man, was not only tolerated by a people so far our superiors in cultivation as were the Greeks [*uns so sehr kulturüberlegenen Volke wie den Griechen*], but was actually entrusted by them with important social functions. The sexual life of each one of us extends to a slight degree—now in this direction, now in that—beyond the narrow lines imposed as the standard of normality. The perversions are neither bestial nor degenerate in the emotional sense of the word.[25]

In Freud's parallel text of psychodynamic theory, which was published the same year as the "Dora" case, he stesses the distinction between inverts and degenerates and argues: "Account must be taken of the fact that inversion was a frequent phenomenon—one might almost say an institution charged with important functions—among the peoples of antiquity at the height of their civilization."[26] Freud notes with approval the turn from ethnocentric marginalization of homosexuals to a historical and ethnographic relativism and again invokes the case of pagan Hellas and Rome: "The pathological approach to the study of inversion has been displaced by the anthropological. The merit for bringing about this change is due to Bloch (1902–3), who has also laid stress on the occurrence of inversion among the civilizations of antiquity."[27]

A third of a century later, when writing to an American mother, Freud offered her the Stoic comfort of historical antiquity:

> I gather from your letter that your son is a homosexual. I am most impressed by the fact that you do not mention this term yourself in your information about him. May I question you why you avoid it? Homosexuality is assuredly no advantage, but it is nothing to be ashamed of, no vice, no degradation; it cannot be classified as an illness; we consider it to be a variation of the sexual function, produced by a certain arrest of sexual development. Many highly respectable individuals of ancient and modern times have been homosexuals, several of the greatest men among them. (Plato, Michelangelo, Leonardo da Vinci, etc.) It is a great injustice to persecute homosexuality as a crime—and a cruelty, too.[28]

V

For the stratum of Austrian secular Jewish intelligensia of the late nineteenth century to which Freud belonged the culture of reference was Hellenic-Roman. The statue of Athena, symbolizing the wisdom of rational law, stands before the classic Greek Parliament building on Vienna's Ringstrasse.[29]

Freud was a philosophical Stoic and lived his personal life by that creed learned from Seneca and Epictetus in his humanistic gymnasium. The Stoics taught the world the conception of the weakness and misery of men, individually and in society. They sought in Stoic philosophy a refuge against the vicissitudes of fortune that they beheld daily and maintained the essential dignity and internal freedom of every human being. Their attitude was tolerant of suicide as a "way out" of incurable discomforts, including the infirmity of old age.[30] The essence of Stoic philosophy as Freud learned it and practiced it was to accept the inevitable with dignity and resolution.

In his personal life, his psychotherapeutic stance, and in his worldview, Freud was submissive to natural law and the cruelties of fate, such as the death of a beloved grandson, or the malignancy that tormented him for the last sixteen years of his life and that eventually killed him. Thus, in 1895 he tells patients who want miracles:

> No doubt fate would find it easier than I do to relieve you of your illness. But you will be able to convince yourself that much will be gained if we succeed in transforming your hysterical misery into common unhappiness. With a mental life that has been restored to health you will be better armed against that unhappiness.[31]

This is Freud, the Stoic, speaking. When, more than three decades later, he was to write of "the great necessities of Fate, against which there is no help [which we must] learn to endure with resignation,"[32] we hear the teachings of the Stoics that Freud had made his personal philosophy of life and death.

The final test for any man who is a Stoic is the way he dies. We have the remarkable account of the last ten years of Freud's life and his ordeal with cancer from Max Schur, his last personal physician. Freud faced his malignancy with full cognizance of the certainty of his death. In Freud's experience, as was generally true in the pre-antibiotic era, death was life's companion. He lived in the presence of death from childhood. He lost an infant brother; in 1914 his beloved half-brother Emmanuel was killed in a railway accident; others close to him who died were his friends Ernst von Fleishl-Marxow and Anton von Freund; his daughter Sophie in 1920, when she was only twenty-six, then her son Heinele in 1923, when he was four or so years old.

Meeting with death is never without denial and ambivalence, both by the patient and the patient's caretakers. In Freud's case the ambivalence was dramatic in his original suspicions of cancer and his inaction and the reassurances and denials from his physician and inner circle. In the spring of 1923 he detected a growth on his right jaw and palate. For two months he did not mention it to a family member, physician, or friend, or take steps to have it examined.[33] When he showed it to his physician,

Felix Deutsch, he did so with the comment "Be prepared to see something you won't like." Upon examination, said Deutsch, "At the very first glance, I had no doubt that it was an advanced cancer."[34]

Freud chose Marcus Hajek to operate on him, a man who "was generally known to be a somewhat mediocre surgeon" and about whom he had misgivings because he was aware of Hajek's ambivalence toward him.[35] It was a decision that nearly cost Freud his life. He was not properly cared for nor hospitalized, and he almost bled to death. The surgeon did not take the usual precautions against the shrinking of the scar, thereby causing Freud hardship for the rest of his life.[36] Hajek did not tell Freud that he had cancer. Both Deutsch and Freud's "Committee," his most trusted disciples, also withheld from him the diagnosis of cancer and the need for a second major operation. Years later, when Ernest Jones told him of the committee's deception, Freud "with blazing eyes . . . asked '*Mit welchem Recht?*' [By what right?]"[37] He was full of reproach toward Deutsch because the accurate diagnosis had been withheld from him and he had been deceived. Very likely, had Freud been confronted with the true diagnosis, he would not have been so casual about his first surgery, agreeing to go to an outpatient clinic with no hospital room, bed, or proper nursing care. Freud wrote to Deutsch invoking his Stoic ideal:

> I could always adapt myself to any kind of reality, even endure an uncertainty due to a reality—but being left alone with my subjective insecurity, without the fulcrum or pillar of the *ananke*, the inexorable, unavoidable necessity, I had to fall prey to the miserable cowardice of a human being and had to become an unworthy spectacle for others.[38]

During the next sixteen years Freud underwent thirty-three operations of the mouth. As ever-greater areas of the jaw, palate, and cheek were removed in increasingly radical operations, he had to learn to live with a huge prosthesis that he termed "the monster." Deutsch notes that Freud "never complained about his misfortune to me; in these years he simply treated the neoplasm as an uninvited, unwelcome intruder whom one should not mind more than necessary."[39]

In 1928 Freud took a new physician, Max Schur. He did so under two conditions: first, that he always be told the truth, and second, "that when the time comes, you won't let me suffer unnecessarily."[40] When, in September 1939, Freud asked Schur to redeem his promise, Schur gave him two centigrams of morphine, which he repeated after twelve hours. Freud did not wake up again.[41]

Freud showed no sign of complaint or irritability. His resignation to fate and his acceptance of unalterable reality neither wavered nor faltered. With the exception of an occasional aspirin, he took no drugs until the very end so that he could think clearly. He continued his psychoanalytic work until July 1939. He died on 23 September, a Stoic pagan to the end, believing in life. Death was the necessary outcome of life.

Death is natural, undeniable, and unavoidable. Freud was unflinching about what he termed

> one of the most aggravating features of our modern medicine. The art of deceiving a sick person is not exactly highly necessary. But what has the individual come to, how negligible must be the influence of the religion of science, which is supposed to have taken the place of the old religion, if one no longer dares to disclose that it is this or that man's turn to die? . . . I hope that when my time comes, I shall find someone who will treat me with greater respect and tell me when to be ready.

Freud unconsciously altered Shakespeare's *Henry IV* (act 5, scene 1), where Prince Hal tells Falstaff: "Why, thou owest God a death" to "You owe Nature a death" (*Du bist der Natur einen Tod schuldig*). To this letter he adds the postscript: "I am deep in Burckhardt's *History of Greek Civilization*."[42]

Freud's attitude toward death: forthright, without sentimentality or self-pity but with a full consciousness of reality, represents the best of what Freud means for a person's attitude toward himself or herself: stoic acceptance. This life is all there is and there is little you can do about it. One must die and that fact should not be obviated or denied. We must live with that realization and die, if possible, with a minimum of suffering and without illusions. This is what the Stoic pagan Freud had to offer—no panacea, utopia, or life after death—as he had said in the beginning of his career as a psychoanalyst almost half a century earlier, all he could offer was the transformation of neurotic misery into the ability to cope with the "common unhappiness" that is our lot as humans.

NOTES

1. For Freud and Judaism, see Robert S. Wistrich, "The Jewish Identity of Sigmund Freud," in *The Jews of Vienna in the Age of Franz Joseph* (Oxford: Oxford University Press, 1989), pp. 537–82, also "The Jewishness of Sigmund Freud," in *Between Redemption and Perdition: Modern Antisemitism and Jewish Identity* (London: Routledge, 1990), pp. 71–85; Lary Berkower, "The Enduring Effect of the Jewish Tradition upon Freud," *American Journal of Psychiatry* 125:8 (February 1969): 1067–73; Martin S. Bergman, "Moses and the Evolution of Freud's Jewish Identity," *Israel Annals of Psychiatry and Related Disciplines* 14:1 (March 1976): 3–26; David Bakan, *Sigmund Freud and the Jewish Mystical Tradition* (New York: Van Nostrand, 1958); Ernst Simon, "Sigmund Freud, the Jew," *Leo Baeck Institute Yearbook*, vol. 2 (London: East and West Library, 1957), pp. 270–305; Peter Loewenberg, "Sigmund Freud as a Jew: A Study in Ambivalence and Courage," *Journal of the History of the Behavioral Sciences* 7:4 (October 1971): 363–69; and "A Hidden Zionist Theme in Freud's 'My Son, the Myops . . .' Dream," *Journal of the History of Ideas* 31:1 (January–March 1970): 129–32; Peter Gay, *A Godless Jew: Freud, Atheism, and the Making of Psychoanalysis* (New Haven: Yale University Press, 1987); Emanuel Rice, *Freud and Moses: The Long Journey*

Home (Albany: SUNY Press, 1990); Yosef H. Yerushalmi, *Freud's Moses: Judaism Terminable and Interminable* (New Haven: Yale University Press, 1991); Dennis B. Klein, *Jewish Origins of the Psychoanalytic Movement* (New York: Praeger, 1981); Leonard Shengold, "Freud and Joseph," in *Freud and His Self-Analysis*, ed. Mark Kanzer and Jules Glenn (New York: Jason Aronson, 1979), pp. 67–86.

Two works that deal with Freud's relation to antiquity from perspectives different from mine are the pioneering essay by Suzanne Cassirer Bernfeld, "Freud and Archeology," *American Imago* 8:2 (June 1951): 107–28; and Marthe Robert, *From Oedipus to Moses: Freud's Jewish Identity*, trans. Ralph Manheim (Garden City, N.Y.: Anchor/Doubleday, 1976).

2. *Encyclopaedia Britannica*, 11th ed. (Cambridge: Cambridge University Press, 1911), 19:449.

3. Lynn Gamwell and Richard Wells, eds., *Sigmund Freud and Art: His Personal Collection of Antiquities* (New York: Abrams, 1989).

4. Peter Gay, introduction to Gamwell and Wells, *Sigmund Freud and Art*, p. 18. See Gay's perceptive section "A Partiality for the Prehistoric" in *Freud, Jews and Other Germans: Masters and Victims in Modernist Culture* (New York: Oxford University Press, 1978), pp. 39–46.

5. Gamwell and Wells, *Sigmund Freud and Art*, p. 158.

6. Freud to Stefan Zweig, Vienna, 7 February 1931, in *Letters of Sigmund Freud*, ed. Ernst L. Freud (New York: Basic Books, 1960), Letter 258, pp. 402–3 (hereafter cited as *Letters*).

7. *The Psychopathology of Everyday Life* (1901), in *Standard Edition of the Complete Psychological Works of Sigmund Freud*, translated under the general editorship of James Strachey in collaboration with Anna Freud, assisted by Alix Strachey and Alan Tyson, 24 vols. (London: Hogarth Press, 1953–1975), 6:167–68 (hereafter cited as *S.E.*).

8. Ibid., p. 169.

9. Ibid., pp. 169–70.

10. Jacques Barzun misused this piece of Freud's self-analysis to attack the use of psychoanalysis in the humanities and social sciences, asking, "If an observable, intimately known living being is to be exempt from an analysis that is not genuinely clinical, what is to be said of essaying it upon the unobservable, never-encountered dead?" *Clio and the Doctors: Psycho-History, Quanto-History and History* (Chicago: University of Chicago Press, 1974), p. 52. What is to be said is that never-encountered dead subjects are not friends and cannot have injured feelings. The difference is between a clinician's insight into a patient's psychodynamics and the patient's self-insight. That difference may constitute years of hard work on both their parts. Freud's self-reproach was not because the interpretation was wrong, as Barzun suggests; rather, it was because to offer interpretations in a social context is a sure way of destroying a friendship. Freud explicitly comments on his luck in cementing the friendship together. It is his indiscretion that almost caused him to lose a friend that Freud regrets, not the inaccuracy of the interpretation. Indeed, Freud's interpretation was probably correct, or his friend would not have taken such umbrage. Cf. Peter Loewenberg, "Some Pills Are Hard to Swallow," *CLIO* 5:1 (Fall 1975): 123–27.

11. "Some Reflections on Schoolboy Psychology" (1914), in *S.E.*, 13:241; "Zur Psychologie des Gymnasiasten," in *Studienausgabe*, ed. Alexander Mitscherlich, Angela Richards, and James Strachey 12 vols. (Frankfurt am Main: S. Fischer Verlag, 1969–1975) 4:237 (hereafter cited as *Studien*).

12. *S.E.*, 13:244; *Studien*, 4:239.

13. "A Disturbance of Memory on the Acropolis" (1936), in *S.E.*, 22:247–48; "Eine Erinnerungsstörung auf der Akropolis," in *Studien*, 4:292–93.

14. See the perceptive treatment of the Freud–Rolland relationship by David James Fisher in "Sigmund Freud and Romain Rolland: The Terrestrial Animal and His Great Oceanic Friend," in *Cultural Theory and Psychoanalytic Tradition* (New Brunswick, N.J.: Transaction Publishers, 1991), pp. 27–78.

15. *The Interpretation of Dreams* (1900), *S.E.*, 194; *Die Traumdeutung*, in *Studien*, 2:205.

16. Freud to Wilhelm Fliess, 21 December 1899, *Briefe an Wilhelm Fliess, 1887–1904*, ed. Jeffrey M. Masson (Frankfurt am Main: S. Fischer Verlag, 1986), Letter 229, p. 430 (hereafter cited as *Briefe an Fliess*); *The Complete Letters of Sigmund Freud to Wilhelm Fliess, 1887–1904*, trans. and ed. Jeffrey M. Masson (Cambridge: Harvard University Press, 1985), p. 390 (hereafter cited as *Letters to Fliess*).

17. *S.E.*, 4:194 n. 1; *Studien*, 2:205 n. 1.

18. Johann Wolfgang von Goethe, *Italienische Reise* (Munich: Wilhelm Goldman Verlag, 1961), p. 78.

19. The theme of the Roman Catholic part of Freud's childhood socialization and adult identity is treated in Kenneth A. Grigg, "All Roads Lead to Rome: The Role of the Nursemaid in Freud's Dreams," *Journal of the American Psychoanalytic Association* 21 (1973): 108–26; Paul C. Vitz, *Sigmund Freud's Christian Unconscious* (New York: Guilford, 1988); and, most elegantly, by Carl E. Schorske in "Politics and Patricide in Freud's *Interpretation of Dreams*," in Finde-Siècle *Vienna: Politics and Culture* (New York: Knopf, 1980), especially pp. 189–93, on Freud's "Rome neurosis." The third act of Giacomo Puccini's *Tosca* takes place in the Castel Sant' Angelo, where Scarpia, Rome's dreaded police chief, holds Tosca and her lover Cavaradossi. In the final scene Tosca leaps from the parapet of the castle terrace to the Tiber some two hundred meters away. Contemporary Roman wags commented on the record-breaking long jump. *Tosca* premiered in January 1900, so could not have been a day residue for Freud's dream.

20. *Interpretation of Dreams*, *S.E.*, 5:422; *Studien*, 2:410.

21. Freud to Fliess, 19 September 1901, *Briefe an Fliess*, Letter 271, pp. 493–96; *Letters to Fliess*, p. 449.

22. Bruno Walter, *Theme and Variations: An Autobiography* (New York: Knopf, 1946), pp. 164–66. See also Emanuel E. Garcia, "Somatic Interpretation in a Transference Cure: Freud's Treatment of Bruno Walter," *International Review of Psychoanalysis* 17:3 (1990): 83–88; and George H. Pollock, "On Freud's Psychotherapy of Bruno Walter," *Annual of Psychoanalysis* 3 (1975): 287–95.

23. Freud to Dr. Chaim Koffler, Keren Hajessod, Vienna, 26 February 1930, Schwadron Collection, Jewish National and University Library, Jerusalem.

24. Dr. Chaim Koffler, Vienna, to Dr. Abraham Schwadron, Jerusalem, 2 April 1930, Schwadron Collection, Jewish National and University Library, Jerusalem.

25. Freud, "Fragment of an Analysis of a Case of Hysteria" (1905), in *S.E.*, 7:50; "Bruchstück einer Hysterie-Analyse," in *Studien*, 6:124–25.

26. Freud, "Three Essays on the Theory of Sexuality" (1905), in *S.E.*, 7:139; "Drei Abhandlungen zur Sexualtheorie," in *Studien*, 5:51.

27. Freud, "Three Essays on the Theory of Sexuality" (1905), in *S.E.*, 7:139 n. 2; "Drei Abhandlungen zur Sexualtheorie," in *Studien*, 5:51 n. 1.

28. Freud to Anonymous, 9 April 1935 (original in English), *Letters*, Letter 277, p. 423.

29. Schorske, "The Ringstrasse, Its Critics, and the Birth of Urban Modernism," *Fin-de-Siècle Vienna*, pp. 24–115. For the design of the Parliament particularly, see pp. 40–46.

30. *Encyclopaedia Britannica*, 25:942–51.

31. Freud, "Studies on Hysteria" (1895), in *S.E.*, 2:305.

32. Freud, "The Future of an Illusion" (1927), in *S.E.*, 21:50; "Die Zukunft einer Illusion," in *Studien*, 9:183.

33. Max Schur, *Freud: Living and Dying* (New York: International Universities Press, 1972), p. 348.

34. Felix Deutsch, "Reflections on Freud's One Hundredth Birthday," *Psychosomatic Medicine* 18:4 (July–August 1956): 280.

35. Schur, *Freud*, p. 351.

36. Ernest Jones, *The Life and Work of Sigmund Freud*, vol. 3 (New York: Basic Books, 1957), pp. 90–91.

37. Ibid., p. 93.

38. Deutsch, "Reflections," p. 282.

39. Ibid.

40. Schur, *Freud*, p. 408.

41. Ibid., p. 529.

42. Freud to Fliess, 6 February 1899, *Briefe an Fliess*, Letter 191, p. 376; *Letters to Fliess*, pp. 343–44.

3

SIGMUND FREUD'S
PSYCHOSOCIAL IDENTITY

Hebraism and Hellenism, between these two points of influence moves our world. At one time it feels more powerfully the attraction of one of them, at another time of the other; and it ought to be, though it never is, evenly and happily balanced between them.

Matthew Arnold

Whoever knows only one thing about Freud knows something wrong, which is to say, knows something that standing alone is out of balance and is therefore only a partial truth. I will place Freud in the fecund creative historical-sociological tradition of those who are marginal to mainstream Western culture; they are *in* Western culture but not *of* it. The excitement of their lives and discoveries is that they are initially peripheral to the larger society, they stand on its boundaries, and therefore they have a cultural vantage point of both clarity of perception and vulnerability—and their discoveries are adopted by the culture to become central to its intellectual corpus. This in/out position of straddling boundaries is also the professional stance of psychoanalysts toward the lives of their analysands.

Today there is a substantial literature and a heated debate about Freud's cultural and social identity. We have before us in the scholarship essentially five understandings of Freud's historico-social identifications: (1) as a secular North German atheist; (2) as a product of Habsburg Austrian culture; (3) as a Jew who secularized Judaism in psychoanalysis; (4) as a person harboring a Christian, particularly Roman Catholic, consciousness; (5) as a Hellenic pagan. To dilate briefly on each of these categories:

1. Freud was a secular atheist and positivistic scientist. This is the interpretation of Peter Gay, whose researches on Freud are prodigious. He pictures Freud as a product of the Germanic cultural world and essentially the product of north German culture:

It was not Asian wisdom that Freud offered the world but German wisdom. Now this, in the cosmopolitan scientific atmosphere of the nineteenth century, meant European wisdom.[1]

In truth Freud could have developed his ideas in any city endowed with a first-rate medical school and an educated public large and affluent enough to furnish him with patients.[2]

Medical Vienna [was] a German city. It was in that city, and that city alone, that Freud developed and felt most at home. . . . The intellectual instrument that led him to his psychoanalytic theories was not Jewish or Austrian.[3]

There is a partial truth, or a distortion, in Gay's analysis. He is speaking of only one of the determinants of Freud's identity. On the issue of cultural influences on Freud, he is discussing Freud's *conscious* identity. An identity, of course, is based on positive and negative, conscious and unconscious psychological identifications.

Freud did have an important North German political orientation in his student days.[4] He revered his Prussian teacher in neurophysiology, Ernst Brücke, whom the colleagues in Berlin called "our Ambassador to the Far East,"[5] and after whom he named his third son, Ernst.[6] But there was also a strong connection to western Europe, to France where Freud had received a fellowship to study in Paris with Jean-Martin Charcot, for whom he named his first son, Martin. His two half-brothers lived in England; he envied them for being able to raise their children in a land relatively free of anti-Semitism.[7] Freud tells us he named his next son Oliver, to honor Cromwell, who had readmitted the Jews to England— "a great historical figure who had powerfully attracted me in my boyhood, especially since my visit to England. During the year before the child's birth I had made up my mind to use his name if it were a son and I greeted the new-born baby with it with a feeling of high *satisfaction*."[8]

Gay is resolute in holding that there is nothing essentially "Jewish" in Freud's ideas, or the structure of his thought.[9] He takes Freud out of the social context of being born of Galician Jewish parents in Moravia and growing up in Habsburg Austria, specifically in Vienna's Second District, the Leopoldstadt, where many of the Eastern European Jews lived. Leopoldstadt had the largest concentration of Jews in Vienna; 48.3 percent of all Viennese Jews lived there. Jews made up 9 percent of the population of the city, but in 1880 accounted for one-third of the people of Leopoldstadt.[10]

For the Eastern European, particularly Jewish, influence in Freud's life and thought, it is necessary to do no more than to read *Jokes and Their Relation to the Unconscious* (1905), which is infused with Eastern European, especially Galician, Jewish humor. It is often referred to among psychoanalysts in training as "the Jewish joke book." The work is filled with Jewish *Schnorrers* (beggars), travelers on trains, bathhouses, and *Schadchens* (marriage brokers). It includes Freud's analysis of the psychology of Jewish humor, which is interpreted as an acceptable mode of expressing hostility and as one-upmanship, as if to say, "We know our faults and can mock them much better than you ever could." Freud writes:

> The jokes made about Jews by foreigners are for the most part brutal comic stories in which a joke is made unnecessary by the fact that Jews are regarded by foreigners as comic figures. The Jewish jokes which originate from Jews admit this too; but they know their real faults as well as the connection between them and their good qualities, and the share which the subject has in the person found fault with creates the subjective determinant (usually so hard to arrive at) of the joke-work. Incidentally, I do not know whether there are many other instances of a people making fun to such a degree of its own character.[11]

As to the fourth point of the cultural compass, the Helleno-Latin world across the Alps in the Mediterranean South, we need refer only to Freud's papers on Michelangelo, da Vinci, the Acropolis, and what Carl Schorske termed his "Rome neurosis."[12] Freud traveled to Italy five times between 1895 and 1898 while he was struggling with his self-analysis and writing *The Interpretation of Dreams*, without being able to reach the Eternal City. He identified with the Carthaginian general Hannibal:

> Like him, I had been fated not to see Rome. . . . Hannibal, whom I had come to resemble in these respects, had been the favourite hero of my later school days. . . . And when in the higher classes I began to understand for the first time what it meant to belong to an alien race, and anti-semitic feelings among the other boys warned me that I must take up a definite position, the figure of the semitic general rose still higher in my esteem. To my youthful mind Hannibal and Rome symbolized the conflict between the tenacity of Jewry and the organization of the Catholic church. And the increasing importance of the effects of the anti-semitic movement upon our emotional life helped to fix the thoughts and feelings of those early days. Thus the wish to go to Rome had become in my dream-life a cloak and symbol for a number of other passionate wishes.[13]

The Freudian case of psychotherapy I find most endearing for his faith in Hellas's curative powers is his prescription for Bruno Walter's hysterical paralysis of his right arm. Freud told him to go directly to Sicily, do nothing for a few weeks but drink in the beauty of the Greek antiquities, and come home and conduct the orchestra—Freud would take the responsibility for any failure.[14]

2. Freud was squarely rooted in the society and politics of Habsburg Austria and particularly the culture of *fin-de-siècle* Vienna. Prior to the First World War Vienna stood at the social and cultural crossroads of Europe. The case that his conscious thought and unconscious dream life were permeated by the class and national struggles of failing Austrian political liberalism was compellingly made and precisely explicated in the researches of Carl Schorske and William McGrath.[15]

3. Freud had a Jewish religious identification that was more pervasive than he recognized or acknowledged. There is a substantial scholarly literature on this theme.[16] This view, stressing Freud's Jewish religious roots rather than ethnic cultural identification, is given its most articulate expression in the recent work of Y. H. Yerushalmi, who polemicizes against Gay and wishes to resuscitate Freud's Jewish religious identity. He locates the particular source of this identity in Freud's Galician Jewish father, Jakob.[17] Whereas Gay wishes to consider only the new and most forward secular position of Freud, Yerushalmi chooses to focus on the traditional themes in Freud's corpus that contain where he emotionally came from: his father, Galicia, and the observant Jewish past.

4. Freud functioned with a series of latent Christian identifications, particularly with Austro-Hungarian Roman Catholicism, as a result of his childhood socialization by a Czech nanny, a peasant woman who took him to church and taught him Christian notions of a heaven and damnation in hell, and the powerful social pressures of Austrian anti-Semitism that inhibited his professional career advancement.[18]

5. Freud had a decisive cultural identification with the classical civilization of Attic Greece. This view emphasizes the importance of Freud's humanistic gymnasium education with its classical languages and philosophy. For the stratum of Austrian secular Jewish intelligentsia of the late nineteenth century to which Freud belonged the culture of reference was Hellenic-Latin.[19] Freud was a Hellenic pagan in four main dimensions of his personality: (1) Most importantly in his oedipal triumph over his poor Jewish merchant father; (2) his admiration and identification with the aesthetics of what he viewed as a superior culture, and the geography of Mediterranean antiquity; (3) his enlightened plea for a tolerant nonjudgmental sexual morality; and (4) his personal philosophy of Stoicism and in the manner in which he faced his terminal illness and death.

In sum, Freud's psychosocial identity was a dynamic interplay of the four points of the European cultural compass of which Vienna was the late-nineteenth-century center, and of the five psychocultural influences that are evident: Germanic science, Austrian liberal politics, Jewish religious values, Habsburg Christian culture, and Hellenic paganism.

II

The definition of Freud's historico-social position that I propose is that Freud was a larger-than-life exemplar of the center of a three-generational late-nineteenth-century process by which large parts of European Jewry embraced Western Enlightenment, science, modernity, religious reform, and secularism. His father, Jakob, was a wandering wool merchant from the Galician shtetl of Buczacz who in his life made the move, which correlated with political emancipation, from religious orthodoxy to Haskalah, which saw Judaism as a religion of universal enlightenment.[20] Jakob Freud's home was religiously observant, though not strictly Orthodox. Ernest Jones says Sigmund "was certainly conversant with all Jewish customs and festivals."[21] Sigmund Freud was of the transition generation of Central European Jewry in the brief heyday of political liberalism when the pace of assimilation was at its maximum. He stood between the observant household of his parents and the totally secularized upbringing of his own children. His wife, Martha, who came from a strictly Orthodox Hamburg home, was forced to give up Sabbath observance and kosher dietary laws when she married him. Freud briefly considered conversion to Protestantism at the time of their wedding in order to avoid an Orthodox Jewish ceremony. His friend and patron Josef Breuer dissuaded him by murmuring, "Too complicated."[22] Sigmund continued the Westernizing momentum of his father by receiving a secular higher education and becoming a free professional, a scientist, and a pathbreaking cultural innovator not just for the Jews but for humankind.

History is always a tension of change and stasis, of new developments and transformations, and of conservative continuities with the past. The position of social marginality was defined by Stonequist:

> Because of his in-between situation, the marginal man may become an acute and able critic of the dominant group and its culture. This is because he combines the knowledge and insight of the insider with the critical attitude of the outsider. His analysis is not necessarily objective—there is too much emotional tension underneath to make such an attitude easy of achievement. But he is skillful in noting the contradictions and "hypocrisies" in the dominant culture. The gap between its moral pretensions and its actual achievements jumps to his eye.[23]

Stonequist explicitly refers to Freud when he analyzes the cultural creativity of Jews as a function of their marginality in society.[24]

I will draw on the understandings of this problem of Jewish cultural creativity in the modern world by three great twentieth-century scholars, a sociologist, an economist, and a historian, that illuminate the particular case of Sigmund Freud and his Jewish heritage. These are the German Jew converted to Protestantism Georg Simmel; the American gentile Thorstein Veblen; and the Polish-Jewish Marxist Isaac Deutscher. Their work is as relevant to our comprehension of the historical Freud as are his own poignant understandings of his cultural position and his relation to nationalism and Judaism.

The earliest description of sociocultural marginality and its implications was by the sociologist Georg Simmel, a Jew who was baptized as a Protestant at birth. He was denied a professorship in Germany until he was fifty-six. When he was a candidate for a chair at the University of Heidelberg, he was successfully attacked in a letter to the Baden Minister of Culture as "surely an Israelite through and through, in his outward appearance, in his bearing, and in his mental style—*Geistesart*."[25] When he finally received a professorship, it was at the boundary of the German

Reich, in territorially ambiguous and culturally marginal Alsace, at the University of Strasbourg. Simmel's sociological analysis reflected the jeopardy and insight, the sense of precarious insecurity and acute perception, of a person between cultures.

It is due to Simmel, who in 1908 first defined "the stranger" as a distinctive phenotype subject to analysis, that we today have the culturally marginal outsider as a category of sociological understanding. The stranger is present but not entirely integrated in the culture. Simmel denoted European Jews as "the classical example" of "the stranger" who is not merely

> the wanderer who comes today and goes tomorrow, but rather as the person who comes today and stays tomorrow. He is, so to speak, the *potential* wanderer: although he has not moved on, he has not quite overcome the freedom of coming and going. He is fixed within a particular spatial group, or within a group whose boundaries are similar to spatial boundaries. But his position in this group is determined, essentially, by the fact that he has not belonged to it from the beginning, that he imports qualities into it, which do not and cannot stem from the group itself.[26]

The stranger is involved in "a specific form of interaction," a special relationship to his culture of residence: he is not merely an outsider, he is also a potential critic. In what we would today term the psychoanalytical object-relations idiom of optimal distance, Simmel spoke of

> that synthesis of nearness and distance which constitutes the formal position of the stranger. . . . He is not radically committed to the unique ingredients and peculiar tendencies of the group, and therefore approaches them with the specific attitude of "objectivity." But objectivity does not simply involve passivity and detachment; it is a particular structure composed of distance and nearness, indifference and involvement.[27]

In 1919 Thorstein Veblen, the Wisconsin-born son of Norwegian immigrant parents, and America's most original native social scientist, penned a profound essay entitled "The Intellectual Pre-eminence of Jews in Modern Europe," in response to the Balfour Declaration. Veblen was a notable philo-Semite who identified with the Jews, hailing them as "the vanguard of modern inquiry" and drawing attention to

> a fact which must strike any dispassionate observer—that the Jewish people have contributed much more than an even share to the intellectual life of modern Europe. So also it is plain that the civilisation of Christendom continues today to draw heavily on the Jews for men devoted to science and scholarly pursuits. It is not only that men of Jewish extraction continue to supply more than a proportionate quota to the rank and file engaged in scientific and scholarly work, but a disproportionate number of the men to whom modern science and scholarship look for guidance and leadership are of the same derivation. . . . [T]hey count particularly among the vanguard, the pioneers, the uneasy guild of pathfinders and iconoclasts, in science, scholarship, and institutional change and growth.[28]

Veblen stresses that it is the departure from one cultural tradition but not yet being fully assimilated or at home in another that is the fragile position of creativity. His point, counter to Yerushalmi and others who elevate Freud's debt to the Jewish religious tradition, would be that Freud *had* to leave religious orthodoxy and its rigidity to become a creative pathbreaker.

> It appears to be only when the gifted Jew escapes from the cultural environment created and fed by the particular genius of his own people, only when he falls into the alien lines of gentile inquiry and becomes a naturalized, though hyphenate, citizen in the gentile republic of learning, that he comes into his own as a creative leader in the world's intellectual enterprise. It is by loss of allegiance, or at the best by force of a divided allegiance to the people of his origin, that he finds himself in the vanguard of modern inquiry.[29]

According to Veblen, among the attributes of the Jewish mind which are requisites "for any work of inquiry" are "a skeptical frame of mind . . . a degree of exemption from hard-and-fast preconceptions, a skeptical animus, *Unbefangenheit*, release from the dead hand of conventional finality." Veblen's identification with the Jews is nowhere clearer than when he writes of their position of restless alienation. There is a heavy price in anxiety to pay for being an innovator and challenger of received orthodoxy. Veblen invokes the myth of the wandering Jew as his metaphor for the intellectual:

> The intellectually gifted Jew is in a peculiarly fortunate position in respect of this requisite immunity from the inhibitions of intellectual quietism. But he can come in for such immunity only at the cost of losing his secure place in the scheme of conventions into which he has been born, and at the cost, also, of finding no similarly secure place in that scheme of gentile conventions into which he is thrown. For him as for other men in the like case, the skepticism that goes to make him an effectual factor in the increase and diffusion of knowledge among men involves a loss of that peace of mind that is the birthright of the safe and sane quietist. He becomes a disturber of the intellectual peace, but only at the cost of becoming an intellectual wayfaring man, a wanderer in the intellectual no-man's-land, seeking another place to rest, farther along the road, somewhere over the horizon.[30]

Isaac Deutscher, author of a monumental trilogy of the life of Leon Trotsky as well as a biography of Stalin and other works on the Soviet Union and Marxism, penned an analysis of what he termed *The non-Jewish Jew*, by which he meant the "great revolutionaries of modern thought: Spinoza, Heine, Marx, Rosa Luxemburg, Trotsky, and Freud."[31] They had in common "something of the quintessence of Jewish life and of the Jewish intellect." These qualities include determinism, a dialectical manner of thinking, a relativity of moral standards, a commitment to knowledge being inseparable from action (praxis), and a belief in the ultimate solidarity of man. Deutscher is the only one of the major theorists of social marginality whom we consider who explicitly sub-sumed Freud's work in his generalizations.

> They are all, from Spinoza to Freud, determinists, they all hold that the universe is ruled by laws inherent in it and governed by *Gesetzmässigkeiten* [conformity to natural laws]. They do not see reality as a jumble of acci-dents or history as an assemblage of caprices and whims of rulers. There is nothing fortuitous, so Freud tells us, in our dreams, follies, or even in our slips of the tongue.[32]

> As Jews they dwelt on the borderlines of various civilizations, religions, and national cultures. They were born and brought up on the borderlines of various epochs. Their mind matured where the most diverse cultural in-fluences crossed and fertilized each other. They lived on the margins or in the nooks and crannies of their respective nations. Each of them was in so-ciety and yet not in it, of it and yet not of it. It was this that enabled them to rise in thought above their times and generations, and to strike out men-tally into wide new horizons and far into the future.[33]

Of Freud, Deutscher said his "mind matured in Vienna in estrange-ment from Jewry and in opposition to the Catholic clericalism of the Habsburg capital."[34] Although Deutscher did not avail himself of Freud's ideas in his historical research, to its detriment I think, he had an appre-ciative and accurate understanding of what Freud was about:

> He transcends the limitations of earlier psychological schools. The man whom he analyses is not a German, or an Englishman, a Russian, or a Jew—he is the universal man who is part of nature and part of society, the man whose desires and cravings, scruples and inhibitions, anxieties and predicaments are essentially the same no matter to what race, religion, or nation he belongs. From their viewpoint the Nazis were right when they coupled Freud's name with that of Marx and burned the books of both.[35]

I wish to correlate the theses of our sociohistorical culture critics with the position Freud created: the unique vantage point of the psychoana-lyst in the clinical situation. Psychoanalysts must be both empathic with and detached from their analysands. They stand with one foot in and one foot out of the emotional field or life space of the analysand in order to have an independent perspective. Psychoanalysts are intimately in-volved in the lives of patients and use their own responses and internal objects as tools of cognition, yet they are also outsiders who must main-tain appropriate boundaries and distance, sometimes connoted as clinical "neutrality," to help analysands gain their full autonomy.

III

When considering Freud's sociocultural identity, we are well advised to consider what he himself had to say about it. He often gave the subject of his Jewish identity candid and explicit attention, as when he describes his encounters with academic anti-Semitism in his autobiography:

When, in 1873, I first joined the University, I experienced some apprecia-
ble disappointments. Above all, I found that I was expected to feel myself
inferior and an alien because I was a Jew. I refused absolutely to do the
first of these things. I have never been able to see why I should feel
ashamed of my descent or, as people were beginning to say, of my "race."
I put up, without much regret, with my non-acceptance into the community; for it seemed to me that in spite of this exclusion an active
fellow-worker could not fail to find some nook or cranny in the framework
of humanity. These first impressions at the University, however, had one
consequence which was afterwards to prove important; for at an early age
I was made familiar with the fate of being in the Opposition and of being
put under the ban of the "compact majority" [the reference is to Henrik
Ibsen's *Enemy of the People*]. The foundations were thus laid for a certain
degree of independence of judgement.[36]

Freud was well aware of his own social marginality as a Jew in Europe,
and of the cultural marginality of psychoanalysis. This comes most clearly
to the fore in his correspondence with his disciple and colleague Karl
Abraham of Berlin. The letters often involve the *Realpolitik* of their infant
psychoanalytic movement. A crisis occurred with the impending de-
fection of Carl Gustav Jung from the psychoanalytic movement in 1908.
Freud pleaded with Abraham for forbearance:

> Please be tolerant and do not forget that it is really easier for you than it is
> for Jung to follow my ideas, for . . . you are closer to my intellectual con-
> stitution because of racial kinship, while he as a Christian and a pastor's
> son finds his way to me only against great inner resistances. His association
> with us is all the more valuable for that. I nearly said that it was only by
> his appearance on the scene that psycho-analysis escaped the danger of be-
> coming a Jewish national affair.[37]

Freud acknowledged to Abraham the structural affinity between
Talmudic reasoning and the logic of psychoanalytic explanation, and
shared his feelings of a special Jewish sensibility for psychoanalysis
as well as his resentment that being Jewish was held against him and
his ideas:

> After all, our Talmudic way of thinking cannot disappear just like that.
> Some days ago a small paragraph in *Jokes* strangely attracted me. When I
> looked at it more closely, I found that, in the technique of apposition and
> in its whole structure, it was completely Talmudic.[38]

> On the whole it is easier for us Jews, as we lack the mystical element.[39]

> I think that we as Jews, if we wish to join in, must develop a bit of
> masochism, be ready to suffer some wrong. Otherwise there is no hitting
> it off. Rest assured that, if my name were Oberhuber, in spite of everything
> my innovations would have met with far less resistance.[40]

When Freud considered the forces of resistance to psychoanalysis for
a French-Swiss Jewish journal, *La Revue Juive* of Geneva, he broached
the subject of the decisive role of his being Jewish:

Finally, with all reserve, the question may be raised whether the personality of the present writer as a Jew who has never sought to disguise the fact that he is a Jew may not have had a share in provoking the antipathy of his environment to psychoanalysis. An argument of this kind is not often uttered aloud. But we have unfortunately grown so suspicious that we cannot avoid thinking that this factor may not have been quite without its effect. Nor is it perhaps entirely a matter of chance that the first advocate of psycho-analysis was a Jew. To profess belief in this new theory called for a certain degree of readiness to accept a situation of solitary opposition—a situation with which no one is more familiar than a Jew.[41]

Freud's most forthright and articulate statement of his Jewish identity was in a message to the Jewish fraternal lodge B'nai Brith, which he had joined in 1895 and for many years regularly attended twice a month. This address alludes to his atheism, a conviction he was to argue at length in the ensuing year in *The Future of an Illusion*,[42] but also stresses his deep and firm commitment to values of Jewish culture:

What bound me to Jewry was (I am ashamed to admit) neither faith nor national pride, for I have always been an unbeliever and was brought up without any religion though not without a respect for what are called the "ethical" standards of human civilization. . . . But plenty of other things remained over to make the attraction of Jewry and Jews irresistible—many obscure emotional forces, which were the more powerful the less they could be expressed in words, as well as a clear consciousness of inner identity, the safe privacy of a common mental construction. And beyond this there was a perception that it was to my Jewish nature alone that I owed two characteristics that had become indispensable to me in the difficult course of my life. Because I was a Jew I found myself free from many prejudices which restricted others in the use of their intellect; and as a Jew I was prepared to join the Opposition and to do without agreement with the "compact majority."[43]

There are two great allegories for the understanding of Freud's identity and the essence of psychoanalysis, one pagan the other Judaic in origin. I think of the great pagan allegory of Aenaeas, who, as he leaves the burning Troy, returns to rescue his aged father by carrying him out on his back, and, leading his son by the hand, goes forth and founds Rome:

But now the fire roars across the walls; the tide of flame flows nearer. "Come then, dear father, mount upon my neck; I'll bear you on my shoulders. That is not too much for me. Whatever waits for us, we both shall share one danger, one salvation." . . . This said, I spread a tawny lion skin across my bent neck, over my broad shoulders, and then take up Anchises; small Iülus now clutches my right hand; his steps uneven, he is following his father; and my wife moves on behind.[44]

The other allegory is the aged Freud in what must have been one of the saddest moments of his life, when psychoanalysis had been destroyed in the Germanophone world and his family and followers were forced to flee into exile. He then derived strength from Jewish history and values of intellection, recalling in *Moses and Monotheism* the sacking of Jerusalem:

> The Jews retained their inclination to intellectual interests. The nation's political misfortune taught it to value at its true worth the one possession that remained to it—its literature. Immediately after the destruction of the Temple in Jerusalem by Titus, the Rabbi Jochanan ben Zakkai asked permission to open the first Torah school in Jabneh. From that time on, the Holy Writ and intellectual concern with it were what held the scattered people together.[45]

When in March 1938, Freud at last conceded that he had to escape Vienna as a refugee, he drew on this story of Jewish spiritual survival and said: "We are going to do the same. We are, after all, used to persecution by our history, tradition and some of us by personal experience."[46]

Freud taught us that we involuntarily carry the past in us whether we will it or not. Our choice is the extent we wish to be aware of our burdens and strengths from our personal and cultural past. For those of us who have learned from Freud, as we stand at the centenary of the birth of psychoanalysis and now face its second century, we may see portions of Freud's past living in his heritage as we realize it.

NOTES

1. Peter Gay, *Freud, Jews and Other Germans* (New York: Oxford University Press, 1978), p. 92.

2. Peter Gay, *Freud: A Life for Our Time* (New York: Norton, 1988), p. 10.

3. Peter Gay, *Reading Freud: Explorations and Entertainments* (New Haven: Yale University Press, 1990), pp. 61, 62–63.

4. William J. McGrath, *Dionysian Art and Populist Politics in Austria* (New Haven: Yale University Press, 1974), pp. 247–48.

5. Siegfried Bernfeld, "Freud's Earliest Theories and the School of Helmholz," *Psychoanalytic Quarterly* 13 (1944): 341–61; quotation, p. 349.

6. For the naming of the Freud children, see Gay, "Six Names in Search of an Interpretation," in *Reading Freud*, pp. 54–73.

7. Peter Loewenberg, "A Hidden Zionist Theme in Freud's 'My Son, the Myops . . .' Dream," *Journal of the History of Ideas* 31:1 (January–March 1970): 129–32.

8. Freud, *The Interpretation of Dreams* (1900), in *Standard Edition of the Complete Psychological Works of Sigmund Freud*, translated under the general editorship of James Strachey in collaboration with Anna Freud, assisted by Alix Strachey and Alan Tyson, 24 vols. (London: Hogarth Press, 1953–1975), 5:447–48 (hereafter cited as *S.E.*).

9. Peter Gay, *A Godless Jew: Freud, Atheism, and the Making of Psychoanalysis* (New Haven: Yale University Press, 1987), pp. 37, 41, 146–147. Professor Gay has suggested that in this sentence I do him an injustice (personal communication, 5 September 1994). I have re-examined his text and I believe my assessment of his position is accurate.

10. Marsha L. Rosenblit, *The Jews of Vienna, 1867–1914: Assimilation and Identity* (Albany: SUNY Press, 1983), p. 76.

11. Freud, *Jokes and Their Relation to the Unconscious* (1905), in *S.E.*, 8:111–12.

12. Carl E. Schorske, "Politics and Patricide in Freud's *Interpretation of Dreams*," in *Fin-de-Siècle Vienna: Politics and Culture* (New York: Knopf, 1980), pp. 189–93.

13. Freud, *Interpretation of Dreams*, in *S.E.*, 4:196–97.

14. See above, pp. 23–24.

15. Schorske, *Fin-de-Siècle Vienna*, pp. 181–207; William J. McGrath, *Freud's Discovery of Psychoanalysis: The Politics of Hysteria* (Ithaca: Cornell University Press, 1986).

16. Sander L. Gilman, *The Case of Sigmund Freud: Medicine and Identity at the Fin de Siècle* (Baltimore: Johns Hopkins University Press, 1993); Jerry V. Diller, *Freud's Jewish Identity: A Case Study in the Impact of Ethnicity* (Cranbury, N.J.: Associated University Presses, 1991); Lary Berkower, "The Enduring Effect of the Jewish Tradition upon Freud," *American Journal of Psychiatry* 125:8 (February 1969): 1067–73; Martin S. Bergmann, "Moses and the Evolution of Freud's Jewish Identity," *Israel Annals of Psychiatry and Related Disciplines* 14:1 (March 1976): 3–26, reprinted in Mortimer Ostow, *Judaism and Psychoanalysis* (New York: Ktav, 1982), pp. 115–42; David Bakan, *Sigmund Freud and the Jewish Mystical Tradition* (New York: Van Nostrand, 1958); Ernst Simon, "Sigmund Freud, the Jew," *Leo Baeck Institute Yearbook*, vol. 2 (London: East and West Library, 1957), pp. 270–305; Peter Loewenberg, "Sigmund Freud as a Jew: A Study in Ambivalence and Courage," *Journal of the History of the Behavioral Sciences* 7:4 (October 1971): 363–69; Emanuel Rice, *Freud and Moses: The Long Journey Home* (Albany: SUNY Press, 1990); Dennis B. Klein, *Jewish Origins of the Psychoanalytic Movement* (New York: Praeger, 1981); Leonard Shengold, "Freud and Joseph," in *Freud and His Self-Analysis*, ed. Mark Kanzer and Jules Glenn (New York: Jason Aronson, 1979), pp. 67–86; Robert S. Wistrich, "The Jewish Identity of Sigmund Freud," in *The Jews of Vienna in the Age of Franz Joseph* (Oxford: Oxford University Press, 1989), pp. 537–82, also "The Jewishness of Sigmund Freud," in *Between Redemption and Perdition: Modern Antisemitism and Jewish Identity* (London: Routledge, 1990), pp. 71–85.

17. Professor Yerushalmi informed me that I do not understand his view of Freud correctly (personal communication, 16 June 1994). In his book Yerushalmi finds "in Freud a sense of otherness vis-à-vis non-Jews which . . . seems to have been primal, inherited from his family and early milieu, and it remained with him throughout his life." In "Monologue with Freud" he postulates Freud's intention for psychoanalysis as "itself a further, if not final, metamorphosed extension of Judaism, divested of its illusory religious forms. . . . I think you believed that just as you are a godless Jew, psychoanalysis is a godless Judaism. But I don't think you intended us to know this." Yosef Hayim Yerushalmi, *Freud's Moses: Judaism Terminable and Interminable* (New Haven: Yale University Press, 1991), pp. 39, 99.

18. Kenneth A. Grigg, "All Roads Lead to Rome: The Role of the Nursemaid in Freud's Dreams," *Journal of the American Psychoanalytic Association* 21 (1973): 108–26; Paul C. Vitz, *Sigmund Freud's Christian Unconscious* (New York: Guilford, 1988); John Murray Cuddihy, *The Ordeal of Civility: Freud, Marx, Lévi-Strauss, and the Jewish Struggle with Modernity* (New York: Basic Books, 1974).

19. See the argument in chapter 2.

20. Bergmann, in Ostow, *Judaism and Psychoanalysis*, p. 116.

21. Ernest Jones, *The Life and Work of Sigmund Freud*, vol. 1 (New York: Basic Books, 1953), p. 19.

22. Ibid., p. 167; vol. 2 (1955), p. 17.

23. Everett V. Stonequist, *The Marginal Man: A Study in Personality and Culture Conflict* (New York: Scribner's 1937), pp. 154–55; see also the section "The Jews," pp. 76–82.

24. Ibid., p. 81.

25. The author of the letter was Dietrich Schaefer, a student of Treitschke's, quoted in Gay, *Freud, Jews and Other Germans*, p. 121.

26. Georg Simmel, "The Stranger" (1908), in *The Sociology of Georg Simmel*, trans. and ed. Kurt H. Wolff, (New York: Free Press, 1950), p. 402.

27. Ibid., p. 404.

28. Thorstein Veblen, "The Intellectual Pre-Eminence of Jews in Modern Europe," *Political Science Quarterly* 34 (March 1919), reprinted in Leon Ardzrooni, ed., *Essays in Our Changing Order* (New York: Viking, 1934), pp. 221–24 passim.

29. Ibid., pp. 225–26.

30. Ibid., pp. 226–27.

31. Isaac Deutscher, *The Non-Jewish Jew and Other Essays*, ed. Tamara Deutscher (London: Oxford University Press, 1968), p. 26.

32. Ibid., p. 35.

33. Ibid., p. 27.

34. Ibid., p. 30.

35. Ibid., pp. 34–35.

36. Freud, "An Autobiographical Study" (1925), in *S.E.*, 20:9.

37. Freud to Abraham, 3 May 1908, in *A Psycho-Analytic Dialogue: The Letters of Sigmund Freud and Karl Abraham*, ed. Hilda C. Abraham and Ernst L. Freud, trans. Bernard Marsh and Hilda C. Abraham (New York: Basic Books, 1965), p. 34.

38. Freud to Abraham, 11 May 1908, ibid., p. 36.

39. Freud to Abraham, 20 July 1908, ibid., p. 46.

40. Freud to Abraham, 23 July 1908, ibid., p. 46.

41. Freud, "The Resistances to Psycho-Analysis" (1925), in *S.E.*, 19:222.

42. *The Future of an Illusion* (1927), in *S.E.*, 21:3–56.

43. Freud, "Address to the Society of B'nai B'rith" (1926), in *S.E.*, 20: 273–74.

44. Virgil, *The Aeneid*, trans. Allen Mandelbaum (New York: Bantam Books, 1961), Book II, pp. 52–53, lines 954–59, 974–79, passim.

45. Freud, *Moses and Monotheism* (1939), in *S.E.*, 23:115.

46. Jones, *Freud*, 3 (1957): 221.

4

THE CREATION OF A SCIENTIFIC COMMUNITY: THE BURGHÖLZLI, 1902–1914

The best things come, as a general thing, from the talents that are members of a group; every man works better when he has companions working in same line, and yielding the stimulus of suggestion, comparison, emulation.

Henry James

The interplay between originality and the acceptance of tradition as the basis for inventiveness seems to me to be just one more example, and a very exciting one, of the interplay between separateness and union.

D. W. Winnicott

Cultural creativity is our most precious possession as a civilization. We need originality in ideas and techniques and wish to nourish it in our institutions. Creativity has been extensively studied in biography and often convincingly located in the development of individuals. But very few, if any, cases of creativity are in isolation. All creations are in a political, social, cultural, and group context. Every author writes for someone, in fantasy or reality, some first reader or first viewer or listener whose response matters. Creative artists, painters, and musicians all compose for an audience. Scientists research and publish with specific peers in mind. Creativity is a psychological function of real or fantasied groups. What makes a creative group?

Some creativity appears to take the form of clusters of gifted people who interact, cross-fertilize, and benefit from the group process, which is often institutionalized. Some of the twentieth-century institutions worthy of study and understanding because we still draw on their genius are the Enrico Fermi Group of nuclear physicists in Rome, 1925–1938, who did their Nobel Prize physics while working, living, and playing in close proximity to one another;[1] the Bauhaus at Weimar and Dessau, 1920–1933, where masters and students lived, worked, and celebrated together and where the modern "international school" of architecture was fashioned;[2] the founders of Cubism, Pablo Picasso and Georges Braque, who lived and worked with others in the Bateau-Lavoir in the Paris Montmartre;[3] groups of early expressionist artists such as the Blaue Reiter in Munich,[4] and Die Brücke in Dresden,[5] where the members lived together and exhibited their art collectively as a group product without signing their paintings; and the "Frankfurt School" of social science, whose sociological institute and psychoanalytic institute coexisted in one building—a working group that remained intact during emigration to Paris, New York, Berkeley, and back to the Frankfurt of the Federal Republic.[6]

We will examine closely a case of this kind of group creativity, seeking its structural preconditions, institutional wellsprings, and intergroup and interpersonal processes. In a Swiss mental hospital eighty years ago a group of mental health workers led by an eminent scientific personality revolutionized modern psychiatry, hospital management, and psychotherapy by applying psychodynamics to what had been the static and hopeless treatment methods for the emotionally crippled and mentally ill. We will look at the leadership, group process, and interpersonal and intrapsychic dynamics of this small coterie in Zurich, 1902–1914, as a case study of the social ecology that is a precondition of creative groups.

II

European psychiatry was stalemated at the turn of the century. It had developed nosological categories based on organic lesions, but the psychiatrist had nothing to offer in the way of therapy or hope. We may hear the message of despair from Emil Kraepelin himself:

> Along with our knowledge has come a lack of confidence in the efficacy of our medical practices. We know now that the fate of our patient is determined mainly by the development of the disease . . . we can rarely alter the course of the disease . . . our ability frequently to predict what will happen keeps us from falsely assuming . . . that our treatment will appreciably influence the outcome of the disease. . . . We must openly admit that the vast majority of the patients placed in our institutions . . . are forever lost.[7]

The Cantonal Psychiatric University Hospital and Clinic of Zurich, known as the Burghölzli, was a place of exciting intellectual ferment and discovery rarely matched in the history of scientific creativity during the decade prior to World War One. The hospital clinic was the scene of intense group interaction that attracted young people from abroad and permitted them to work in concert on a new project. It was the first public mental hospital where psychoanalysis was taught and practiced. Eugen Bleuler was the director, and the chief resident (*Oberarzt*) was C. G. Jung (1875–1961). Sigmund Freud wrote in 1914:

Nowhere else did such a compact little group of adherents exist or could a public clinic be placed at the service of psychoanalytic researches, or was there a clinical teacher who included psycho-analytic theories as an integral part of his psychiatric course. The Zurich group thus became the nucleus of the small band who were fighting for the recognition of analysis. The only opportunity of learning the new art and working at it in practice lay there. Most of my followers and co-workers at the present time came to me by way of Zurich, even those who were geographically much nearer to Vienna than to Switzerland. . . . Representatives of all the most important nations congregate in Switzerland, where intellectual activity is so lively. . . . [A] focus of infection there was bound to be of great importance for the spread of the "psychical epidemic," as Hoche of Freiburg has called it.[8]

Zurich became the world's leading psychoanalytic training and research center. Fritz Meerwein, who himself had been an assistant at the Burghölzli, delivered this historical evaluation:

In no other psychiatric clinic did the great strands of psychiatric history flow together in such fruitful hybrids and climaxes as at the Burghölzli. . . . The first scientific fertilization of psychiatry through the thought of Freud took place particularly at the Burghölzli and continues to be effective until today. . . . It is established that the Burghölzli at that time became an absolute center of clinical psychoanalytic research and therapy and that this "School of Zürich" won rapid international recognition.[9]

Well, he should have said this, for the leading theorists and clinicians who came to Freud out of the Burghölzli workshop included Karl Abraham (1884–1925) from Germany, who was assistant there from 1904 to 1907; Hermann Nunberg (1884–1970) and Gustav Bychowski (1895–1972) from Poland; Johan H. W. von Ophuijsen (1882–1950) from the Netherlands; Ludwig Binswanger (1881–1966), Franz Riklin (1878–1938), and Alphonse Maeder (1882–1971) from Switzerland; Sabina Spielrein (1886–1941) from Russia; Otto Gross (1877–1919) and Max Eitingon (1881–1943) from Austria; Abraham A. Brill (1874–1948) from the United States. Edouard Claparede (1873–1940) from Geneva and Ernest Jones (1879–1958) from England were also frequent visitors. This was a cluster of gifted mental health workers gathered at a time of a crisis of sterility and innovation such as has rarely existed in the history of science.

III

What was there in the cosmopolitan intellectual and cultural life, and in the sociopolitical context, of Zurich at this particular time that brought these people to this city and allowed them to be creative there? We will explore the composition and operation of this creative group from three perspectives: the political and cultural ambiance of Zurich, the scientific and institutional leadership of the Burghölzli, and the social, interpersonal, and psychodynamic group process.

The city of Zurich lies in a valley at the north end of a long lake cut by a glacier before it retreated to the high Alps. The city bestrides the bright green Limmat River, which flows north from the lake to join the Rhine. The gently rising hills and small plain on the left bank contain the bourgeois streets with exclusive watch and leather shops, banks, and confisceries, which has made Zurich synonymous with luxury and reliability. The right bank of the Limmat, the old city [*Altstadt*], rises through steep narrow streets filled with bohemian cafes, bookshops, theaters, and boutiques to the two great educational institutions of Zurich, the Swiss Federal Institute of Technology, Zurich (ETH), and Zurich University, which stand adjacent halfway up to the forest-topped mountain known as the Zurichberg.

Behind the right bank of the Limmat, a series of hills runs along the east margin of the city. There, about two miles south of the Zurichberg still on the right bank across the city on a hill of its own are the grounds of the Cantonal Psychiatric Hospital Burghölzli. The grounds include a parklike hilltop where the patients take walks and a hospital farm, including a working dairy, that stand in bucolic contrast to the now densely populated residential district of Switzerland's largest city.

Zurich was a small but rapidly growing city by European standards at the turn of the century. In 1897 it had 151,994 inhabitants; by 1905, 169,410.[10] A monument to Ulrich Zwingli stands in front of the Wasserkirche, the old Protestant church, to commemorate the reformer of Zurich who in 1519 kindled the German-Swiss Reformation and in 1531 went forth from the city to die in battle. Zurich in the early twentieth century was not only a center of the silk, textile, machine, and metal industries, it was also a cradle of revolutions in European science, culture, and politics. Its cultural and political climate before World War One made it a seedbed for the development of new ideas and divergent points of view in many fields. This was the cosmopolitan city that was hospitable to, and fostered the work of, writers like James Joyce, scientists such as Albert Einstein, and revolutionaries such as V. I. Lenin. In a Zurich cafe in 1916 Tristan Tzara invented the word *Dada*, seeking with his followers to scandalize opinion and shake up bourgeois lethargy. The manifestos of surrealism were drafted and proclaimed here.[11]

The right to political asylum was guaranteed by the Swiss Federal Constitution of 1848.[12] Among Russian revolutionaries, Herzen and Bakunin sought refuge in Switzerland; they were followed by Plekhanov, Axelrod, and Vera Zasulich. The leadership, bank accounts, and newspaper of the German Social Democratic Party fled to Zurich to escape persecution under Bismarck's antisocialist laws in the years 1878 to 1890. German socialist leaders, including Wilhelm Liebknecht, August Bebel, Eduard Bernstein, and Karl Kautsky, fled to Switzerland. The party newspaper, *Der Sozialdemokrat*, was legally published in Zurich. The first issue came off the press on 28 September 1879. It and successive issues were smuggled over the border and illegally distributed by the

Socialist "Red Postal Service" in Bismarck's Reich. The German socialist club had a good library, a reading room, and a lecture hall, where the
foundations of what would become the world's largest socialist party, the
prewar German SPD, were built. The German Social Democratic Party
held its congresses outside Germany, including in Wyden Castle,
Switzerland, in 1880 and St. Gallen, Switzerland, in 1887. Important
theoretical and administrative issues were settled in the party's Zurich
conference in 1882.[13] A historian of anarchism records that "Zurich was
in those years the only city with a German-speaking population where
anarchists could present their views without having to think of the
Damocles sword of possible persecution that always threatened their
comrades in Germany and Austria."[14]

No German university in the late 1860s allowed women the full
matriculation necessary for certification as physicians. The only German-
language university where the study of medicine by women was possible
was Zurich University, and in 1870 it admitted its first German female
matriculant.[15] The institution became a particular haven for Eastern
Europeans, Jews, and women, who were barred from securing higher
education in Russia. These students often were attracted to the most
militant oppositional ideology of their generation, Marxism. In May 1873
a Russian government decree ordered the 103 Russian women studying
in Zurich to return home. The decree accused the women of sexual immorality and political radicalism, asserting they had been "carried away
by communist theories of free love and under cover of fictitious marriage
[were pushing] their disregard for fundamental moral principles and of
feminine chastity to the extreme." Further, it charged the women medical students with the sin of sins, studying abortion: "Some of these girls
have fallen so deep that they are making a special study of that branch of
obstetrics which in all countries is punished by criminal law and despised
by honest people." Twenty-five of the women completed their studies
begun in Zurich; most by the classic mode of adapting to an autocratic
regime—they accommodated to the letter of the law by obtaining their
medical degrees from Bern, which was not declared off-limits by the
Czarist government.[16]

Those who made the long journey from Russian Poland to Zurich included Rosa Luxemburg, who came to enroll in the University of Zurich
in 1889 and stayed there until 1898. Luxemburg lived in rooms at Uni-
versitätsstrasse 79, on the hill above the handsome buildings of the
university and the ETH. She was proud of her rooms, which were comfortably furnished and cheap, and offered a view of the lake and the
forested mountains. In 1890 she enrolled in the faculty of philosophy
and took courses in the sciences and mathematics.[17] In 1892 she moved
to the law faculty and studied public law and political science under Professor Julius Wolf (1862–1937), whom she cited and attacked the rest of
her life. He considered her his outstanding pupil and was to write about
her in his autobiography:

Rosa Luxemburg was the most gifted of my students during my Zurich years, although she came to me from Poland and Russia as a completed Marxist. I gave her academic stirrups with her doctorate in government [*Staatswissenschaft*]. She wrote a first-rate dissertation about the industrial development of Poland.[18]

Many of the friendships she made in her early years in Switzerland remained with her all her life; so did her enmities—for example, with Georgi Plekhanov.

A Russian physician, N. E. Osipov (1877–1934), studied at the Burghölzli, and introduced psychoanalysis in Moscow. He became head of the university clinic in Moscow and there expounded Freud's ideas and those of the Zurich school. As early as 1908 he wrote the article "The Psychology of Complexes and Experiments in Association at the Zurich Clinic."[19]

Benito Mussolini, then a young revolutionary socialist, lived in Zurich and Bern in 1903–1904. Alexandra Kollontay, later to be the Soviet ambassador to Norway and Mexico, studied economics at the University of Zurich from 1898 to 1901. Karl Radek, a Pole who was to head the Comintern in Germany, worked in a library in Zurich.[20] V. I. Lenin lived in Zurich and preferred it to Bern because "there were a large number of revolutionary-minded young foreigners in Zurich." He also liked the libraries, especially their lack of bureaucracy, "no red tape, fine catalogues, open shelves and the exceptional interest taken in the reader." He saw the Swiss library system as a model for the future Soviet society. Yet, he did not like Switzerland, terming it "a country of health resorts."[21]

The Russian anarchist Peter Kropotkin also wrote of the life of the Russian emigré students in Zurich, their zeal and their yearning for a revolution at home:

The famous Oberstrass, near the Polytechnic was a corner of Russia, . . . the students lived as most Russian students do, especially the women; that is, upon very little. Tea and bread, some milk, and a thin slice of meat cooked over a spirit lamp, amidst animated discussions of the latest news from the socialistic world of the last book read,—that was their regular fare. Those who had more money than was needed for such a mode of living gave it for the common cause, the library, the Russian review which was going to be published, the support of the Swiss labor papers. As to their dress, the most parsimonious economy reigned in that direction. Pushkin has written in a well-known verse, "What hat may not suit a girl of sixteen?" Our girls at Zurich seemed defiantly to throw this question at the population of the Old Zwinglian city: "Can there be a simplicity in dress which does not become a girl, when she is young, intelligent, and full of energy?"With all this, the busy little community worked harder than any other students have ever worked since there were universities in existence, and the Zurich professors were never tired of showing the progress accomplished by the women at the university, as an example to the male students.[22]

Americans, too, were impressed by Switzerland. The social critic Henry Demarest Lloyd visited Switzerland twice, in 1901 and 1902, and found the answer to its culture in the freedom and decentralization of Swiss political institutions:

> Students of politics are generally agreed that Switzerland contains a larger variety of instructive experiments in political and economic democracy than any other living nation. Nowhere else has the direct personal participation of the body of citizens in acts of government been applied in so many different ways. . . . The direct participation of a simple citizen in acts of government, and the application of the federal principle, are the keynotes to Swiss democracy. . . . The only democracy in the world which cannot be betrayed is the Swiss.[23]

Florence Kelley, who became a leading social reformer and the first chief state factory inspector in the United States, enrolled in Zurich's Swiss Federal Institute of Technology (ETH) in 1883. She, too, admired Swiss political institutions, writing: "Swiss people were the freest in the whole range of civilization. It was their proud boast that they, like England and the United States, could admit the oppressed of all the earth." She describes student life:

> Zurich in those days was a small and simple city, with many steep and narrow streets, some of them beautifully curved, and lined with impressive remnants of old walls. There was abundant music, and a little repertory theater subsidized by the city. The forest, owned by the canton and maintained according to the highest standards of forestry then known, extended down from the top of the Zurichberg almost to the Polytechnicum. It was an enchanting forest with broad allees cut as fire safeguards, and between the endless rows of pines, wild flowers such as I had never seen. Here we students walked by the hour arguing in English, French or German. For me, conversation in Russian was a dead loss because I have never succeeded in learning the language.
>
> From the edge of the woods there was visible on every clear day a group of snowcaps, since, alas! concealed at that point by apartment houses, Zurich having become Switzerland's most important commercial center. Then, however, it was a joke among the polyglot students that the Russians were so busy with the future that they never knew whether the snowcaps were clear and lovely or shrouded in fog, any beauty that survived despite our modern capitalist civilization being unworthy their notice.[24]

Oskar Pfister (1873–1956) was the pastor of the Prediger Kirche in the center of the old city of Zurich and in 1908 first encountered Freud's work. Pfister applied psychoanalysis to his pastoral work and to education. He carried on a vigorous correspondence with Freud and published numerous books and papers on psychoanalytic technique, religion and hysteria, the psychology of art, philosophy and psychoanalysis, psychoanalysis in pastoral work, Christianity and anxiety, and on the role of sexuality in the etiology of the neuroses.[25] He replied to Freud's *The Future of an Illusion* with his own tract, *The Illusion of a Future*, in which he carried on a disputation with Freud in a scientific spirit and without rancor.[26]

IV

The ascendancy of the Burghölzli begins with the work of Auguste Forel (1848–1931). Forel was the initiator of what is known as the "Swiss Period" in the history of psychiatry. Coming from Morges on the Lake of Geneva in French Switzerland, he studied with Theodor Meynert in Vienna, in Munich, and with Bernheim and Liebeault in Nancy. Forel attained worldwide recognition but remained unheralded in his own home canton of Vaud. He was never given a psychiatric position in French Switzerland. Forel was a leading advocate of hypnosis and of alcoholic abstinence in psychiatry. In 1879 he became the director of the Burghölzli and professor of psychiatry in Zurich. Freud wrote a positive review of Forel's book on hypnotism in 1889.[27] Forel introduced Freud to Bernheim, and Freud visited the latter at Nancy in the summer of 1889. Adolf Meyer (1866–1950), who became the dean of American psychiatrists, was among Forel's students at the Burghölzli, as was Eugen Bleuler.[28]

Bleuler (1857–1939) was Switzerland's foremost psychiatrist in the early twentieth century. He was a son of a farm family in the town of Zollikon on the eastern shore of the Lake of Zurich. His father was a merchant. Growing up, he had a severely psychotic person, his catatonic sister, in his immediate environment,[29] which influenced his interest in medicine and psychiatry. Bleuler's son Manfred (1903–1994), who was also the director of the Burghölzli, from 1942 to 1969, lived on family land that belonged to his grandfather in Zollikon, which is no longer a farming community but part of the "gold coast" of fine suburbs along the lakeshore.[30]

The first professors of psychiatry in Zurich and directors of the Burghölzli hospital prior to Forel were all Germans. The farming population of the canton complained that these men spoke only High German and were not able to communicate with the patients in the Swiss German dialect. Bleuler wished to become a psychiatrist who would understand mental patients and be comprehended by them. He studied medicine in Zurich, serving his residency at the Waldau mental hospital in canton of Bern. He studied with the Charcot in Paris and became an assistant to Forel at the Burghölzli. At age twenty-nine, he was awarded the directorship of the asylum Rheinau, a small mental hospital in the canton of Zurich. In 1898 he became professor of psychiatry and director of the Burghölzli. His international reputation rests on his theory and description of schizophrenia, which he defined to replace the term *dementia praecox*, now no longer in use. Bleuler coined the term *depth psychology* (*Tiefenpsychologie*) for psychoanalysis as the psychology of the unconscious.[31]

The leader of the Burghölzli group, Bleuler attracted others to come to study in Zurich. Bleuler was unusually free of preconceptions. He was aware of the stalemate in which psychiatry found itself at the end of the nineteenth century and he sought new models of explanation for mental phenomena. He welcomed Freud's ideas and defended them against the virulent attacks launched particularly by the leaders of German psychiatry, Gustav Aschaffenburg, Alfred Hoche, Wilhelm Weygandt, and Max Isserlin.

Bleuler's major work is *Dementia Praecox or the Group of Schizophrenias* (1911), in which he defines the primary symptom of schizophrenia as looseness of associations, similar to what happens in dreams or daydreams. He views secondary schizophrenic symptoms as "splits" in the ego. He organized the symptoms into permanent or fundamental splits (*Spaltungen*) between various mental functions. The consequences of dissociation include autism—the loss of contact with reality, the split between feeling and intellect, and the inappropriateness of affect. He made determined efforts to understand the apparently incoherent "word-salad" of schizophrenics and their "absurd" delusions. In Bleuler's classification of the symptoms of schizophrenia, the famous four "A's" were (1) disturbance of associations, (2) affective indifference and inappropriateness, (3) autism, and (4) ambivalence, a term he coined and that Freud adopted as a "happy choice" of Bleuler's, and that has since come into a general usage for the description of opposing feelings of approximately equal strength.[32]

Bleuler's concept of schizophrenia included various acute conditions that had previously been considered disease entities of their own. This is more than a taxonomic quibble. Bleuler demonstrated that if patients with these acute syndromes, including melancholic, manic, and catatonic conditions, delusions, twilight states, stupors, deliria, and *Benommenheit* (clouded, abstracted, doped states of mental inertia), receive proper intensive care they have good chances of recovery. Alternatively, if they are neglected or improperly treated, they will evolve toward chronic schizophrenia. He introduced an optimistic approach that schizophrenia could be stopped or regressed at any phase of its evolution.

Bleuler strove to establish an emotional rapport (*affektiver Rapport*) with each patient. His teaching on the therapy of schizophrenia emphasized the creative intuition of the therapist, including breaking routine, sometimes surprise, and engagement of the patient in a human relationship. His therapeutic techniques included early hospital discharge, change of clinical environment, sudden and unexpected transfers of the patient to another ward, and assigning responsibility to the patient. He developed programs of occupational therapy in the hospital nursery, the farm, and a dairy, programs that still function today. Bleuler created a strong program of leisure-time activities for patients, including concerts, dances, lectures, and theater. Early in his career at the Burghölzli Secundärarzt C. G. Jung was in charge of the social program.

Bleuler's therapeutic principle was that a sound, strong personal relationship between staff and patient is requisite. He fostered a sense of human community and therapeutic socializing with patients. It was not unusual for patients to take meals with the doctors and to participate in the research projects. Dr. Manfred Bleuler, who grew up in the director's apartment on the first floor of the hospital, described how his father would go into the kitchen and prepare vegetables with patients, and how once he took a dangerous patient with him to the barn to chop wood. A door opened from the Bleuler dining room directly onto the women's ward. Staff members lived close to the patients, like a large family, and were available at all hours.[33] He recalls that patients from the turbulent ward were invited to a family afternoon coffee at a nicely set table.[34]

For Eugen Bleuler the symptoms of psychosis were always restitutive; there was hope for improvement. He encouraged flexibility in treatment and awareness of the role of what today we call countertransference:

> The manner in which each individual case is handled must be left to the physician. Consideration must be given, not only to the patient's personality but also to that of the physician himself. A method, which has proven valuable in the hands of one physician, may result in failure in the hands of another. The principal rule is that no patient must ever be completely given up, the doctor must always be prepared to take action, and to offer the patient the chance to abandon his pathological way of thinking.[35]

Bleuler devoted much time and detailed care to patient and staff welfare. If one had to be in mental hospital in the early twentieth century, the Burghölzli was a very good place to be, because the director was involved in every phase of the staff's efforts and the patient's welfare.

Bleuler conducted an extensive correspondence with the petty and precise Swiss cantonal bureaucracy concerning the details of patient comfort and care, such as in one case, getting a dress made for a patient. For instance, there are letters requesting authorization for a given doctor or staff person to take meals at the hospital. Such appeals were not perfunctory; the case for each meal had to be individually made. A sample letter from 1913 reads:

> To the high Sanitätsdirection, Zurich.
> Highly respected Mr. Regierungsrat!
> Our voluntary physician, Frau Dr. Morgenstern, conducts important researches in our laboratory, which have not only scientific, but also great practical significance. She lives with her family, but cannot leave her work at any time and therefore must now and then eat here. I now wish to respectfully request your permission that the meals which she takes here not be billed to her. We must be thankful for aid in these tasks for which we would not otherwise have the time.[36]

After World War One, Bleuler engaged also in extensive correspondence with the alien police (*Fremdenpolizei*) to forestall deportation of his foreign doctors. He had to demonstrate that no Swiss doctor was available for each position at issue. Sometimes he would have to organize a *démarche* by the officials of the *Gesundheitsdirektion* and the Alien Police of the Canton of Zurich to the federal officials in Bern in the doctor's behalf. For example, in June 1919, Dr. Wlassak, an Austrian national, was being ordered to leave Switzerland. Although for the previous six years he had been a cantonal official and *Privatdozent* at the Burghölzli, he was then working on an unsalaried basis and not even taking his meals at the hospital. Bleuler wrote:

> We can do no other than protest against such an action. We strongly urge you to join our protest to the responsible authorities. . . . We hope that the atrocity of this deportation does not occur. I will stand good for costs, including possible telegraphing to Bern.
> Should there be further steps which we can or must undertake, kindly advise us. One cannot allow such a case to stand unchallenged, even if a *fait accompli* has occurred.[37]

Small wonder that Bleuler asked for a one-month leave in the fall of 1914 and seven weeks in the fall of 1915 so he could write a psychiatric textbook. He appealed: "Such a work is simply impossible during the service as a director which often leaves me only a few usable hours during the entire semester."[38] Bleuler's creativity is remarkable in view of the burden of detail that he carried as an administrator.

Bleuler was supportive of psychoanalytic clinical methods and research while directing the hospital, teaching, and writing his synthesis of schizophrenia. He published an early defense of Freud and psychoanalysis in 1910, and systematically countered the prevailing attacks on psychoanalysis with verve and conviction. His answer to the criticisms of Freud's method was that they were not derived from actual experience with the psychoanalysis of patients and self. His work is still a pleasure to read for its astute and measured responses based on clinical evidence and particularly his self-analysis and personal life. He compared Freud's naysayers to those who had opposed Semmelweis without testing his theories. To say, as did Hoche, that a treatment is "impermissible for a physician" (*ärztich unerlaubt*) precludes judging the therapy and makes the critic incompetent to participate in the discussion. Bleuler writes as a convinced adherent of psychoanalysis, always using the collective "we" when making his case for it.

The complex and still-relevant issues of the psychoanalytic guild—its institutionalization as a closed group, its passion for a cause, the rigidity that comes from what Freud in another place called "a situation of solitary opposition,"[39] its ability to have scientific disputation without personal rupture or rejection—are raised and exposed in the Bleuler-Freud correspondence, which lasted from 1904 to 1937.

The correspondence began when Bleuler sent descriptions of several of his dreams to Freud, asking for help in interpreting them. Bleuler was convinced of the existence of the dynamic unconscious, of infantile sexuality, and that repressed sexuality is converted into anxiety. He conveys the excitement of discovery and the breaching of personal boundaries in the early years of psychoanalysis as he tells Freud how he encouraged the interpretation of his dreams to become a group enterprise at the Burghölzli:

> In one case I laid my dream before the Assistants and my wife. In my presence we got nowhere. Then I had to leave the room for a longer period and when I returned, they had laid out the dream, but so that it could in no way represent my thought: they had very clearly imposed the complexes of my wife who had taken the lead in the analysis. This was in the beginning. Such lapses no longer occur with us. According to our experience when an interpretation or a portion of one is clear, the dreamer according to our experience usually has the distinct feeling of rightness: "the explanation fits."

Bleuler was convinced by Freud's theory of the sexual etiology of neurosis and felt he could demonstrate it in himself: "I once experienced in myself the nucleus of a depression . . . which from beginning to end was ascribable to an ungratified sexual drive, with all the certainty which one may have from a single case."

When writing of his sexual drive being early and clear, Bleuler crossed out the word *mother* (*Mutter*), replacing it with *wife* (*Frau*). The excitement and curiosity about the newly discovered meaning of the psychology of slips is apparent when Bleuler notes: "The many errors and corrections in this letter are symptoms of a complex which I recognize in myself since I started writing with a typewriter close to a year ago."[40] Fortunately, Bleuler shared with Freud the texts of some of his dreams, asking for help in interpreting them: "I cannot crack these nuts. . . . I am turning to the master himself, naturally not in the hope that you will solve everything for me, but thinking of the possibility that by a hint you could show me the way by which I will find the solution."[41]

Bleuler's dreams grant us a direct view of the instinctual emphasis of dream interpretation during the first decade of psychoanalysis. His focus is on his sexual drives and impulses:

> *Revolver: Fredi* [Manfred] *inherited my early sexuality? The lady in gray is an Englishwoman, she also has a resemblance to an Englishwoman (American woman) who has sexually excited me, unconsciously when awake, later in dreams unconsciously. Later she was charged with having a sexual relationship with an orderly. Justifiably?? She appeals to me less and less. Recently I asked myself whether she has become older or stupider or both. (conscious: Negro). He had no feelings.*
>
> You may not publish this dream. I stand quite nakedly exposed before my doctors. They would recognize me immediately. Also my wife. I once interpreted a dream and afterwards it was false, even though everything fitted nicely. I discovered that the event which I interpreted only occurred after the dream. What am I now thinking when I believe I am thinking nothing? Revolver (external cause: itching at the critical spot = genitals, or is the itching a consequence?) Typing. No progress in interpretation. Revolver. Nannie. Englishwoman. Lady in gray. Miss S = the Englishwoman. Did I tell this to my wife? Sometimes I think I did, sometimes not. Revolver. I do not know how far I will get. Is it my revolver? Pocket = vagina. I do not

know whether it belongs to me or to her? Does the P. felt underneath the clothes have the meaning of a nannie? That is like an enlightenment. Why did it appear legitimate. Why me behind the Negro? I killed him; he had no feelings. Affects. I know of no specific situation where this occurred, but it is possible, I almost believe, that it happened. At this point I can go no further. Do I have too little power over the nannie because of this? I do not think so. Is Hardi (the younger) therefore displaced by Fredi (the elder), because I up to now have only feared for Fredi. Stalemate. What is the meaning of these stalemates? That something is correct? I thought that the lost boy was somewhere in a field, sugarcane field, dead or alive; however, in the dream I did not think that it was mine. Could the name of my boy not stand for any small boy? Then it would merely mean: "what have you done with the child?" Yes or no: "where is the child?" The form: what did you do with Fredi? already occurred to me earlier in place of the right thought, easier than the right thought. The attempt to move forward in this way may fail because I should write everything down, which is impossible. Thus I make the wrong choice.[42]

In taking up the argument of the sectarianism of psychoanalysis,[43] Bleuler said that although it may exist, and that the anti-Freudians also constitute a sect, sectarianism is no counterproof of the truth of an idea. He pointed to the personal psychological grounds and complexes that he was aware of in some of the opposition.

Many of the arguments Bleuler countered are still heard in polemics against psychoanalysis and psychotherapy today. For example, he cited Mendel (1910), who pleaded, "Do not rob us of our holy feelings, our love and honor for our parents, the joyful love of our children by dragging them in the filth of your fantasies through the constant pushing of disgusting sexual motives." Bleuler responds with the hope that such appeals will remain unheard in the forums of science. There are no aesthetic or ethical arguments against a truth in science; only facts and logic count. Those who cannot tolerate the truth should stay away from science; those who wish to engage in science cannot be concerned with what is holy or disgusting but, rather, must be singularly concerned with where the truth lies. It should be clear, suggested Bleuler, which side is offering religion and which side science. The heaviest attacks against Freud were directed at his view of the role of sexuality in human life and emotions. In that connection Bleuler responded: "He who has no sexual drive is a cripple [*wer keinen Sexualtrieb hat, ist ein Krüppel*]. It is no disgrace to have a sexual drive."[44] He relates his personal experience with schizophrenics, which validated Freud and greatly surprised Bleuler: of the hundreds of patients whom they had analyzed at the Burghölzli, not a single one was without a sexual complex.[45]

Bleuler made the same point about Freud's concept of infantile sexuality: "He who does not see infantile sexuality is simply blind to an everyday occurrence." He was most candid in drawing on his own unconscious and life experience. In this he was following Freud's example of subjective self-revelation as a criterion of conviction in the mental sciences. He told of the special pleasure of the child in touching the other sex, especially when naked, and in love relationships that do not end in coitus but that in other respects are in no way different from young love. There is a very special tone in the interest in the genitalia of the other sex. After defining the phenomenology of childhood sexuality, Bleuler drew on his own experience: "Those who can observe children know this, and those who can recall their own youth know this as well. I have the absolute certain memory of sexual feelings from the fourth year on. I entered school at six years; all 62 classmates, male and female, were in this respect the same."[46]

Bleuler showed his capacity for biting irony when he presented the Oedipus complex:

> It is of course the summit of unintelligibility, of lack of piety, the disgusting product of a debauched fantasy. . . . But this oedipus complex exists despite this strong scientific contrary evidence, and in fact it is found, if one looks for it, with such regularity, that the assumption that it is the property of all humans who are raised by parents of the opposite sex is most likely correct.
>
> As I first read about it, I had exactly the same feelings as most of our critics. Eventually—over about four years—I have demonstrated it in myself in a very crude form, and in fact from indications from my puberty, that is to say evidence that dates long before Freud's publication.[47]

Bleuler discussed his dreams, which he had not been able to interpret prior to the concept of the Oedipus complex. He brings evidence from his object choice in marriage and from his family life and children:

> I consciously discovered important similarities between my wife and my mother long after my marriage, but before I knew my oedipus complex. Such similarities in her were also independently noted by other people who know nothing of Freud. And in the, to be sure, rare dreams in which my wife briefly appears, she is usually condensed with my mother. (She is 12 years younger than I am.) I have observed the oedipus complex from the first year (inclusive) in my older son and my daughter with absolute certainty.[48]

Bleuler's arguments were often sophisticated. To the critics of psychoanalytic symbol interpretation, he pointed out "that the Freudian meanings are essentially supplied by the patients themselves, that they are related to the symptoms through many connections, and also in that to a certain degree they represent the same types from patient to patient."[49] He stressed the importance of having full command of the method in order to test it. He told of his experiments in dream interpretation with his own dreams and artificially constructed dreams.

Bleuler showed an early keen awareness of the importance of listening to the patient's body language, to what decades later Wilhelm Reich would term "character armor":

> With a sick person even more frequently than a healthy person words are merely a matter of indifference which are used on grounds of convenience,

whereas that which the patient expresses—I am consciously not saying: "that which the patient wishes to express"—is by his tone of voice, body movements and all which is related to them. The same answer which the patient gives in words, he may also give in grunts, a shrugging of shoulders, or rapid breathing; such expressions are often precisely the critical ones; whether words accompany them or not is entirely irrelevant.[50]

V

Carl Gustav Jung soon became the spokesman and leader of the psychoanalytic group at the Burghölzli. He became Freud's designated heir as leader of the psychoanalytic movement. Jung had become an assistant at the Burghölzli in 1900.[51] He was a son of the city of Basel, the descendant of Protestant ministers and professors. Of his move, he said:

> I was glad to be in Zurich, for in the course of the years Basel had become too stuffy for me. . . . When I came to Zurich I felt the difference at once. Zurich relates to the world not by intellect, but by commerce. Yet here the air was free, and I had always valued that. Here you were not weighed down by the brown fog of centuries.[52]

Jung was an assistant to Bleuler from 1901 to 1905. He then became *Oberarzt* at the Burghölzli and with his family moved into the apartment above Bleuler on the third floor of the main building, where they lived until 1909.

Jung broke many lances in vituperative professional debates on behalf of psychoanalysis. He defended Freud's theory of hysteria in a reply to Gustav Aschaffenburg published in November 1906. Jung was consistently psychoanalytic, particularly on the role and importance of sexuality—the very issue on which he would later break with Freud. Here he called sexuality "an essential component of the psyche":

> We know only that one meets sexuality everywhere. Is there any other psychic factor, any other basic drive except hunger and its derivatives, that has a similar importance in human psychology? I could not name one. It stands to reason that such a large and weighty component of the psyche must give rise to a correspondingly large number of emotional conflicts and affective disturbances and a glance at real life teaches us nothing to the contrary.[53]

Jung met squarely Aschaffenburg's charges of psychoanalytic "immorality" in dealing with sexual fantasies. He responded: "Whenever morals get mixed up with science one can only pit one belief against another belief . . . there are at least a great many cases where discussion of sexual matters not only does no harm but is positively helpful."[54]

In that same month, November 1906, Jung had a confrontation with Alfred Hoche at a congress of South-West German psychiatrists in Tübingen. Jung and Aschaffenburg had a further "duel" at the First International Congress of Psychiatry and Neurology in Amsterdam in September 1907.[55]

During these years Jung conducted his famous association experiments that provided empirical confirmation of the theory underlying Freud's method of free association.[56] This was Jung's most important scientific contribution to psychoanalysis. In work with his colleague and cousin Franz Riklin,

> complexes of ideas referred to as emotionally charged are shown up in the experiment by characteristic disturbances, and their presence and quality can be inferred precisely from these disturbances. . . . With the association experiment we always combine a second, which we call the reproduction test. This test consists in making the subject state how he responded to each stimulus word in the first test. Where memory fails we usually find a constellation through a complex. The reproduction technique also allows a more detailed description of the complex disturbances.[57]

After 1909 Jung broke with Bleuler, which casts Jung's break with Freud in 1911–1912 in a new light. What we see is a two-phase process of rupture toward autonomy. First Jung turned on Bleuler while acting as Freud's disciple, then he severed his relationship with Freud. All the while Bleuler and Freud maintained their relationship of scientific respect while disagreeing on the political aspects of the psychoanalytic movement. Although we have known about the Jung break with Freud in detail since the publication of their correspondence in 1974, historians have known virtually nothing about Jung's relationship with Bleuler. It has been shrouded in secrecy and deleted from Jung's autobiography and letters. As Henri Ellenberger perceptively pointed out, "It is extraordinary that in his autobiography the name of Bleuler is not mentioned once."[58] However, when we look at Jung's references to the Burghölzli, we see all the feelings toward Bleuler displaced to the institution:

> With my work at Burghölzli, life took on an undivided reality—all intention, consciousness, duty, and responsibility. It was an entry into the monastery of the world, a submission to the vow to believe only in what was probable, average, commonplace, barren of meaning, to renounce everything strange and significant, and reduce anything extraordinary to the banal. Henceforth there were only surfaces that hid nothing, only beginnings without continuations, accidents without coherence, knowledge that shrank to ever smaller circles, failures that claimed to be problems, oppressively narrow horizons, and the unending desert of routine. For six months I locked myself within the monastic walls in order to get accustomed to the life and spirit of the asylum, and I read through the fifty volumes of the *Allgemeine Zeitschrift für Psychiatrie* from its very beginnings, in order to acquaint myself with the psychiatric mentality.[59]

Jung's unpublished correspondence is revealing on this score because it is so vituperative about Bleuler; these passages and letters were excised from the published Jung correspondence. For example, this letter from 1911 to Alphonse Maeder:

Naturally the affair with [Hans W.] Maier was only a facade. . . . There is no trace of good will behind this, only poison [*Gift*]. My personal affect is based on the fact that the resistances in the main are directed against me. Bleuler unmistakably demonstrated this to me. All of us, Freud, Binswanger, Riklin, you and I have tried to handle the affair cleanly. None of us succeeded, instead the carriage was shoved deeper into the dirt because he wants it in the dirt. So nothing will help. We will have to separate from the Burghölzli.[60]

During this time of Jung's relationship with his former patient Sabina Spielrein, Jung wrote to the American psychoanalyst Trignant Burrow about a colleague named Honegger who had committed suicide. According to Jung, Honegger cut off his fiancée, fell in love with a woman patient, broke with Jung, grew conscious of his awful mistake, and committed suicide. Jung also refers to "my former father Bleuler" in this letter of 1911.[61] In that year, we can also find early reference to Jung's fundamental difference with Freud on sexuality despite due recognition of Freud's mentorship: "After all and in spite of the views of our master even, I still believe that it is not necessary to hurt through extravagant sexual speech, as many men of the Vienna school like to do."[62]

At the end of 1911 Jung wrote to his colleague Alphonse Maeder: "I must balance Bleuler's influence, who of course wishes to dilute it. We are, however, not bound to the Burghölzli if they do all they can there to allow psychoanalysis to die out."[63] The Swiss Psychoanalytic Society under Jung left the Burghölzli, although Bleuler continued to teach psychoanalysis in the institution. Within a year Jung and Freud were in the midst of their split, in which Jung left the psychoanalytic movement to found his own movement and institutions.

The controversies over admission to psychoanalytic societies, and what kinds of higher academic degrees should be prerequisites for membership—with which we are so familiar today—began early in the psychoanalytic movement. In 1910 Jung and Sándor Ferenczi exchanged information about psychoanalytic courses and seminars they were teaching in Zurich, Vienna, and Budapest. Jung wished to limit membership in the International Psychoanalytic Association to those with a higher academic graduate degree, as had already been done in Zurich. This, he said, gave the Zurichers good grounds for keeping out patients and students. However, after correspondence with Freud, Jung conceded that such a restriction to university graduates would not work for the International. In Zurich the public was now for the first time warming up to psychoanalysis. Jung was already sowing distrust against the Viennese when he wrote to Ferenczi that

the Viennese have brought us to a fine fix pursuant to the *Correspondence Letter of the International Association*. They publish their meeting reports and literature twice—once in the *Correspondence Letter* and again in the *Central Journal*—so as to be a double publication and to rob the *Letter* of its importance and to make it completely purposeless. We should have forthrightly said at the Nuremberg Congress that if we are founding a central journal then the *Correspondence Letter* should be shut down.[64]

Jung presented his theoretical and clinical differences with Freud to an international medical congress in London in 1913. Speaking in English and as a representative of international psychoanalysis, he outlined the Freudian theory of the infantile etiology of neurosis, urging his audience to become personally acquainted with the fundamental works on psychoanalysis, then available only in German. He stated that Freud's theory, although worked out in great detail, was neither very clear nor easily accessible. He reviewed Freud's actual trauma theory of hysteria of 1895: that hysteria and the related neuroses have their origin in a sexual trauma of early childhood. While tracing the shift to Freud's later sexual fantasy theory, Jung used the unfortunate term that the patient "invented" the story of a "so called trauma," suggesting it was a conscious lie. He referred to manifestations of these fantasies in "early bad habits," which Freud called "infantile sexual perversities." Jung did not use the term *masturbation*.

Jung explicated the Freudian theory of phase specificity of the neuroses according to the stage of infantile development in which the fixation took place and discounted the theory because he had often personally proved that the infantile fantasies exist in normal people as well. He posed the question, Why does the infantile neurotic conflict break out at a given moment in time?

> I ask what the necessary task is which the patient will not accomplish. The whole list of his infantile fantasies does not give me any sufficient etiological explanation since I know that the phantasies are only puffed up through the regressive libido, which has not found its natural outlet into a new form of adjustment to the demands of life.
>   You may ask why the neurotic has a special inclination not to accomplish his necessary tasks. Here let me point out that no living being adjusts itself easily and smoothly to new conditions.[65]

In this 1913 paper Jung appears as a forerunner of modern psychoanalytic ego psychology with its emphasis on the presenting life crisis, adaptation and adjustment, and the potential for regression in a crisis situation. His position was neither mystical nor racial. There is much in it that would be entirely acceptable to modern psychoanalytic clinicians, such as attention to the time specificity of the onset of symptoms: "The moment of the outbreak of the disease is by no means indifferent; as a rule it is most critical. It is usually the moment where a new psychological adjustment, a new adaptation is demanded. Such moments are favorable occasions for the outbreak of neurosis."[66] We note Jung's focus on adjustment and adaptation a quarter of a century prior to Anna Freud (1936) and Heinz Hartmann (1939). A question therefore arises: Was the rupture with international Freudian psychoanalysis theoretically necessary? I believe the break was largely due to interpersonal dynamics and minimally due to differences in theory. If the emotional situation had permitted the psychoanalytic movement of 1913 to assimilate Jung's ego psychology of that time, Heinz Hartmann, Ernst Kris, Rudolph Loewenstein, David Rapaport, and George Klein would not have had to go through the strenuous efforts to open psychoanalytic theory to ego psychology and adaptation a quarter of a century later. To the extent that the contribution of Freud to modern culture includes the object-relational insight that individuals make their own outer worlds to conform to inner fantasies, Jung in 1913 was a precursor of object-relations theory and of ego psychology.

VI

The social organization of the hospital was a critical precondition to making creativity possible. When we examine the living and working situation of the director, the *Oberarzt*, the assistants, and the staff, we see that informal networks and relationships were vital in making the Burghölzli a great research institution and clinical hospital. The setting, the hospital farm, the apartments, assistants' rooms, club rooms, and wards were specific institutional structures that promoted intense interaction and creativity. The medical director and his family lived on the first floor of the main building. The women's ward was immediately outside Bleuler's apartment. The *Oberarzt* and his family lived on the second floor. Doctors and patients mixed socially, were often invited to meals and coffee privately. The staff interacted psychoanalytically, analyzing one another's dreams routinely at mealtimes and in study groups that met at the hospital. A group process existed that is accountable for the spirit and mutual creativity of those who worked in the institution. This process invites an exploration of the issues of group conflict, competitiveness, and their resolution in this setting.

Among the most important accounts is that of Ludwig Binswanger, who was a young doctor at the Burghölzli in 1906:

> Eugen Bleuler had already in the clinical semesters aroused my admiration for his personality and developed my "inherited" love for psychiatry to the utmost. . . . I still see him before me always jotting notes on little slips of paper which he pulled from his vest pocket. Karl Abraham, my predecessor on the Men's Ward, was personally somewhat reserved, however his high intelligence and his sensitive, often ironic nature exerted an important influence on his younger colleagues. . . . C. G. Jung, the Chief Resident Physician of the clinic, with whom I wanted to do my doctorate, was a real fiery spirit who took his student's breath away with his temperament and the wealth of his ideas. . . . He supported me, not only with his counsel and his knowledge, but also through his participation as an experimental subject. If I reckon the year at the Burghölzli as by far the most pivotal year of my psychiatric education, it is because the Burghölzli already then (1906) stood in the center, in fact was carried by the intellectual movement that stemmed from Vienna and bore the name psychoanalysis and whose origins went back to a single name, that of Sigmund Freud.[67]

Binswanger was delighted to be invited by Jung to accompany him and his wife on their first visit to Freud in Vienna in February 1907.

Under Bleuler, the Burghölzli made a conscious effort not to be inbred in its personnel policy. Both by comparison to other university clinics such as Vienna, Munich, and Berlin before World War One, and longitudinally to the present, the Burghölzli was open to foreign doctors, including appointments as assistants for such non-Swiss as Karl Abraham from Germany and A. A. Brill from the United States in the 1902–1912 period. Currently, by contrast, of thirty house physicians at the Burghölzli, twenty-nine are Swiss, and only one, a German, is a foreigner.

An example of Bleuler's tolerant nonparochial attitude was his letter to the Health Ministry nominating Abraham of Berlin for a residency at the Burghölzli in 1904. He wrote:

> As you will recall, Dr. Abraham is very well recommended by his chief and he has had many years of independent psychiatric experience at the institution in Dalldorf. He wishes to come here because his race prevents his advancement. I hope that we treat this with contempt; as to the North German idiom, it is a shortcoming which should not weigh too heavily. A little freshening up through new ideas is good for every institution, above all for a clinic. An excellent foreigner is to be preferred to a slipshod native under any circumstances.[68]

These were exciting times in psychiatry. Abraham wrote to Freud in 1907: "In Zurich I have breathed freely. No clinic in Germany could have offered me a fraction of what I have found here. . . . No less than twenty doctors appeared at the second meeting of our 'Freudian Association' here; some came quite a long distance from hospitals in the country."[69] Ernest Jones describes one of these meetings:

> It was well attended, and even von Monakow, the distinguished Professor of Neurology at the University of Zurich, had climbed the mountain on a winter's evening to participate eagerly in a discussion on the symbolism of dreams. They were amused when I remarked that if only his respectable colleagues knew about it they would say he might as well climb the Brocken to attend a Witches' Sabbath.[70]

A. A. Brill of New York, who took Abraham's place as an assistant to Bleuler at the Burghölzli in 1907 wrote over thirty years later:

> It would be impossible to describe how I felt when I entered the ranks of this enthusiastic group, I repeat what I have often stated in the past— namely, that no such group of psychiatric workers ever existed before or since. Under the benevolent but penetrating eye of our "Herr Direktor" all of us worked zealously and assiduously.[71]

Brill describes his enthusiasm on his first contact with the Burghölzli:

> After attending the first staff meeting, I felt inspired. The way they looked at the patient, the way they examined him, was almost like a revelation. They did not simply classify the patient. They took his hallucinations, one by one, and tried to determine what each meant, and just why the patient

had these particular delusions. In other words, instead of registering phenomenon, they went into the dynamic elements which produce those phenomena. To me, that was altogether new and revealing.[72]

Bleuler always greeted newly appointed residents personally and carried their suitcases to the residents' rooms. He was the personification of work and duty, exacting toward himself and his staff.

Bleuler displayed an unlimited devotion to the patients. The first rounds on the wards before the daily staff meeting took place at 8:30 A.M., when the residents reported on their patients. Two or three times a week at 10:00 A.M. a staff meeting was directed by Bleuler, at which there was a common discussion about the case histories of new patients. He made short visits to the wards four to six times daily. Evening rounds were between 5:00 and 7:00 P.M. There were no secretaries; residents wrote up their own case histories, often working until 11:00 P.M. Hospital doors were closed at ten o'clock. A junior resident who planned to be away and then return after that hour would have to borrow a key from a senior resident.

Alphonse Maeder recounted the atmosphere of his residency at the Burghölzli:

> The patient was the focus of interest. The student learned how to talk with him. Burghölzli was in that time a kind of factory where you worked very much and were poorly paid. Everyone from the professor to the young resident was totally absorbed by his work. Abstinence from alcoholic drinks was imposed on everyone. Bleuler was kind to all and never played the role of the chief.[73]

Jakob Wyrsch reported on the relationship of the residents to the director:

> Bleuler never blamed a resident. If something had not been done, he would just inquire about the reasons for the omission. There was nothing dictatorial in him. He often came to the residents' room after lunch and took coffee with them. Then he would ask about new developments in medicine or surgery, not to test the knowledge of the residents, but just to keep himself informed.[74]

Brill described the intensity of the group process:

> In the hospital the spirit of Freud hovered over everything. Our conversation at meals was frequently punctuated with the word "complex," the special meaning of which was created at that time. No one could make a slip of any kind without immediately being called on to evoke free associations to explain it. It did not matter that women were present—wives and female voluntary internees—who might have curbed the frankness usually produced by free associations. The women were just as keen to discover the concealed mechanisms as their husbands.[75]

The ordeal of having every slip scrutinized sounds as though it was often unpleasant, amounting to constant confrontation. To make the social pleasures of everyday life, such as mealtimes, into an analytic marathon, must often have been downright obnoxious. Thus Brill:

> We observed and studied and noted whatever was done or said about us with unfailing patience and untiring interest and zeal. We made no scruples, for instance, of asking a man at the table why he did not use his spoon in the proper way, or why he did such and such a thing in such and such a manner. It was impossible for one to show any degree of hesitation or make some abrupt pause in speaking without being at once called to account. We had to keep ourselves well in hand, ever ready and alert, for there was no telling when and where there would be a new attack. We had to explain why we whistled or hummed some particular tune or why we made some slip in talking or some mistake in writing. But we were glad to do this if for no other reason than to learn to face the truth.[76]

Philip Rieff noted Brill's military simile of functioning amidst constant unanticipated "attacks": "The warfare of the Freudians among themselves was not entirely for the sake of truth, I suspect. Aggression appears even among professional students of aggression."[77]

An important variable when looking at a creative group is how its members handle competitiveness, rivalry, and envious feelings. A feature of the leadership of Eugen Bleuler at the Burghölzli is that he made it possible for his subordinates and coworkers to become scientific and group leaders. He was neither jealous of nor competitive with his colleagues. Bleuler allowed a role differentiation, a split between the psychoanalytic scientific leadership and his administrative control of the institution.[78] He permitted subordinates, such as his clinical director and chief resident physician (*Oberarzt*) C. G. Jung, to take the lead in a weekly psychoanalytic discussion group, pursue their own research, and develop their scientific ideas freely.

VII

The atmosphere of excitement and collaboration at the Burghölzli began to fall apart with Jung's departure in 1909. He went into private practice, withdrew from the institution, and—hard as it may be for us to appreciate now—took an absolutist stance in championing psychoanalysis. Either one accepted all of it and was willing to go to the wall for it, or one was an enemy.

Jung's posture alienated Bleuler, who had withdrawn from the Swiss Psychoanalytic Society by 1910 and carried on a searching dialogue with Freud on the issues of totalism and relativism that plagued the early psychoanalytic movement, and still plague it today.

Bleuler was publishing psychoanalytically and was pleased when Freud approved of his work:

> I am very happy that you found my "Sexuality of Children"—for which I had not enough time—not too amateurish. I was somewhat surprised that you saw in this a great change in my views since 1905. It is true that since

then some things became clearer to me and I succeeded to assimilate your views. Essentially, however, my views are the same as at that time. The only change of which I am conscious is that I now consider anal eroticism a fact, while in those days I had no understanding for it.[79]

Bleuler's respect for Freud and his sense of excitement at a rapidly developing field are expressed in a letter of December 1909:

> Many thanks for your "Notes Upon a Case of Obsessional Neurosis." [This was presumably the "Rat-Man" case but Bleuler referred to it as *Alltagsleben & die Zwangsgedanken*.] It is a real task to digest it. Your views have developed so fast that it is difficult for me to follow them. I will, however, spare no effort. The great difficulty consists in that I seldom see such cases and when I have an opportunity to see one I have no time to analyze the case. I had, however, succeeded in many respects to limp along behind you and to hope that my weak legs this time too will allow me to reach the goal.[80]

Bleuler refused to join the newly formed International Psychoanalytical Association. Freud sought to retain his adherence to the organized psychoanalytic movement by pointing out that Bleuler's withdrawal from the Swiss Psychoanalytic Society was fueling the opposition:

> If it is your intention—which would be proper because of your official position, your personal relations and your wisdom—to preserve the bridge of communication between psychoanalysis and academic psychiatry, then with your absence from the society and its yearly meetings and with your withdrawal from active participation you achieve just the opposite of what you want to achieve. The intransigent attitude (within the Psychoanalytic Society) will gain the upper hand and the relationships to our opponents will deteriorate. Of course, should you not want to change your attitude, we shall have to go ahead without you, but this will not help our cause, and your withdrawal will render our opponents the advantage of making the caricature they draw of the psychoanalytic movement more believable.[81]

Freud was even willing to let Bleuler shape the psychoanalytic movement's "foreign policies" in order to secure his allegiance. He saw Bleuler as the potential channel to acceptance by academic psychiatry and did not like the policy of sectarian isolation for psychoanalysis. He also had a high respect for Bleuler's scientific work:

> I make you then a concrete proposition: Please let me know what changes you want to have in the Association to make it acceptable to you, and what modifications of our foreign policies toward our opponents you consider as correct. I personally will try and will use my influence upon others to give the greatest possible consideration to your wishes and ideas and thus make it possible for you to implement them.[82]

Bleuler explained his reluctance to join the movement in a candid and tempered letter that pointed out the difference between a "cause" to its founder and a relativized scientific view:

> The greater one evaluates the significance of the cause one supports, the more one can accept the disadvantages. I know from my own experience,

as well as from experiences of others, that I would only do harm and would not help should I participate in a fashion which is against my feelings. I can't simply go along; it is expected from me that I cooperate. There would be always a false note in my speeches and writings, which would harm the cause and would unavoidably paralyze me. There is a difference between us, which I decided I shall point out to you, although I am afraid that it will make it emotionally more difficult for you to come to an agreement. For you evidently it became the aim and interest of your whole life to establish firmly your theory and to secure its acceptance. I certainly do not underestimate your work. One compares it with that of Darwin, Copernicus and Semmelweis.

I believe too that for psychology your discoveries are equally fundamental as the theories of those men are for other branches of science, no matter whether or not one evaluates advancements in psychology as highly as those in other sciences. The latter is a matter of subjective opinion. For me, the theory is only one new truth among other truths. I stand up for . . . [psychoanalysis] because I consider it valid and because I feel that I am able to judge it since I am working in a related field. But for me it is not a major issue, whether the validity of these views will be recognized a few years sooner or later. I am therefore less tempted than you to sacrifice my whole personality for the advancement of the cause.[83]

Jung's successor as Bleuler's *Oberarzt* at the Burghölzli, Hans W. Maier, was asked to resign from the Swiss Psychoanalytic Society because Jung said he "stole" from psychoanalysis without identifying with it. He came to the meetings of the society, but Jung said:

> I am fed up with Maier's posturing. He steals me blind and plumes himself with feathers which he gathers as our guest. He must decide whether he will join us or not. If he does not join us, then he is absolutely superfluous in our meetings. The choice of another meeting place [not the Burghölzli] should also be seriously considered if Maier should not join.[84]

Jung was enforcing a closed-door policy that admitted only members to the group's scientific discussions. Bleuler's reply to Freud put the case for an open-door policy and pointed out the scientific and pragmatic costs of the policy Jung was pursuing:

> "Who is not with us is against us", the principle "all or nothing" is necessary for religious sects and for political parties. I can understand such a policy, but for science I consider it harmful. There is no ultimate truth. From a complex of notions one person will accept one detail, another person another detail. The partial notions, A and B, do not necessarily determine each other. I do not see that in science if someone accepts A, he must necessarily swear also for B. I recognize in science neither open nor closed doors, but no doors, no barriers at all. For me, Maier's position is as valid or invalid as of anyone. You say he wanted only the advantages of [of being a member], but wanted to make no sacrifice. I cannot understand what kind of sacrifice he should have made, except to sacrifice one part of his views. You would not demand this from anyone. Everyone should accept views only as far as they are his own views; if he accepts more he is insincere; you are, of course, of the same opinion.

I do not believe that the Association is served by such intransigence. This is not a "Weltanschauung." . . . You think my resignation from the Society will harm psychoanalysis more than my joining helped in the past. So far as I can see, I am the only one who loses.

As I told you before, my joining did not help at all and I can with some justification foretell that my resignation will do no harm either. Psychoanalysis as a science will prove its value with me or without me, because it contains a great many truths and because it is led by persons like you and Jung.

The introduction of the "closed door" policy [however], scared away a great many friends and made of some of them emotional opponents. My joining did not change that in the least, and neither will my resignation change this fact. Your accusation that I should have considered the harm I am causing the society by my resignation seems to me, therefore, not valid.

He [Jung] believed in closed doors, while I considered it wrong; he considered this principle as vital for psychoanalysis; it was, therefore, his obligation to get rid of me. I cannot blame him for this no matter how painful his hostile attitude towards me is. At present nothing can be done about this. One can beg for money, but not for love. I would be most happy if this situation would ever change. We [Bleuler and Freud] could, however—although not in the psychoanalytic society—collaborate scientifically as we did until last Christmas. I wish that the future will justify the prevailing policy to have closed doors, although this time I cannot believe in this wish of mine.[85]

Two and a half years later Bleuler defined psychoanalysis as a humanity and Freud as an artist whom he admires as a discoverer:

Scientifically I still do not understand why for you it is so important that the whole edifice [of psychoanalysis] should be accepted. But I remember I told you once that no matter how great your scientific accomplishments are, psychologically you impress me as an artist. From this point of view it is understandable that you do not want your art product to be destroyed. In art we have a unit which cannot be torn apart. In science you made a great discovery which has to stay. How much of what is loosely connected with it will survive is not important.[86]

Twelve years later Bleuler congratulated Freud on the publication of his *Autobiography* and affirmed his personal and institutional commitment to psychoanalysis:

Noteworthy, but for me disturbing, are your sentences concerning the differences in our views. For you they appear so significant that you cannot understand that I still stand for psychoanalysis; I consider these differences quite unimportant side issues. . . . Your essential theories were for me self-evident after I fully understood them. . . . Moreover, I am still sending patients to be psycho-analyzed. . . . In spite of the objections of my colleagues I stress in my clinic the significance of psychoanalysis; my theoretical lecture course for years consists essentially in a course about psychoanalysis and I consider your teaching the greatest advancement in

the science of psychology. With old reverence for the work and its originator,
Your thankful, Bleuler.[87]

VIII

Let us look at a case history from the Burghölzli of our period—that of Sabina Spielrein, who was a patient from 17 August 1904 to 1 June 1905. Brought as a nineteen-year-old by her parents from Rostov on the Don, Russia,[88] she was the eldest child of a cultured Jewish family that included three younger brothers and a sister. Her history is remarkable because she began as a patient, became a scientific researcher at the Burghölzli, and finally a psychiatrist and psychoanalyst who significantly contributed to the literature.[90] She was also C. G. Jung's patient, collaborator, pupil, lover, and mistress.[91]

Aldo Carotenuto has published her letters to Jung, her diary, her correspondence with Freud, and an interpretation of her relationship to Jung during the years 1909 to 1912, but has not written about her treatment as a patient in the Burghölzli, 1904–1905. It is clear from her diary and letters that Jung had a passionate love affair with his patient; Carotenuto calls it a "psychotic countertransference."[92] He dates Jung's realization that he was in love with Sabina to the beginning of 1908.[93] We can now definitively establish from Jung's correspondence with Freud in the Burghölzli archives that he was aware of a highly erotized transference by Sabina as early as 1905. He was troubled by it and saw it as a problem. He responded to it by cutting Sabina off from contacts with her family, by gratifying her love, and by gratifying himself.

Jung discussed the case of Sabina in his reply to Gustav Aschaffenburg at the First International Congress of Psychiatry and Neurology in Amsterdam, in September 1907, diagnosing her as a case of "psychotic hysteria."[94] Her symptoms included the inability to look anyone in the face, attacks of depression alternating with fits of weeping, laughter, and screaming. She kept her head bowed and stuck out her tongue "with every sign of loathing" if anyone touched her.[95] She described herself at the time of admission: "I was still a baby of 19 then, and ran around in very simple dresses and with a long, dangling braid, since I wanted to elevate my soul above my body."[96]

The hospital record begins with Sabina's getting settled. Jung asked for a report from her previous physician in Interlaken.[97] He wrote to her mother at a Zurich hotel for Sabina's two suitcases.[98] Three days later Bleuler wrote to the mother on Sabina's behalf asking for the manuscripts of her writings to be sent over to her at the hospital.[99]

Fees for foreign patients at the Burghölzli were set on an *ad hoc* basis. Bleuler corresponded with the cantonal health ministry in regard to fees,[100] suggesting that because of the great demands on the staff by

Sabina's case, her fee be set at ten francs a day, which was high. (In 1901 Bleuler's annual salary as director was 7,000 Swiss francs; in 1909 Jung's salary as a resident was 2,500).[101] Bleuler noted that the family seemed wealthy.

Bleuler also corresponded with Sabina's parents concerning arrangements for having Sabina's measurements taken by the seamstress of the hospital or a seamstress in town to make a dress for her, and considered which would result in the best fit.[102]

At the end of September 1904 Bleuler reported on Sabina's condition to her father. He was pleased to relate that although her condition had not appreciably changed, the staff had been able to interest her in the scientific work of the hospital, which had diverted her from her sick ideas. "In the mornings she often participates with great interest in our case consultations, in the afternoon she usually goes for a walk with her attendant. She frequently uses these opportunities for childish tricks, but they are all of quite harmless nature."[103] Sabina commented on her collaboration with Jung on his scientific experiments and his encouraging response: "He gave me some work to do on his first paper, 'The Reaction-Time Ratio in the Association Experiment.' We had numerous discussions about it, and he said, 'Minds such as yours help advance science. You must become a psychiatrist.'"[104]

On 12 October 1904 Bleuler asked her parents for an answer to Sabina's last letter of October, saying she was awaiting reports from home with great tension (*grosser Spannung*). She was somewhat quieter and could better concentrate on her work, and "walks alone in our great park now and then." He related the happy fact that she had decided to begin the study of medicine the next spring in Zurich.[105] At the end of October Bleuler reported that she was helping one of the doctors on a scientific project that interested her very much. He stressed that she should stay in Zurich where she was familiar with things, that she should not return to Russia for a long time to come, and that she should not meet with her family before commencing her studies.

> Your daughter needs a fully independent and autonomous development, namely she must be fully freed from her passionate anxieties about the family and from all the inhibiting factors that accompany family life. This can only be achieved by living for a prolonged period in a new and strange environment where she can completely give herself to a captivating project.[106]

The next monthly letter to the parents was from Jung, who wrote that while he had been away in military service for three weeks, Sabina's condition had been stable, and that since his return she had been making progress. She still had all kinds of ideas that kept her from regular work, but recently she had taken part in a social event at Bleuler's home for the first time and with success. Her self-control was much better, although there were still days when she yielded to childish impulses.[107]

In January 1905 Bleuler reported that writing to her parents excited Sabina, and therefore he believed it would be good if she did not write them at all in the coming months. To relieve her of the responsibility, the hospital had forbidden her to write her father. She was then attending lectures in science and working in the anatomy laboratory.[108] Jung supplemented this the same month with an account of how the idea that she had to congratulate her father on his birthday emotionally excited her—so much so that Jung forbade future letters to her father. Her improvement continued, and a voluntary meal at the table of the resident physicians constituted a substantial success. A visit by her mother would be approved, but a meeting with the entire family would be premature.[109] Bleuler's report of the next month related that meals at the resident physicians' table had become part of her daily routine, a further success. Sabina was spending several hours every day in scientific work. Largely freed of hysterical symptoms, she might soon be considered as recovered.[110]

In April 1905 Jung and Bleuler equipped Sabina with the certifications she needed to study medicine at the University of Zurich: Jung's report affirmed that she would stay in Zurich for a longer time and planned to study at the university;[111] Bleuler's deposition certified that she was not insane (*ist nicht geisteskrank*) but was in treatment for nervousness with hysterical symptoms, and he recommended her matriculation.[112]

Sabina was concerned that her father would misinterpret her not writing as a lack of feeling. Jung wrote to assure him that such was not the case, explaining that pictures and memories of home upset her. It was a peculiarity of her neurosis that a number of obsessional ideas that disquieted and provoked her were attached to her father. He went on to say that her condition was very satisfactory. She attended classes daily, was punctual everywhere, and felt honor bound to participate fully. Her behavior was still not quite normal, but much better than at the time of her father's last visit. The staff believed Sabina could soon leave the Burghölzli and begin a self-sufficient existence.[113] A week later Bleuler wrote her father to deflect parental requests that Sabina look after a brother who was studying in Zurich. For the foreseeable future she must remain absolutely *free* (underlined in the original) of any responsibility toward members of her family. She had found herself an apartment and would move in the next few days.[114]

On 7 June 1905 Jung wrote to Mr. Spielrein that Sabina had moved, but there was the unfortunate circumstance that her older brother lived nearby:

> It is of the utmost importance for the health of Miss Spielrein that she have as little contact as possible with her brother. Therefore it would be most welcome if you could induce your older son to attend a university other than Zurich. Also it is of greatest importance for the continued improvement of your daughter if the contacts with the younger brother could be restricted as far as possible. . . . We assume that your younger son is only here temporarily and ask that you bear this situation in mind when you

place your older son somewhere. It would then perhaps be desirable if both brothers moved into the same apartment.

You will now send the money directly to your daughter; however if you wish a certain supervision in this respect, I am pleased to be of service and receive the money for Miss Spielrein.[115]

Psychotherapists may be legitimately concerned about a patient's renewed contact with a pathogenic situation and hence prescribe a program of isolation. The strategy of treatment may call for a minimizing of the influence of parents and family so as not to reenforce the former neurotic patterns and to give the newly won adaptations a chance to gain strength and be successful. What is critical in the case of Sabina is the timing. Jung is imposing the strictures on contact with her brothers and parents after her dismissal from the Burghölzli, when she is in her own apartment, apparently well, and studying medicine. In light of what we know about his affair with her, we may say he was setting the stage for it by severing all contact between her and her family except what came through him as a conduit—including monetary remittances, which he was willing to disburse to her. What we see in this case is Jung, with Bleuler's concurrence, systematically cutting ties between his patient and her family. He forbade her writing to her parents, discouraged their visits, and even suggested that her two brothers continue their studies someplace other than Zurich. All this naturally heightened Sabina's dependency on him and the transference to him because it deprived her of emotional interchange with other persons close to her. Such a policy does not, of course, alter the patient's inner bonds and ties, which is the task of dynamic psychotherapy. Sabina's parents were still with her as inner objects in her emotional life.

We also see in the case of Sabina the high level of personal and professional involvement of the director and staff, the degree of engagement and maximum involvement of the patient in the life of the institution. She was invited to work on and identify with the institute's research. As she got better, she attended social functions in Bleuler's home and ate with the medical staff. Eventually, she fully identified and became a doctor and healer herself. No wonder she got better! She was offered new supportive introjects and identifications. She found full acceptance rather than exclusion, and a new identity.

The last reference we have to the case in the Burghölzli Archive is an extensive report by Jung, given to Sabina's mother for transmission to Freud, in which he mentions the patient's name. The letter is headed "Report on Miss Spielrein to Professor Freud in Vienna, given to Frau Spielrein for possible use."

The daughter of Mrs. SPIELREIN, Miss SABINA SPIELREIN, a student of medicine, suffers from hysteria. The patient is heavily burdened hereditarily. Father and mother are hysterics, especially the mother. A brother of the patient is heavily hysteric since earliest childhood. The patient will shortly be twenty years old. About three years ago the illness strongly came into the foreground. The pathogenic experiences of course reach far back into her childhood. I have quite completely analyzed the picture of the illness according to your method, including very good results in the beginning.

The analysis by and large showed:

The corporal punishment which her father applied to the patient on her behind between her fourth and seventh years has unfortunately associated itself with the patient's premature and now very strong sexual feelings. The sexuality already expressed itself very early in that the patient began to masturbate by pressing together the upper part of her thighs. The masturbation always occurred after punishments administered by her father. Eventually blows were no longer necessary to induce the sexual excitement, rather it sufficed merely to be threatened, even by otherwise mildly violent situations such as curse words, threatening hand motions, etc. In the end she could no longer look at her father's hands without being sexually aroused. She could not bear to see him eat because she had to think of how the food is excreted and beating on the buttocks, etc. These associations also related to the younger brother who also has masturbated vigorously for a long time. Threats or minor abuses of the boy excited her, and she had to masturbate when she saw him being punished.

Eventually she was excited by all situations even remotely recalling suggestion of coercion, i.e.: if someone said to her she must obey. As soon as she was alone she was plagued by compulsions, e.g.: she had to imagine all kinds of tortures. The same occurred in her dreams, thus she often dreamt, for example, that she was eating dinner sitting on the toilet and all that she ate immediately came out of her behind while a great mass of people was observing her; another time she was being whipped in front of a large crowd of people.

Because of this her situation at home naturally became untenable. After numerous great excitements she was brought to Switzerland about a year ago, first to a sanitorium where the physician was not at all up to her absolutely demonical moods and tempers. She drove all the people there to despair. Finally it was no longer feasible in the private sanitorium and she was brought to us in the mental hospital. Here she was terribly unruly in the beginning, provoking the attendants to their limits of endurance. With the progress of her analysis her situation visibly improved and at last she revealed herself as a highly intelligent and talented person of great sensibility. Her character definitely has something ruthless and mean about it. Also any feeling for tactful timing and external appearances is lacking. Naturally much of this must be ascribed to Russian peculiarities.

Her condition improved so substantially that she was able to study last summer semester. She naturally suffers when she is together with her relations, which her mother especially does not wish to understand, but which in all of the above context is certainly very understandable. (By the way, Mrs. Spielrein knows the most important part of her daughter's complex.)

The patient had the bad fortune [*Malchance*] to fall in love with me during the treatment. She now always revels in her love in front of her mother in an ostentatious manner. A secret hostile pleasure in shocking her mother plays a not inconsiderable role in this. Therefore her mother now wishes, in case of need, to place her in another treatment, with which I am of course in agreement.[116]

In closing, Jung refers to the heated transference situation and prepares Freud for the accusations from Sabina, her mother, and Mrs. Jung that are to come. Jung's personal relationship with Sabina jeopardized his position at the Burghölzli and led to his rupture with Bleuler and his departure from the University of Zurich.

The end of the Burghölzli group in its great period of breakthrough and discovery came with the departure of Jung after his affair with Spielrein became known to Bleuler in 1909. Jung's leaving the Burghölzli was followed by his break with Freud. In December 1909 Jung wrote to Sándor Ferenczi: "I do not feel like a usurper. . . . Whether I am recognized as 'heir-apparent' or not can for a time anger or please me or *vice versa*. Since I have renounced the academic career . . . I do not wish to measure myself against Freud."[117] On Christmas Day 1909 Jung described Freud's new work on the obsessional neurosis, presumably the "Rat Man" case,[118] as "wonderful" but very difficult to comprehend. Jung had had to read it over three times. He asks: "Am I particularly dumb?" He attributed his difficulty to Freud's style, asserting that a chasm existed between Freud's lectures and his writing.[119]

The ending of a creative working group is as important to understand and as worthy of study as its beginning. Here we see how the psychological assumptions and social processes that held the group together and kept it functioning are torn asunder. The divisive forces of rivalry, competitiveness, desire for control, and intolerance of ambiguity and of theoretical pluralism were all continuously present. The adhesive forces of excitement over intellectual discoveries and the social-group process of following an idealized leader and standing in opposition to rival groups held the Burghölzli group together for a decade. Between 1902 and 1914 the institutional team worked as a scientific cohort pursuing clinical research and treatment in psychodynamics and carrying the insights of psychoanalysis to the world.

IX

In our study of the dynamics of the Burghölzli group we may profit from the work of Ludwik Fleck in Poland a half century ago.[120] Fleck was a practicing immunologist in Lwów who became an "internalist" historian of science.[121] He defined the useful concept of the "thought collective" (*Denkkollektiv*) as "a community of persons mutually exchanging ideas or maintaining intellectual interaction." Such a group is "the special 'carrier' for the historical development of any field of thought, as well as for the given stock of knowledge and level of culture."[122] A "thought collective" has a "thought style" that is "the entirety of intellectual preparedness or readiness for one particular way of seeing and acting and no other. . . . The thought style may also be accompanied by a technical and literary style characteristic of the given system of knowledge."[123]

Fleck's case example was the scientific group led by August von Wassermann that in the 1860s developed the blood serum test for syphilis. Fleck wrote about the empathic understanding between Wassermann and his researchers in language reminiscent of Henry Thoreau's personal drummer and of Sigmund Freud's description of the unconscious as an instrument for clinical listening. Freud asked the psychoanalyst to

> turn his own unconscious like a receptive organ towards the transmitting unconscious of the patient. He must adjust himself to the patient as a telephone receiver is adjusted to the transmitting microphone.[124]

Fleck described the preverbal preconscious and nonrational empathy between Wassermann and his group in similar terms:

> Wassermann heard the tune that hummed in his mind but was not audible to those not involved. He and his co-workers listened and "tuned" their "sets" until these became selective. The melody could then be heard even by unbiased persons who were not involved.[125]

What Fleck called *Gestaltsehen*, the perception of the total context, requires learned judgment and an apprenticeship:

> The ability directly to perceive meaning, form, and self-contained unity is acquired only after much experience, perhaps with preliminary training. . . . The optimum system of a science, the ultimate organization of its principles, is completely incomprehensible to the novice.[126]

And Fleck, as Freud often did, used the metaphors of battle and military advance and occupation for the progress of science:

> The vanguard does not occupy a fixed position. It changes its quarters from day to day and even from hour to hour. The main body advances more slowly, changing its stand—often spasmodically—only after years or even decades.[127]

The Burghölzli group considered itself the vanguard, the heroic band locked in arduous combat on issues of great import—a cause that would determine the future. Ernest Jones's account of the scientific battles was in the idioms of the jousting of medieval knights or of a street gang of juvenile toughs:

> Friedlaender, Hoche and Raimann aimed their shafts directly at Freud; Abraham had to contend with Oppenheim and Ziehen; Jung with Aschaffenburg and Isserlin; and Pfister with Foerster and Jaspers; while Vogt and I had a corner to ourselves. In America Brill had to face the New York neurologists, Dercum, Allen Starr and Bernard Sachs; Putnam was harried by Joseph Collins and Boris Sidis; while I had a wide choice there which was soon extended when I returned to England in 1913.[128]

The members of the Burghölzli group had the cipher, they were the initiates who had the code, they understood, they were the scientific brotherhood with the esoteric clues to human motivation, conflict, and behavior. When Gustav Aschaffenburg made an obvious public slip at the Amsterdam International Congress of Psychiatry and Neurology in September 1907 by putting himself in the place of Freud as Breuer's coauthor, Jones writes: "He did not appear to have noticed it himself, and perhaps Jung and I were the only people to have done so, or at least to perceive its significance; we could only smile across at each other."[129] They knew the esoteric code to deciphering slips, they could share knowing glances across the meeting room because they were members of the thought collective who shared a common group experience and a group boundary against outsiders.

When Jung wrote to Freud from Amsterdam during this meeting, he had only to allude to the slips to make his point. His level of vituperation is at least up to that of the two men's critics:

> What a gang of cut-throats we have here! Their resistance really is rooted in affect. Aschaffenburg made two slips of the tongue in his lecture ("facts" instead of "no facts"), which shows that unconsciously he is strongly infected. Hence his furious attack. . . . A ghastly crowd, reeking of vanity. . . . I am glad you have never been caught in the bedlam of such a mutual admiration society. I constantly feel the urgent need of a bath. What a morass of nonsense and stupidity![130]

The Burghölzli group was a scientific "thought collective" that had a defined "thought style" setting it off from the traditional psychiatry of its time. Its members communicated in a special restricted esoteric language based upon a period of apprenticeship and initiation. They shared common perceptions structured by the psychoanalytic theory of Sigmund Freud.

X

D. W. Winnicott has given us the useful psychodynamic concept, the "transitional object," by which he means that children of six months to a year become attached to a soft object such as a blanket or stuffed toy.[131] The object is excitedly loved and mutilated, it must never change, it seems to the infant to give warmth, to move, to have texture, and to have a vitality or reality of its own. This blanket or teddy bear or whatever it may be stands for the breast or the mother or the first relationship; the transitional object is symbolic of the mother and her breast. Although it is real, it is important that here the child is distinguishing between fantasy and fact. It is not a hallucination. The child is beginning to distinguish between inner objects and the outer world, between subjective creativity and perception. The transitional object is the beginning of the capacity for symbol formation and representational thought. It is not inside the child, the "me," nor is it outside—it is not part of the repudiated world—the "not me," which the child recognizes as truly external, beyond his or her magic omnipotent control. Yet it is not an internal object; it is a me, an extension, occupying a space between inner and external reality. This is the place of play and of the first phase of cultural and scientific creativity.

We may, I think, appropriately view the Burghölzli as a holding environment in Winnicott's sense of being a secure space in which individuals in the group could be playful and safely try out ideas. They could allow the most intimate "me" content of their preconscious and unconscious processes to become the "not me" in an intermediate area of experience that he defines as the sphere of the transitional object:

> This intermediate area of experience, unchallenged in respect of its belonging to inner or external (shared) reality, constitutes the greater part of the infant's experience, and throughout life is retained in the intense experiencing that belongs to the arts and to religion and to imaginative living, and to creative scientific work.[132]

The point when a new idea is launched, when the manuscript is given over to its first reader, when the artist shows a painting or sculpture for the first time, is absolutely critical because until that moment the creation was still a part of the self. Now, it has become a transitional object. The idea, text, or creation stands between the observer and the creator's self. It is a me-extension moved from the inner world of nothing-but-me into a world of people and objects outside the me's omnipotent control. The use of this space happens only when there is a feeling of confidence in the relationship that the fragile new parts of the self will be sheltered. Here there is an exciting weave of subjectivity and objective observation, it is an area that is intermediate between the inner reality of the individual and the shared reality of many supportive people.

The Burghölzli, like other rare institutions that truly foster new thought and praxis, provided a creative space where its workers were protected in an intermediate area of experience, between the inner and the external shared reality. This is the essential precondition of creativity. The intense group process of the Burghölzli in the Bleuler years was one of personal interpenetration. Boundaries between individuals and between administration, staff, their families, and patients were dissolved in an ongoing group process of regressive fusion. The personal boundary in important aspects came to be the institution itself, which stood in creative competition with the outside world of static psychiatry and hostile opposition to the depth-psychological ideas of the Burghölzli.

The regressive group phenomenon was exciting and exhilarating. It provided intense emotional closeness coupled with scientific cross-fertilization and stimulation. We can see A. A. Brill still being attached to the experience and mourning it thirty years after leaving the Burghölzli. The sense of creative regression, of room to play (*Spielraum*), and of a forum in which new things flourished also had its attendant dangers. Transferences and countertransferences were acted out, as in the case of C. G. Jung and Sabina Spielrein.

Johan Huizinga, who first advanced the *ludic* concept of culture, noted the esoteric and limiting quality of play. One plays within boundaries that distinguish the player from "outsiders" who do not share the mystique and knowledge of play.

> The exceptional and special position of play is most tellingly illustrated by the fact that it loves to surround itself with an air of secrecy. Even in early childhood the charm of play is enhanced by making a "secret" out of it. This is for *us*, not for the "others." What the "others" do "outside" is no concern of ours at the moment. Inside the circle of the game the laws and customs of ordinary life no longer count. We are different and do things differently.[133]

Huizinga maintained that "civilization is, in its earliest phases, played. It does not come *from* play like a babe detaching itself from the womb: it arises *in* and *as* play, and never leaves it."[134] Erik Erikson proposed "the theory that the child's play is the infantile form of the human ability to deal with experience by creating model situations and to master reality by experiment and planning."[135] Child psychoanalyst Robert Dorn gives to the term *Spielraum*, or play space,

> meanings related to flexible ego attitudes toward ideas and concepts, things and people, fantasies of course, and oneself. In both literal and figurative terms it represents an ability to come close, handle, touch, feel, "play with" the new, different, strange, unusual, unexpected, forbidden, etc. There is both inner (psychic) and outer space and time for playing with ideas and concepts in both the adult and child, just as the small child plays with himself, little toys, and as he grows older, with other children.[136]

Psychoanalyst and literary critic A. D. Hutter locates the critical space of creativity in the act of writing itself. As in psychoanalysis, in written composition the act of creation takes place in the transition from nonverbal to preverbal to words. Hutter declares: "It is through writing that we dare to externalize and 'objectify' ourselves—undoubtedly why writing is so difficult and so filled with what we loosely call 'writer's block.' . . . Filling up that page requires a certain kind of courage, especially when it will be examined by someone else and perhaps criticized."[137]

Hutter has pinpointed the critical point of the "first" reader. All works are written with some fantasied reader in mind. In the case of students, it is the professor; for scientists and professionals, it is the community of peers, coworkers, and rivals; for writers, it is the editor. Behind these figures in the here and now stand the early parental imagoes for whom the toddler "creates" his or her first gifts. This is why the first reader of a manuscript, the first "receiver" of an idea, the first one to listen and respond to a nascent thought is so critically important—as Fliess was to Freud, and as the members of any dyad or working group are to each other and to one another. That first person or persons provide the vital "holding space" where "mirroring"[138] takes place, where in the shared intimacy of a relationship that has been tested for reliability what has been brought to the encounter is reflected and given back and found to be acceptable. According to Winnicott, "Psychotherapy is not making clever and apt interpretations; by and large it is a long-term giving the patient back what the patient brings. It is a complex derivative of the face that reflects what there is to be seen."[139]

Our ability to create depends upon our capacity to "play," which Hutter defines as "to experiment with and interact with an object outside of the self and to use this interaction to expand the boundaries of the ego and of the cultural space which each of us creates and inhabits."[140] This is the Burghölzli's cultural play space: safe and a good holding environment for the first finding, leaking, spilling, and reflection of ideas and clinical therapeutic methods. As Winnicott put it: "We experience life in the area of transitional phenomena, in the exciting interweave of subjectivity and objective observation, and in an area that is intermediate between the inner reality of the individual and the shared reality of the world that is external to individuals."[141]

In the group play space of the Burghölzli we see the interplay between separateness and union, between regressive fusion among staff and in some cases between staff and patients. This was, to paraphrase Ernst Kris, a regression in the service of creativity.[142] Creativity occurred in the institutional space where individuals could comfortably allow themselves the freedom to regress, to share their unconscious associations, slips, dreams, and behavior, in the service of individual growth and creativity in their mutual scientific enterprise of furthering the psychoanalytic understanding of self and others.

XI

Kant instructed us to pose questions of phenomena, not like students who wish to be told what the teacher wills but like the sitting judge who demands answers to questions he or she puts to witnesses.[143] From a historical examination of the functioning of the group of psychiatric clinicians at the Burghölzli just after the turn of the century, we may conclude that there are six preconditions of creative scientific institutions:

1. A political-social ecology of exceptional cultural openness that is structured institutionally. This includes the avoidance of institutional inbreeding, open recruitment, and placing material resources at the service of the creative enterprise.
2. The art or science appears to be in a situation of stasis or stalemate. There is an urgent need for new concepts and models or synthetic paradigms to explain and subsume more data that give promise of filling the need of the discipline and moving it forward.
3. A leadership model with a split function between the administrative and scientific or research leadership. The institutional leader must be able to tolerate intellectual independence and growth of

subordinates, and must also be a scientist conversant with the group work.

4. The group has inner cohesion because it is competitive with other scientific centers or schools. Its members feel themselves a spearhead, an enthusiastic unified group, the cutting edge of an advancing cause against an entrenched conservative opposition.

5. There is deeply involved personal concern for the work—in this case patient care and therapy—that entails and includes the dangers of loosened boundaries and transference and countertransference acting out.

6. The group process is one of intense social interaction. Members live together, sharing meals and recreation as well as a work agenda, a situation that is both abrasive and stimulating. The boundaries between workers are dissolved by personal interpenetration. The personal and group boundary becomes the institution itself, which is individually regressive but confers the exhilaration of group regression and may be regression in the service of creativity.

Isak Dinesen once said, "An answer is a rarer thing than is commonly imagined." Perhaps answers are not as important as commonly imagined, either. Perhaps questions matter more. Without supplying a total answer, I have posed a salient contemporary question: What are the preconditions of institutional creativity? To the extent that creativity is a value that we seek to foster in our institutions and our lives, this is a question worth asking. What were the factors of cultural and political ecology, leadership, and institutional group setting that made it possible eighty years ago for a small cohort in Zurich to stimulate themselves and others, to strike sparks in the mental sciences that ignited fires from whose heat we still draw inspiration, warmth, and intellectual nurture? The partial answer is a happy combination of cultural diversity, a permissive but structured political-social setting, an urgent scientific need, a synthetic paradigm that filled that need, a leader of stature who could tolerate independence among his subordinates, a struggle against determined external opposition that for a time unified the group and kept divisive forces of envy and competition in check, and, finally, an intense group interaction that acted as an abrasive and a stimulant, permitting the creative enterprise to move forward.

NOTES

1. Gerald Holton, "Striking Gold in Science: Fermi's Group and the Recapture of Italy's Place in Physics," *Minerva: A Review of Science, Learning, and Policy* 12:2 (April 1974): 159–98; reprinted in *The Scientific Imagination: Case Studies* (Cambridge: Cambridge University Press, 1978), pp. 155–98. Laura Fermi, *Atoms in the Family* (Chicago: University of Chicago Press, 1954); Emilio Segre, *Enrico Fermi: Physicist* (Chicago: University of Chicago Press, 1970).

2. Hans M. Wingler, *The Bauhaus: Weimar, Dessau, Berlin, Chicago* (Cambridge: MIT Press, 1969); Frank Whitford, ed., *The Bauhaus: Masters and Students by Themselves* (Woodstock, N.Y.: Overlook Press, 1993).

3. William Rubin, *Picasso and Braque: Pioneering Cubism* (New York: Museum of Modern Art, 1989); John Golding, *Cubism: A History and Analysis, 1907–1914*, 3d ed. (Cambridge: Harvard University Press, 1988); Edward F. Fry, *Cubism* (New York: Oxford University Press, 1966, 1978); Edward Burns, ed., *Gertrude Stein on Picasso* (New York: Liveright, 1970; Boston: Beacon Press, 1985); Gerald Kamber, *Max Jacob and the Poetics of Cubism* (Baltimore: Johns Hopkins University Press, 1971); Mary M. Gedo, *Picasso: Art as Autobiography* (Chicago: University of Chicago Press, 1980); Francis Steegmuller, *Apollinaire: Poet among the Painters* (New York: Farrar, Straus, 1963); Françoise Gilot and Carlton Lake, *Life with Picasso* (New York: McGraw-Hill, 1964); Daniel-Henri Kahnweiler, *Mes galeries et mes peintres: Entretiens avec Francis Cremieux* (Paris: Gallimard, 1961); Kahnweiler, *Juan Gris: sa vie, son oeuvre, ses écrits* (Paris: Gallimard, 1946); Kahnweiler, "Naissance et développement du cubisme," in *Les Maîtres de la peinture française contemporaine*, ed. Maurice Jardot and Kurt Martin (Baden-Baden: Woldemar Klein, 1949); Dora Vallier, "Braque, la peinture et nous," *Cahiers d'art* 29:1 (October 1954).

4. Armin Zweite, *The Blue Rider in the Lenbachhaus, Munich* (Munich: Prestel-Verlag, 1989).

5. Donald E. Gordon, *Ernst Ludwig Kirchner* (Cambridge: Harvard University Press, 1968).

6. Martin Jay, *The Dialectical Imagination: A History of the Frankfurt School and the Institute of Social Research, 1923–1950* (Boston: Little, Brown, 1973).

7. Emil Kraepelin, *One Hundred Years of Psychiatry*, trans. W. Baskin (New York: Citadel Press, 1962), pp. 117, 150, as quoted in Hannah S. Decker, *Freud in Germany: Revolution and Reaction in Science, 1893–1907* (New York: International Universities Press, 1977), p. 64.

8. Freud, "On the History of the Psychoanalytic Movement" (1914), in *Standard Edition of the Complete Psychological Works of Sigmund Freud*, translated under the general editorship of James Strachey in collaboration with Anna Freud, assisted by Alix Strachey and Alan Tyson, 24 vols. (London: Hogarth Press, 1953–1975), 14:27 (hereafter cited as *S.E.*).

9. Fritz Meerwein, "Psychotherapie," in *Hundert Jahre Kantonale Psychiatrische Universitätsklinik Burghölzli, Zurich, 1870–1970* (Zurich: former and current staff, 1970), pp. 44, 46. This, and all subsequent translations, unless otherwise indicated, are mine.

10. Karl Baedeker, *Die Schweiz* (Leipzig: Verlag von Karl Baedeker, 1897), p. 33; *Baedeker la Suisse* (Leipzig: 1905), p. 46.

11. For the cultural background of early-twentieth-century Zurich, I am indebted to the suggestive chapter "Zurich: The Peaceful Cradle of European Revolution," in Lewis S. Feuer, *Einstein and the Generations of Science*, 2d ed. (New Brunswick: Transaction Publishers, 1982), pp. 4–14.

12. For the liberal bourgeois political culture of mid-nineteenth-century Zurich, see Gordon A. Craig, *The Triumph of Liberalism: Zurich in the Golden Age, 1830–1869* (New York: Scribner's, 1988).

13. Vernon Lidtke, *The Outlawed Party: Social Democracy in Germany, 1878 to 1890* (Princeton: Princeton University Press, 1966), pp. 89–100, 135–38, 267–72.

14. Max Nomad, *Dreamers, Dynamiters, and Demagogues* (New York: Waldon Press, 1964), p. 15.

15. James C. Albisetti, "The Fight for Female Physicians in Imperial Germany," *Central European History* 15:2 (June 1982): 101.

16. J. M. Meijer, *Knowledge and Revolution: The Russian Colony in Zurich, 1870–1873* (Assen: Van Gorcum, 1955), pp. 141, 146.

17. J. P. Nettl, *Rosa Luxemburg* (London: Oxford University Press, 1966), 1:60–65; Elżbieta Ettinger, *Rosa Luxemburg: A Life* (Boston: Beacon Press, 1986), pp. 41–71.

18. Julius Wolf, "Selbstbiographie," in *Die Volkswirtschaftslehre der Gegenwart in Selbstdarstellungen,* ed. Felix Meiner (Leipzig: Verlag Felix Meiner, 1924), p. 12. See also Verena Stadler-Labhart, *Rosa Luxemburg an der Universität Zürich, 1889–1897* (Zurich: Verlag Hans Rohr, 1978), pp. 20–21.

19. Aldo Carotenuto, *A Secret Symmetry: Sabina Spielrein between Jung and Freud,* trans. Arno Pomerans, John Shepley, and Krishna Winston (New York: Pantheon Books, 1982), pp. 197; 228 n. 27.

20. Warren Lerner, *Karl Radek: The Last Internationalist* (Stanford: Stanford University Press, 1970), p. 8.

21. Feuer, *Einstein,* pp. 10–11. The author can corroborate that the exceptional service and helpfulness of Swiss libraries and archives has not changed in the past century. For an insightful fictional account, based on documents, of Lenin's Zurich years, see Alexander Solzhenitsyn, *Lenin in Zurich,* trans. H. T. Willetts (New York: Farrar, Straus and Giroux, 1976).

22. Peter Kropotkin, *Memoirs of a Revolutionist* (1899) (Boston: Houghton Mifflin, 1930), p. 269.

23. Henry Demarest Lloyd, *A Sovereign People: A Study of Swiss Democracy,* ed. John A. Hobson (New York: Doubleday, Page and Co., 1907), pp. 1, 7, 211.

24. Florence Kelley, "My Novitiate," *Survey* 58:1 (1 April 1927): 34.

25. David Lee, "Zurich's Two Schisms and the 'Analysenpfarrer'" (paper delivered at the Association Internationale d'Histoire de la Psychanalyse conference Schisms in the History of Psychoanalysis, Berlin, 24 July 1994).

26. Oskar Pfister and Sigmund Freud, *Briefe 1909–1939,* ed. Heinrich Meng and Ernst L. Freud (Frankfurt a M.: S. Fischer Verlag, 1963); *Psycho-analysis and Faith: Letters,* trans. Eric Mosbacher (London: Hogarth Press, 1963). See also Hans Zulliger, "Oscar Pfister: Psycho-analysis and Faith," in Franz Alexander, Samuel Eisenstein, and Martin Grotjahn, eds., *Psychoanalytic Pioneers* (New York: Basic Books, 1966), pp. 169–79.

27. Freud, "Review of August Forel's Hypnotism" (1889), in *S.E.,* 1:89–102.

28. Thomas Haenel, *Zur Geschichte der Psychiatrie: Gedanken zur allgemeinen und Basler Psychiatriegeschichte* (Basel: Birkhäuser Verlag, 1982), pp. 38–42.

29. John Kerr, *A Most Dangerous Method: The Story of Jung, Freud, and Sabina Spielrein* (New York: Knopf, 1993), p. 41.

30. Hans W. Maier, "Eugen Bleuler zur Feier seiner 25 jährigen Tätigkeit als Ordinarius der Psychiatrie und Direktor der Psychiatrischen Klinik in Zürich, April 1923," *Zeitschrift für die gesamte Neurologie und Psychiatrie,* Band 82 (Berlin: Julius Springer, 1923), p. 1. Manfred Bleuler interview, 25 August 1983.

31. Henri F. Ellenberger, *The Discovery of the Unconscious: The History and Evolution of Dynamic Psychiatry* (New York: Basic Books, 1970), p. 562 n. 308.

32. "*Dem glücklichen, von Bleuler eingeführten Namen Ambivalenz,*" Freud, *Drei Abhandlungen zur Sexualtheorie,* in *Studienausgabe,* ed. Alexander Mitscherlich, Angela Richards, and James Strachey, 2 vols. (Frankfurt am Main: S. Fischer Verlag, 1971), 5:104. Freud, *Three Essays on Sexuality* (1905), in *S.E.,* 7:199.

33. Manfred Bleuler, personal communication to the author, 25 August 1983.

34. *"An schön gedecktem Tisch,"* in Manfred Bleuler, "Geschichte des Burghölzlis und der psychiatrischen Universitätsklinik," in *Zürischer Spitalgeschichte* (Zurich: Regierungsrat des Kantons Zürich, 1951), p. 396.

35. Eugen Bleuler, *Dementia Praecox or the Group of Schizophrenias*, trans. Joseph Zinkin (New York: International Universities Press, 1950), pp. 481–82.

36. Bleuler to Sanitätsdirektion, 18 December 1913, Sanitätsdirektion, Kantonal Staatsarchiv, Zurich, Carton 322/2, Folder 4. See also Bleuler's letters regarding Dr. Hansen, 16 June 1921; Dr. Josef Freidenfeld, 18 April 1922; Dr. Annau, 30 December 1924; and the specific charges for meals levied on each physician staff member. The rates varied from free meals through 2.5 to 5. Swiss francs a day. Burghölzli Administration to Direktion des Gesundheitswesens, 20 December 1922.

37. Bleuler to Direction des Gesundheitswesens, 2 June 1919, Sanitätsdirektion, Kantonal Staatsarchiv, Zurich, Carton 322/2, Folder 4, for Dr. Wlassak, an Austrian; see also Bleuler's letter on behalf of Dr. Waldberg, 16 April 1921, in which he justifies to the Alien Police the need for having foreigners like Dr. Waldberg because it is impossible to fill the position with a Swiss.

38. Bleuler to Sanitätsdirektion, 16 July 1914, Sanitätsdirektion, Staatsarchiv, Zurich, Carton s. 322/2, Folder 2. Bleuler was awarded his leave at the meeting of the Executive Council of Zurich, 23 July 1914, *Protokoll des Regierungsrates 1914*, 1644 Burghölzli Urlaub.

39. Freud "Resistances to Psychoanalysis" (1925), in *S.E.*, 19: 222.

40. Bleuler to Freud, 14 October 1905, Freud Collection, B 4, Library of Congress, Washington, D.C.

41. Bleuler to Freud, 9 October 1905, Freud Collection, B 4, Library of Congress, Washington, D.C.

42. Typescript of Dreams, Bleuler to Freud, Freud Collection, B 4, Library of Congress, Washington, D.C.

43. *Die Psychanalyse Freuds: Verteidigung und kritische Bemerkungen* (Leipzig: Franz Deuticke, 1911). Reprinted from the *Jahrbuch für Psychoanalytische und Psychopathologische Forschungen*, vol. 2.

44. Ibid., p. 20.

45. Ibid., p. 23.

46. Ibid., p. 26.

47. Ibid., p. 27.

48. Ibid., pp. 27–28.

49. Ibid., p. 42.

50. Ibid., pp. 48–49.

51. Bleuler to Sanitätsdirektion, Zurich, 15 May 1901; *Protokoll des Regierungsrates*, 13 August 1901, where Jung was formally named II Assistant Physician.

52. C. G. Jung, *Memories, Dreams, Reflections*, ed. Aniela Jaffe, trans. Richard and Clara Winston, rev. ed. (New York: Vintage, 1965), p. 111.

53. C. G. Jung, "Freud's Theory of Hysteria: A Reply to Aschaffenburg" (1906), in *The Psychoanalytic Years*, trans. R. F. C. Hull, Leopold Stein, and Diana Riviere (Princeton: Princeton University Press, 1974), p. 34.

54. Ibid., p. 38.

55. Ernest Jones, *The Life and Work of Sigmund Freud*, vol. 2 (New York: Basic Books, 1955), pp. 111–12.

56. C. G. Jung, "Psychoanalyse und Assoziationsexperiment," *Journal für Psychologie und Neurologie* 7 (1906): 1–2, 1–24.

57. C. G. Jung, *Psychoanalysis and Association Experiments* (1906), trans. R. F. C. Hull, Leopold Stein, and Diana Riviere (Princeton, N.J.: 1974), pp. 5–6.

58. Ellenberger, *Discovery of the Unconscious*, p. 667. This is not quite true; see Jung, *Memories, Dreams, Reflections*, p. 255.

59. Jung, *Memories, Dreams, Reflections*, p. 112.

60. Jung to Alphonse Maeder, 28 November 1911, C. G. Jung Nachlass, Swiss Federal Institute of Technology (ETH) Archive, Zurich, #1056: 20 (hereafter cited as ETH Archive).

61. C. G. Jung to Trignant Burrow, 28 June 1911, Trignant Burrow Papers, Yale University Archives, New Haven.

62. Jung to Burrow, 16 December 1911, Burrow Papers.

63. Jung to Alphonse Maeder, end of 1911, C. G. Jung Nachlass, ETH Archive, #1056: 21.

64. Jung to Sándor Ferenczi, 31 October 1910, C. G. Jung Nachlass, ETH Archive.

65. Manuscript Hs 1055: 472, C. G. Jung Nachlass, ETH Archiv, p. 22.

66. Ibid., pp. 12–13.

67. Ludwig Binswanger, *Erinnerungen an Sigmund Freud* (Bern: Francke Verlag, 1956), pp. 9–10.

68. Bleuler to Sanitätsdirektion, 20 November 1904, Sanitätsdirektion, S 322.2 (3), Mappe 3, Kantonal Staatsarchiv.

69. Karl Abraham to Sigmund Freud, 13 October 1907, in *A Psycho-Analytic Dialogue: The Letters of Sigmund Freud and Karl Abraham, 1907–1926*, ed. Hilda C. Abraham and Ernst L. Freud (New York: Basic Books, 1965), p. 11.

70. Ernest Jones, *Free Associations: Memoirs of a Psycho-Analyst* (New York: Basic Books, 1959), p. 164.

71. A. A. Brill, trans. and ed., *The Basic Writings of Sigmund Freud* (New York: Random House, 1938), p. 26.

72. A. A. Brill, "Psychological Factors in Dementia Praecox, an Analysis," *Journal of Abnormal Psychology* 3 (October–November 1908): 223, as quoted in Nathan G. Hale, Jr., *Freud and the Americans: The Beginnings of Psychoanalysis in the United States, 1876–1917* (New York: Oxford University Press, 1971), p. 203.

73. Ellenberger, *Discovery of the Unconscious*, p. 667.

74. Ibid.

75. Brill, *Basic Writings of Sigmund Freud*, p. 27.

76. Ibid., p. 57.

77. Philip Rieff, introduction to *Dora: An Analysis of a Case of Hysteria* (New York: Collier Macmillan, 1963), p. 19 n. 5.

78. The differentiation into instrumental and expressive roles in small groups was first conceptualized by R. F. Bales, *Interaction Process Analysis* (Cambridge: Harvard University Press, 1950), and Bales and Philip E. Slater, "Role Differentiation in Small Decision-Making Groups," in *Family, Socialization, and Interaction Process*, by Talcott Parsons, R. Freed Bales, et al. (Glencoe, Ill.: Free Press, 1955). Parsons applied this role differentiation to the traditional nuclear family in "The Incest Taboo in Relation to Social Structure and the Socialization of the Child," in *Social Structure and Personality* (New York: Free Press, 1964), pp. 57–77.

79. Bleuler to Freud, 8 May 1909, as quoted in Franz Alexander and Sheldon T. Selesnick, "Freud-Bleuler Correspondence," *Archives of General Psychiatry* 12 (January 1965): 6.

80. Bleuler to Freud, 23 December 1909, ibid.

81. Freud to Bleuler, 28 September 1910, ibid., p. 3.

82. Freud to Bleuler, 27 October 1916, ibid., p. 4.

83. Bleuler to Freud, 19 October 1910, ibid., p. 5.

84. C. G. Jung to Alphonse Maeder, End of 1911, C. G. Jung Nachlass, #1056: 21, ETH Archive.

85. Bleuler to Freud, 11 March 1911, *Archives of General Psychiatry* 12, 5–6.

86. Bleuler to Freud, 5 November 1913, ibid., 6.

87. Bleuler to Freud, 17 February 1925, ibid., 8.

88. C. G. Jung to Dr. Heller, Interlaken, 18 August 1904, Burghölzli Archiv, Zurich Copybook 59, Letter 427 (hereafter cited as BA).

89. For a discussion of Spielrein's life and psychoanalytic contributions, see Adeline van Waning, "The Works of Pioneering Psychoanalyst Sabina Spielrein: 'Destruction as a Cause of Coming into Being,'" *International Review of Psychoanalysis* 19:4 (Winter 1992): 399–414.

90. Sabina Spielrein, *Sämtliche Schriften* (Freiburg i. Br.: Kore, Verlag Traute Hensch, 1987).

91. While Carotenuto presents the relationship as platonic, I am convinced by Spielrein's explicit language that the relationship was sexual. Bruno Bettelheim agrees in his carefully argued "Scandal in the Family," *New York Review of Books*, 30 June 1983, 39–44, as do David James Fisher, "The Analytic Triangle," *Partisan Review* 51:3 (1984): 473–80, and Martin A. Silverman, *Journal of the American Psychoanalytic Association*, Supplement, 33 (1985): 205–9.

92. Carotenuto, *A Secret Symmetry*, p. 160; in the foreword William McGuire terms it "symbolic love" on Jung's part, p. x.

93. Ibid., p. 167.

94. C. G. Jung, "The Freudian Theory of Hysteria" (1908), *The Psychoanalytic Years*, p. 50, para. 53, and "hysterical psychosis" on p. 51, para. 59.

95. Ibid., p. 51, para. 57.

96. Sabina Spielrein to Freud, 13 June 1909, in Carotenuto, *A Secret Symmetry*, p. 101.

97. Jung to Dr. Heller, Interlaken, 18 August 1904, BA, Book 59, #427.

98. Jung to Frau Spielrein, 24 August 1904, BA, Book 59, #450.

99. Bleuler to Mrs. Spielrein, 27 August 1904, BA, Book 59, #461.

100. Bleuler to Sanitätsdirektion, 28 August 1904, BA, Book 59, #466.

101. *Protokoll des Regierungsrat Zurich*, 13 August 1901, and 1 July 1909, Kantonalarchiv, Zurich.

102. Bleuler to Mrs. Spielrein, 14 September 1904, BA, Book 60, #52.

103. Bleuler to Herr Spielrein, 26 September 1904, BA, Book 60, #104.

104. Sabina Spielrein to Freud, 13 June 1909, as quoted in Carotenuto, *A Secret Symmetry*, p. 101.

105. Bleuler to Herr Spielrein, 12 October 1904, BA, Book 60, #180.

106. Bleuler to Herr Spielrein, 25 October 1904, BA, Book 60, #251.

107. Jung to H. A. Spielrein, 28 November 1904, BA, Book 60, #395.

108. Bleuler to H. A. Spielrein, 6 January 1905, BA, Book 61, #96.

109. Jung to Frau Spielrein, 22 January 1905, BA, Book 61, #189.

110. Bleuler to Frau Spielrein, 13 February 1905, BA, Book 61, #281; the letter is damaged.

111. Jung memorandum, 19 April 1905, BA.

112. Bleuler, Ärztliches Erzuegnis, 27 April 1905, BA; see Sabina Spielrein, *Anmeldung zur Immatrikulation für die medizinische Fakultät, Universität Zurich*, 25 October 1909, Matrikel No. 20031.15546, Kantonal Staatsarchiv, Zurich.

113. Jung to Herr Spielrein, 23 May 1905, BA, Book 62, #320.

114. Bleuler to Herr Spielrein, 31 May 1905, BA, Book 62, #361.

115. Jung to Herr Spielrein, 7 June 1905, BA, Book 62, #397–398.

116. Jung to Freud, 25 September 1905, BA, Book 63, #471–472. Bernard Minder points out that erotized transferences were not new to Jung and that he had in fact reported two patients in love with him prior to Sabina. Why then did he write of a "*Malchance*" in her case? "Jung an Freud 1905: Ein Bericht über Sabina Spielrein," *Gesnerus* 50 (1993): 119.

117. Jung to Ferenczi, 6 December 1909, C. G. Jung Nachlass, ETH Archive, #1056: 10.

118. Freud, "Bemerkungen über einen Fall von Zwangsneurose" (1909), trans. as "Notes upon a Case of Obsessional Neurosis," in *S.E.*, 10:151–318.

119. Jung to Ferenczi, December 25, 1909, C. G. Jung Nachlass, ETH Archive, #1056: 11.

120. Ludwik Fleck, *Genesis and Development of a Scientific Fact* (Chicago: University of Chicago Press, 1979), translation by Fred Bradley and Thaddeus J. Trenn of *Entstehung und Entwicklung einer wissenschaftlichen Tatsache: Einführung in die Lehre vom Denkstil und Denkkollektiv* (Basel: Benno Schwabe, 1935).

121. See Robert S. Cohen and Thomas Schnelle, eds., *Cognition and Fact: Materials on Ludwik Fleck* (Dordrecht: D. Reidel, 1986). particularly Cohen and Schnelle's "Introduction," pp. ix–xxxi, and Schnelle's biographical essay "Microbiology and Philosophy of Science, Lwów and the German Holocaust: Stations of a Life—Ludwik Fleck, 1896–1961," pp. 3–36.

122. Fleck, *Genesis and Development*, p. 39.

123. Ibid., pp. 64, 99.

124. Freud, "Recommendations to Physicians Practicing Psychoanalysis" (1912), in *S.E.*, 12:115–16.

125. Fleck, *Genesis and Development*, p. 86.

126. Ibid., pp. 92, 104.

127. Ibid., p. 124.

128. Jones, *Freud*, 2:110.

129. Ibid., p. 112; cf. Steven Shapin, *A Social History of Truth: Civility and Science in Seventeenth-Century England* (Chicago: University of Chicago Press, 1994), pp. 3–41.

130. Jung to Freud, 4 September 1907, in *Freud/Jung Letters*, ed. William McGuire; trans. Ralph Manheim and R. F. C. Hull (Princeton: Princeton University Press, 1974), No. 43 J, p. 83.

131. D. W. Winnicott, "Transitional Objects and Transitional Phenomena" (1953), "Creativity and Its Origins," (1971) and "The Location of Cultural Experience" (1967), in *Playing and Reality* (London: Tavistock, 1971), pp. 1–30, 76–100, 112–21.

132. Winnicott, *Playing and Reality*, p. 14.

133. Johan Huizinga, *Homo Ludens: A Study of the Play Element in Culture* (Boston: Beacon Press, 1950), p. 12.

134. Ibid., p. 173.

135. Erik H. Erikson, *Childhood and Society*, 2d ed. (New York: Norton, 1963), p. 222.

136. Robert M. Dorn, "The Geography of Play, Child Analysis and the Psychoanalysis of the Adult," *International Journal of Psychoanalytic Psychotherapy* 3:1 (1974): 108.

137. Albert D. Hutter, "Poetry in Psychoanalysis: Hopkins, Rossetti, Winnicott," *International Review of Psychoanalysis* 9 (1982): 310.

138. Mirroring is the reflection of himself or herself that the child sees when the mother or others are looking at him or her, i.e., love, approval, joy, disinterest, annoyance, disgust, rejection. Winnicott puts it: "What does the baby see when he or she looks at the mother's face? I am suggesting that, ordinarily, what the baby sees is himself or herself." *Playing and Reality*, p. 112. Heinz Kohut refers to "the gleam in the mother's eye, which mirrors the child's exhibitionistic display" and confirms the child's self-esteem. *The Analysis of the Self: A Systematic Approach to the Psychoanalytic Treatment of Narcissistic Personality Disorders* (New York: International Universities Press, 1971), p. 116.

139. Winnicott, *Playing and Reality*, p. 117.

140. Hutter, "Poetry in Psychoanalysis," p. 314.

141. Winnicott, "Creative Activity and the Search for the Self," in *Playing and Reality*, p. 64.

142. Ernst Kris, *Psychoanalytic Explorations in Art* (New York: International Universities Press, 1952; New York: Schocken Books, 1964), pp. 303–18.

143. Immanuel Kant, *Kritik der reinen Vernunft* (1787), in *Werke*, 11 vols. (Berlin: B. Cassirer, 1922), 3:16.

II

POLITICAL LEADERSHIP AND THE IRRATIONAL

5

GLADSTONE, SIN, AND
THE BULGARIAN HORRORS

Psychoanalysis has a lesson, not only for historians but for the world: an individual is an integral unity—is all of a piece on many levels of consciousness that dynamically interact. This is not merely a statement of conviction, it is demonstrable with great clinical intensity, and it is equally evident in the empirical study of history.[1] Whereas the psychoanalyst has the richness of a daily interaction, the historian has the context and longitudinal picture of a life.

We now know the permutations of the life of William Ewart Gladstone (1809–1898), the "Grand Old Man" of English Liberalism who was the leader of four ministries—more than those of any other prime minister in British history—with greater completeness than any of his contemporaries. We have before us the preeminent Victorian's theology, writings, political acts, and personal life from childhood to old age—nearly ninety years—for historical research and interpretation.[2]

The facts of Gladstone's life and career are well documented. He was born in Liverpool in 1809, the fourth son of a wealthy merchant family of Scottish ancestry on both sides. His father's fortune came from grain trading, shipping, and major slaveholding West Indian plantations. We tend to forget the truly staggering profits made by early industrial and commercial entrepreneurs in the age of Marx's capital accumulation by surplus value. John Gladstone's balance sheet in the war year 1812–1813 shows that he allocated two fifths of his income for a high standard of living and three fifths for savings and investment:

> Income: £45,051
> Expenses: £17,630
> Profit: £27,421[3]

In 1815 the family moved from Rodney Street, Liverpool, to Seaforth, a large estate with a farm and a village, facing the estuary of the Mersey. John Gladstone, who had been born and raised a Presbyterian, wanted an evangelical low church whose ministry and message he could control, so he built and endowed churches in both Liverpool and Seaforth.[4] He was elected an MP for Lancaster in 1818, and became Sir John, a baronet with title to pass to his eldest son, in 1846. His father left William a rich landed gentleman; in 1868 William estimated that his inheritance was "about £120,000."[5]

William's mother, Anne Robertson, conveyed to him her evangelical religious sensibilities, which included intense piety, a deep personal sense of sin to act as a spur to devotion and self-improvement, and a distrust of church mediation. When her eldest son, Tom, was flogged at Eton, she wrote him, "Flogging, like physic, is bitter, but it is wholesome."[6] She was a hypochondriacal invalid (biliousness, weakness, constipation, headaches, toothaches, and rheumatism). As the family moved from one spa to another, in the words of Checkland, "Mrs. Gladstone's couch became a kind of moveable shrine."[7] She was shy, full of social fears and uncertainties, taboos, and inhibitions, fearing public appearances and London social life. Mr. Canning, a close friend of John Gladstone's, stayed away from Seaforth out of solicitude for her health.[8]

His father was forty-five and his mother thirty-seven when William was born. Because of the mother's incapacitation, her place as caretaker was taken by her eldest child, Anne, who was William's godmother and seven years his senior. Anne became indispensable to both parents and to William, to whom she also became a foster mother who inculcated piety and evangelical strictness, together with liveliness, appreciation of himself, sympathy, and common sense.

Gladstone attended Eton and Christ Church, Oxford, where he was beaten for priggishness in his rooms by "a party of men" for reporting their disturbance in chapel.[9] He became president of the Oxford Union and graduated with a "double first" in classics and mathematics. Although he was a member of the Church of England, he had an evangelical Calvinist conscience that drove him to hard work and gave him no peace from his sexual lusts. In the 1830s he gradually moved to a High Church Anglo-Catholicism.[10]

Gladstone went to Parliament as a Tory member for the Duke of Newcastle's pocket borough of Newark in 1832, at the youthful age of twenty-three.[11] He was a proslavery spokesman in the Commons, defending his father's views, and negotiated in the committees regulating compensation of slave owners when abolition became law at the end of 1833; John Gladstone received compensation of £93,526 for 2,039 slaves in his possession.[12] In 1839 William married Catherine Glynne, who had wealth and shared his religious convictions and political interests.

Gladstone was elected a member of Parliament for Oxford University in 1847; was Chancellor of the Exchequer in 1852; became a Liberal in 1859. Gladstone's first, so-called Great, ministry (1868–1874), achieved the disestablishment of the Anglican Church in Ireland. In 1880 he waged the Midlothian ("Little Englander") campaign, which brought him again to office. The hallmarks of his second ministry (1880–1885) included the Irish Coercion Act, British control of Egypt, and the Third Reform Bill. In 1886 Gladstone's third ministry split the Liberal Party over Irish home rule. He formed his fourth ministry (1892–1894); it too failed to pass home rule, this time blocked in the House of Lords. Gladstone resigned as prime minister for the last time in 1894 and died of cancer of the palate and cheekbone, in great pain and under morphine sedation, in 1898.

II

From Gladstone's long and eventful career I have chosen to focus on the important policy position he took on the Near Eastern question in the late 1870s, centering on what is commonly known as the the "Bulgarian Agitation." The integrity of the inner life and the public man is clearly demonstrated in Gladstone's writing and political policies on the Near Eastern crisis in the years 1876 to 1878. Traditional British policy was to keep the Russians out of the Dardanelles and the Mediterranean, keep the lifeline to India and the Far East open (Gibraltar, Malta, Suez), and to that end support the Ottoman Empire. Holding back Russian expansion at Turkish expense is the reason Britain fought the Crimean War (1854–1856).

In May 1876 the Ottoman Empire brought in Circassian irregular troops to crush brutally a revolt of Bulgarian nationalists. As the news filtered out from the Balkans through journalists and consular reports, public sympathy was aroused and opposition to the Tory government's Eastern policy was organized. Initially, Gladstone stayed clear of the agitation. But, as he recalled two decades later, in 1876, when he thought the Bulgarian question "for the moment dead, and had postponed action upon it, tidings of an intended working men's meeting in Hyde Park" led him to "at once perceive that the iron was hot and that the time to strike had arrived."[13] We see that what excited Gladstone and moved him to action was not repugnance at the atrocities but the insight that they were the key to an emotional political mass movement. He himself put it dramatically: "Good ends can rarely be attained in politics without passion: and there is now, the first time for a good many years, a virtuous passion."[14] Aggression was harnessed to high Christian moral purpose in a political campaign that would return him to office. There was in Gladstone abundant hostility and moral righteousness.[15]

Gladstone wrote three widely read pamphlets on the "Eastern Question": *The Bulgarian Horrors* (1876), *Lessons in Massacre* (1877), and *The Paths of Honour and of Shame* (1878).*The Bulgarian Horrors* is a document of political demagoguery, moral indignation, and florid hyperbole in which Gladstone indicts Britain with "moral complicity with the basest and blackest outrages upon record within the present century, if not within the memory of man." He wrote of

shame . . . horror, pain, and indignation . . . of a gigantic wrong . . .
crimes and outrages, so vast in scale as to exceed all modern example, and
so unutterably vile as well as fierce in character, that it passes the power
of the heart to conceive, and of tongue and pen adequately to describe
them. These are the Bulgarian Horrors . . . abominations . . . a broad line
of blood . . . a lurid glare . . . the horror and infamy of massacre . . .
excesses, than which none more abominable have disgraced the history of
the world . . . elaborate and refined cruelty—the only refinement of which
Turkey boasts!—the utter disregard of sex and age—the abominable and
bestial lust—and the utter and violent lawlessness. . . . [M]urdering, burning, impaling, roasting, men, women, and children indiscriminately, with
the extremest refinements of cruelty. . . . [S]cenes, at which hell itself
might almost blush. . . . Satanic orgies . . . unbounded savagery . . . unbridled and bestial lust . . . ferocious passions . . . horrible outrages.[16]

Then came Gladstone's famous coda:

Their Zaptiehs and their Mudirs, their Bimbashis and their Yuzbachis,
their Kaimakans and their Pashas, one and all, bag and baggage, shall, I
hope, clear out from the province they have desolated and profaned. This
thorough riddance, this most blessed deliverance, is the only reparation we
can make to those heaps on heaps of dead; to the violated purity alike of
matron, of maiden, and of child; to the civilization which has been af-
fronted and shamed; to the laws of God or, if you like, of Allah; to the
moral sense of mankind at large. There is not a criminal in an European
gaol, there is not a cannibal in the South Sea Islands, whose indignation
would not rise and overboil at the recital of that which has been done,
which has been too late examined, but which remains unavenged; which
left behind all the foul and all the fierce passions that produced it, and
which may again spring up, in another murderous harvest, from the soil
soaked and reeking with blood, and in the air tainted with every imagin-
able deed of crime and shame.[17]

Lessons in Massacre was even more sadomasochistic in its lurid
pornography. Here Gladstone stood, in the words of Ann Saab, "defenseless before the temptation of demagoguery."[18] He dwells on

deeds of blood and shame. . . . [A] man, who . . . had been burned with
hot irons upon the breast. . . . [B]urning, the heaps of unburied corpses of
women and children . . . savage and filthy brutality. . . . [A] boy had his
forearms flayed . . . a child was cut to pieces (and his flesh offered for
sale—to whom?) . . . "unspeakable atrocities" on females. . . . [A man] was
partially hung, his toes just touching the ground, and kept so until he
fainted. . . . Four hundred men, heavily chained, were "mercilessly beaten
by their escort." . . . [G]ross maltreatment of a boy, including . . . "beating him unmercifully over the head." . . . [A girl] of thirteen or fourteen,
was twice violated, the second time "before her father's eyes." . . . [T]he
women . . . unable to repair to the field, as the Turks violate them; a man
sent to the place to work at harvest, but the Turks attempt to violate *him
as well as* his mother. . . . [M]any women had been ravished, often in the
presence of their relations. . . . [A]bominations hard to believe, and in
some cases far too foul to name . . . plunder, murder, rape, and bestiality.

. . . [*V*]*iolation, followed by the murder, of a girl of fourteen, in the presence of her mother.* . . . [T]he great anti-human specimen of humanity . . . which can convert human life into one huge mass of misery, uniform and unredeemed . . . lost alike to truth, to mercy, and to shame.[19]

Thereon followed *The Paths of Honour and of Shame* (1878), whose opening lines read: "If this age has pride, and if its pride requires a whipping, the needful discipline is perhaps not far to seek."[20] His political opponent, Prime Minister Benjamin Disraeli, termed Gladstone "a sophistical rhetorician, inebriated with the exuberance of his own verbosity."[21]

Russia perceived the diplomatic situation as exceedingly favorable for a war against Turkey because Britain was "bound by the outburst of humanitarian sentiment."[22] The czar declared war on Turkey on 24 April 1877, initiating the fourth Russo-Turkish war of the nineteenth century, and pushed forward until by the end of January 1878 Russian armies were at the gates of Constantinople. The British sent their fleet through the Straits as a counterpoise and warning. The British ambassador to Constantinople, Sir Austen Henry Layard, wonderfully expressed the arrogance of the British imperial temper:

It is the most monstrous piece of folly that we should be ready to sacrifice the most vital interests of our country, India, our position as a first-class Power, the influence that we have hitherto exercised in the cause of human liberty and civilisation, rather than stand shoulder to shoulder with the Turks, *because some Bashibazuks have murdered some worthless and unfortunate Bulgarians!*[23]

The Treaty of San Stefano on 3 March 1878 legitimated Russian gains at Turkey's expense, including autonomy for a large Bulgaria under Russian occupation, which incorporated Macedonia and a seaport on the Aegean. Three days later the Austrians called for a congress of the powers to revise the treaty. The Berlin Congress, 13 June–13 July 1878, with Bismarck acting as "honest broker," carved up the Ottoman Empire, but largely undid the Russian gains in Europe, compensating Russia with the Asian Ottoman lands of Kars, Batum, and Ardahan; the Austrians received a mandate to occupy and administer Bosnia and Herzegovina; Britain got Cyprus, a further protection of its Eastern Mediterranean interest; and the French were permitted to occupy Tunis. Disraeli returned home to popular acclaim, boasting of having achieved "Peace with Honour!"[24]

III

In the Bulgarian Agitation Gladstone was reenacting on an international political stage fantasies and behaviors in the realm of sin, pain, sadism, sex, and rescue that he had expressed and acted out earlier on the smaller, more intimate, in some cases secret, stage of his personal life.

Gladstone seriously injured himself in a hunting accident in 1842; his finger was amputated without anesthetic. His diary recounts the event and its aftermath of pain.

> Went to shoot . . . & after firing one barrel at a partridge, while reloading, found the forefinger of my left hand shattered by the discharge of the 2d barrel—wh must I fear have been at full cock.

He related his pain and survival to divine intervention:

> Thankfulness to my Almighty Father who thus delivered [me][25] guilty and unworthy as I am. . . . I have hardly ever in my life had to endure serious bodily pain: this was short.[26]

Two days later he concluded that he had desired the pain to remind him of his human fragility and mortality:

> This silly & carnal temper has I hope received a rebuke from the Divine mercy in the slight loss I have endured. But also I really reached[27] [wanted] some lesson however little in bodily pain lest I should forget or hold only a dead remembrance of that part of the lot of mortality.[28]

Six days after the amputation he rationalized his pain as being beneficial because it quelled his bodily lusts. He was guilty and loaded with offenses:

> Suppose my little loss have had the effect of barring out wholly or in part during the last week carnal & worldly thoughts. And suppose, which surely ought not to be the case, that this should be the whole of the good resulting from it. Yet that one shade of sin the less should have passed over the soul is a benefit cheaply purchased indeed by the loss of a finger.[29]

Three months later he was aware of the pleasure he derived from pain:

> Eth[ics] Has it been sufficiently considered, how far pain may become the ground of enjoyment. How far satisfaction and even an action delighting in pain may be a true experimental phenomenon of the human mind. May not such virtue often exist, as shall find when the lower faculty is punished or straightened, a joy in the justice and in the beneficial effects of that chastisement, which shall do more than compensate and counteract even at the moment the suffering of the punishment itself?[30]

During his first ministry Gladstone had an intense relationship with a beautiful evangelical former courtesan, one Laura Thistlethwayte. In the fall of 1869 and winter of 1870 letters to her appear almost daily in the diary. They were sent in special envelopes to avoid the private secretaries. This is one of the two areas that Gladstone kept secret from his wife, Catherine.[31] His infatuation took up much of his time in letters and meetings. A few samples of Gladstone's most interesting entries on this affair:[32]

> *19 October 1869:*
> The letter of yesterday from Mrs. Th. caused me to ruminate in a maze. But I believe all is right with her.

20 October:
A letter from Mrs. T. much wounded disturbed me. I have a horror of giving inner pain to a woman.

21 October:
Wrote to Mrs. Thistlethwayte (but with no power of sending).

22 October:
8 1/2 A.M. Wrote again to Mrs. Thistlethwayte, from whom came touching, but bewildering letters.

25 October:
8 1/2 A.M. Wrote to Mrs. Thistlethwayte. Narrative and letters taken together I am indeed astonished, though interested, & bound in honour to do the best I can for her if she really needs it.

28 October:
Wrote to Mrs. Thistlethwayte: in great gravity of spirit. Duty and evil temptation are there before me, on the right & left. But I firmly believe in her words "holy and "pure", & in her cleaving to God.

November 10:
Saw Mrs. Th. 5 1/4–7 1/4.

November 11:
Dined with the Thistlethwaytes . . . X.[33]

November 12:
Mrs Thistlethwayte called here & looked at the *family* pictures. . . . With Mrs. Th. to whom I read Helen's notable paper on ambition.

November 13:
I made a few verses, by way of translation, for Mrs. Th. Dined with the Queen as did C.[34]

November 17:
Went at 10 [P.M.] to see Mrs Th. I was lionised over her pretty room.[35]

November 18:
Mrs. Thistlethwayte 4 1/2–6: we talked of deep matters.

December 11:
Off at 10.30 with A. K[innaird] to join Mrs. Th. and her party at Waterloo. We reached Boveridge [the Thistlethwayte's country house near Cranborne, Dorset] in heavy rain between 2 & 3. Saw the fine *stud*. And walked a little about the place. . . . Saw Mrs Th. several times.

December 12:
Mrs Th. came to my rooms aft. & at night. Walk with her.

December 13:
Went with Mrs Th. who drove to the "meet" at Mr. Churchills. . . . Rode back with her. Also she came with us to Fordingbridge station. How very far I was at first from understanding her history and also her character.

December 19:
Much conversation with C. & some with Jane respecting Mrs Th.

December 29 [Gladstone's sixtieth birthday]:
My review this year includes a prominent object L[aura] T[histlethwayte]: the extraordinary history, the confiding appeal, the singular avowal. It entails much upon me: and as I saw most clearly of all today, first to do what in me may lie towards building up a true domestic community of life and purpose there.

January 6, 1870:
Wrote a letter to Mrs Th. which I may reserve for further consideration.

January 17:
Read . . . L.T.s Autobiographical MS.—some three hours.

January 18:
[T]hree more hours were spent on continuing the reperusal of Mrs T.s really marvellous & most touching tale.

January 19:
Finished the L.T. MS. and reviewed my unsent letter of the 6th which expresses the firm desire of my better mind to build up her married life into greater fulness and firmness not withstanding the agonies out of which it came & in which it grew.

January 20:
Rose early and wrote to Mrs Thistlethwayte a letter covering that of the 6th.

Gladstone wore a ring given to him by Mrs. Thistlethwayte, writing her: "I will have it engraved: 'L.T. to W.E.G.'" She insisted on only "L." He gave her his annotated copy of Tennyson.[36]

The earl of Derby, a Conservative M.P., noted the relationship in his journal:

11 December 1869:
Strange story of Gladstone frequenting the company of a Mrs. Thistlethwaite, a kept woman in her youth, who induced a foolish person with a large fortune to marry her. She has since her marriage taken to religion, and preaches or lectures. This, with her beauty, is the attraction to G. and it is characteristic of him to be indifferent to scandal. But I can scarcely believe the report that he is going to pass a week with her and her husband at their country house—she not being visited or received in society.

14 December:
Malmsbury called . . . and confirmed the story of Gladstone's going to visit the Thistlethwaites! A strange world! He also says that the Liberal party expect him (G.) either to die or break down.[37]

And the Tory Lord Carnarvon said, "Gladstone seems to be going out of his mind. Northcote has just told me that Gladstone's last passion is Mrs. Thistlethwayte. He goes to dinner with her and she in return in her preachments to her congregation exhorts them to put up their prayers on behalf of Mr. G's reform bill."[38]

Gladstone's "rescue work" with prostitutes whom he met on the London streets late at night was well known and regarded at the time as eccentric and politically dangerous. He said: "These talkings of mine are certainly not within the rules of worldly prudence." He referred to them as "the chief burden of my soul." He was subjected to attempted blackmail by threatened exposure to the press. Undeterred, Gladstone immediately went to the police and the courts.[39]

Gladstone also read what he regarded as pornography: Petronius, Restoration poems, bawdy French fables.[40] The means and seductions of evil were insidious. Although he rationalized that he was seeking enlightenment, he succumbed to his own wicked prurience. He tells of frequenting bookshops where

> the eye may range over books which do not contain polluted matter, with an expectation that itself pollutes. . . . I found two vile poems, and of these with disgust I hope but certainly with a corrupt sympathy I read parts under that very pretext, repudiated by myself as being *for me* a sheer and wicked delusion, of acquiring a knowledge of the facts of nature & manners of men.[41]

He could manage only in a foreign tongue to record his feelings of shame in his diary [translated from the Italian]:

> I began to read it, and found in some parts of it impure passages, . . . so I drank the poison, sinfully—I have stained my memory and my soul—which may it please God to cleanse for me, as I have need. Have set down a black mark against this day.[42]

> I have found beastlinesses under the most innocent headings; I should have sheered off at the first hints of evil—may these be the last of such base explorations.[43]

> Having fallen yet again among impurities: how strong and subtle are the evils of that age, and of this. I read sinfully, although with disgust, under the pretext of hunting solely for what was innocent; but—criminal that I am—with a prurient curiosity against all the rules of pious prudence, and inflaming the war between the better qualities of man and the worse.[44]

Gladstone marked an X in his diaries when he read pornography, in some cases underlined three times. He listed his temptations and their antidotes *seriatim*. As "*Channels*" for stimulation he systematically listed, apparently in ascending order: "1 Thought, 2 Conversation, 3 Hearing, 4 Seeing, 5 Touch, and 6 Company." Under the category "*Incentives*" he used Greek letters [Πρόζτι] to write prosti[tute], as in "Curiosity of knowledge . . . prosti[tute]," "see in form prosti[tute]," "see in movement prosti[tute]," "see in language prosti[tute]." Among "*Remedies*" he listed "immediate pain," "not . . . to look over books in bookshops except known ones," and "Ditto as to looking into printshop windows."[45]

He was often in the Commons until midnight. His conversations with prostitutes became regular in May 1849 and lasted for the next forty years, including during his prime ministerships. His wife knew about them, the "fallen women" were invited to his home, and their names are noted in his diary. On Sundays he often went into their lodging houses for talks and tea long into the night. For example, he records: "My trusts are Carnal or the withdrawal of them would not leave such a void. *Was* it possibly from this that thinking P.L. [a prostitute] would look for me as turned out to be the fact, I had a second interview & conversation indoors here: & heard more history: yet I trusted without harm done."[46]

Not until 1975, when Oxford University Press published Gladstone's complete diaries, did the world know how sexually aroused and how guilty the "rescue work" with prostitutes made him. He was a secret flagellant who scourged himself in punishment for sexual temptation. This is the second area he kept from his wife. His notes were kept on a separate sheet, later listed in his diary, and finally entered by a symbol resembling a whip [♄]. He became addicted to the whip and used it when sexually aroused or guilty: "Went to E[lizabeth] C[ollins]'s [a prostitute]—received (unexpectedly) & remained 2 hours: a strange & humbling scene—returned & ♄ "[47] This was followed two days later by: "Fell in with E. C. & another mixed scene somewhat like that of 48 hours before— ♄ afterwards."[48]

Gladstone was deeply conflicted about his contact with "fallen women" and doubted his own motives and efficacy. Indeed, it disturbed his sleep. By his own estimate, he spoke with at least eighty prostitutes; in getting them to abandon their trade he had a possible success rate of one:

> This morning I lay awake till four with a sad & perplexing subject: it was reflecting on & counting up the numbers of those unhappy beings, now present to my memory with whom during now so many years I have conversed indoors and out. I reckoned from 80 to 90. Among these there is but one of whom I know that the miserable life has been abandoned *and* that I can fairly join that fact with influence of mine.[49]

Gladstone believed in humankind's generic sinfulness and in his own personal depravity. A few days prior to his twenty-first birthday he recorded in his diary:

> I, the sinner, the twofold sinner, the sinner within & without, sinner within my rankling passions, (passions which I dare not name—shame forbids it & duty does not seem to require it—) and sinner without in the veil of godliness and of moderation too which I have cast over them—(and my moderation adds to my sin because it renders me much less suspected than if I were a bold and manly character—) I, the hypocrite, and the essence of sin, am indeed deceitful above all things and desperately wicked, desperately wicked.[50]

When he was seventy-eight years old he declared, "I believe in a degeneracy of man, in the Fall—in *sin*—in the intensity and virulence of sin. No other religion but Christianity meets the sense of sin, and sin is the great fact in the world to me."[51]

Of Gladstone's theological competence, Cardinal Newman said, "He talks of divinity as a clergyman talks of geology."[52] This theology included a literal belief in the Crucifixion, with an emphasis on the centrality of God's inflicting pain on his innocent Son. To modern Christians who preferred a symbolic interpretation, he responded that their error was to "presuppose . . . that *pain is essentially or at least universally an evil.* . . . But this, it seems to me, ought to be denied. Pain is not in its nature an evil in the proper sense, nor is it invariably attended with evil as a consequence." The effect of pain is to "energize . . . feelings of self-mortification and self sacrifice."[53] His character was riven by severe conflicts, which are succinctly characterized by J. H. Plumb: "He was deeply and genuinely, indeed almost painfully, religious and at the same time powerfully and, to himself, distressingly sensual, a conflict that drove him to self-flagellation on the one hand and to the pursuit of whores in the street on the other."[54]

IV

Gladstone's instinctual drives and defenses are exposed and evident as only those of a pre-twentieth century character could be.[55] His life and conflicts read as though they were plotted to fit Freud's structural model, with powerful id in conflict with punitive superego. The Freudian theory had its origin in the bourgeois Victorian culture of the late nineteeth century, and is of splendid utility when considering Gladstone. His ego functioning is equally clearly delineated. In the Bulgarian agitation it was politically excellent. He was able to take the high moral ground, find the enemy in the evil Turks, immensely project in religious idioms that appealed to his Liberal nonconformist national constituency, and return to power in the moral crusade of the Midlothian campaign and election of 1880.

Pornography, the prostitutes, and Mrs. Laura Thistlethwayte were sexually needed and exciting objects for Gladstone that he attacked and attempted to repress by beating himself. His aim was to desexualize and idealize the prostitutes by depriving them of their exciting and frustrating libidinal qualities. He reenacted his childhood romance with the exciting and rejecting temptress whom he would rescue and protect from his stern and punitive father. He split the internal image of his mother into two: the sexually tempting and exciting image that was also frustrating and rejecting, his mother and his sister Anne in the first instance, which became the fantasies of his pornography, and Mrs. Thistlethwayte. The "bad," "evil" image became the Disraeli government, which he pictured as cold, uncaring, manipulative, and insensitive, with no humanitarian feeling for those who suffered; and the cruel, raping, butchering Turks in whom he could see no positive functions for British diplomacy nor any good human qualities.

Inner fantasies and conflicts affect, in ways subtle and manifest, the policies, conduct, indeed, the discourse and imagery of all humankind. In such respects was Gladstone affected, particularly in the Balkan crisis of the late 1870s. When the individual is a major historical or cultural figure, our precisely interpreting and comprehending these relationships enriches our understanding of the person; the person's choices, decision making, the very language of presentation and symbolism; and the dynamics of political power. No political personality better conveys the psychodynamic unity of character than Gladstone, the embodiment of nineteenth-century Liberalism, who has been fittingly called "the Ayatollah of Victorian Christianity."[56]

NOTES

1. The idea that literary and theological production, state policy, and the most intimate inner life are integrally interwoven and psychologically determined in both their apparently "rational" and "irrational" aspects is anathema to many historians, whose refrain is "The crucial distinction for purposes of explanation is between rational and irrational actions. The first can be accounted for in terms of the norms operative in a particular culture; it is only in the case of the second that we are warranted in going beyond these to look for unconscious motives and intentions." Gerald Izenberg, "Psychohistory and Intellectual History," *History and Theory* 14 (1975): 146–47. For other examples of this line of argument, see Jacques Barzun, *Clio and the Doctors: Psycho-History, Quanto-History and History* (Chicago: University of Chicago Press, 1974); and David E. Stannard, *Shrinking History: On Freud and the Failure of Psychohistory* (New York: Oxford University Press, 1980).

2. Richard Shannon is unique among biographers to have treated Gladstone's first fifty-six years with psychoanalytical sophistication. *Gladstone, 1809–1865*, vol. 1 (London: Hamish Hamilton, 1982). Peter Gay and Judith Hughes have also dealt with Gladstone psychoanalytically. Gay interprets fantasies of rescue and reparation. *Freud for Historians* (New York: Oxford University Press, 1985), pp. 188–89; and *The Bourgeois Experience: Victoria to Freud*, vol. 2, *The Tender Passion* (New York: Oxford University Press, 1986), pp. 384–88. Hughes's appraisal, in the context of comparison with the contemporaneous German imperial leadership, is generally admiring. She holds, for example, that Gladstone

> did not in an effort to avoid anxiety cut off feelings, thereby administering an anesthetic to his emotional life. . . . If Gladstone's strenuous involvement with prostitutes figured as a symptom of his mental distress, it also offered therapeutic gain. . . . He did not require outward success to confirm his sense of personal worth.

Emotion and High Politics: Personal Relations at the Summit in Late Nineteenth-Century Britain and Germany (Berkeley: University of California Press, 1983), pp. 24–28, passim. Although my interpretation differs from Hughes's, her well-argued theses were a stimulus to writing this chapter.

3. S. G. Checkland, *The Gladstones: A Family Biography* (London: Cambridge University Press, 1971), p. 77.

4. Ibid., pp. 78–80.

5. Ibid., Appendix II, "The Gladstone Fortune," p. 416.

6. Catherine Gladstone to Tom Gladstone, 20 February 1819, as quoted ibid., p. 135.

7. Ibid., p. 86.

8. Ibid., p. 87.

9. Shannon, *Gladstone*, 1:26.

10. For Gladstone's religious development in the 1830s, see Perry Butler, *Gladstone, Church, State, and Tractarianism: A Study of His Religious Ideas and Attitudes, 1809–1859* (Oxford: Oxford University Press, 1982), pp. 49–60; and Peter J. Jagger, *Gladstone, The Making of a Christian Politician: The Personal Religious Life and Development of William Ewart Gladstone, 1809–1832* (Allison Park: Pickwick Publications, 1991), pp. 126–39.

11. John Morley, *The Life of William Ewart Gladstone* (New York: Macmillan, 1903), 1:88.

12. Joyce Marlow, *The Oak and the Ivy: An Intimate Biography of William and Catherine Gladstone* (New York: Doubleday, 1977), p. 14.

13. Shannon, *Gladstone and the Bulgarian Agitation, 1876* (London: Thomas Nelson and Sons, 1963), p. 100.

14. Ibid., pp. 106–7.

15. As Richard Shannon reminds us:

The . . . point that needs to be made about Gladstone, but never is, is that he was a man whose vent for aggressiveness was unsurpassed by any contemporary statesman. His savaging of Cornewall Lewis in 1857 shocked those who witnessed it (Edward Stanley was certain that Gladstone was off his head); and Gladstone's other victims—Palmerston, Disraeli, and latterly Chamberlain—had every reason for diagnosing a vindictiveness which went far beyond the merits of particular political cases.

R. T. Shannon, "Adversaries from the Cradle," *Times Literary Supplement*, 6 January 1984, p. 9. Cf. Shannon, *Gladstone*, p. 331.

16. William E. Gladstone, *The Bulgarian Horrors and the Question of the East* (London: John Murray, 1876), pp. 9–19 and 30–56 passim.

17. Gladstone, *Bulgarian Horrors*, pp. 61–63 passim.

18. Ann Pottinger Saab, *Reluctant Icon: Gladstone, Bulgaria, and the Working Classes, 1856–1878* (Cambridge: Harvard University Press, 1991), p. 79.

19. William E. Gladstone, *Lessons in Massacre; or the Conduct of the Turkish Government in and about Bulgaria since May, 1876* (London: John Murray, 1877), pp. 6–29, 47–56, and 76–79 passim.

20. W. E. Gladstone, "The Paths of Honour and of Shame," *The Nineteenth Century* 3:13 (March 1878): 591–604; quotation, p. 591.

21. Richard Shannon, *The Age of Disraeli, 1868–1881: The Rise of Tory Democracy* (London: Longman, 1992), p. 307. Ann Saab comments appropriately on the social level of Gladstone's audience and its members' inner lives but not on the personal life of the man who created the texts:

It was a picture of an oppressive ruling class which had many symbolic associations for Britons, at a time when the luxury, corruption, and immorality of the "Upper Ten Thousand" were a standing grievance with the Nonconformist middle and working classes. The repelled yet fascinated prurience on which Gladstone drew, and which also attracted readers to the newspaper accounts of the massacres, was not unrelated to the titillated revulsion which greeted tales of sexual misdemeanors in high places in England.

Saab, *Reluctant Icon*, p. 92.

22. Richard Millman, *Britain and the Eastern Question* (Oxford: Clarendon Press, 1979), p. 266.

23. Layard to Derby, 2 January 1878, in R. W. Seton-Watson, *Disraeli, Gladstone and the Eastern Question: A Study in Diplomacy and Party Politics* (London: Macmillan, 1935), p. 244.

24. B. H. Sumner, *Russia and the Balkans, 1870–1880* (Oxford: Clarendon Press, 1937); W. N. Medlicott, *Bismarck, Gladstone, and the Concert of Europe* (London: Athlone Press, 1935); Seton-Watson, *Disraeli, Gladstone and the Eastern Question*; Barbara Jelavich, *The Ottoman Empire, the Great Powers, and the Straits Question, 1870–1887* (Bloomington: Indiana University Press, 1973).

25. Gladstone's slip or perhaps uncompleted thought. The original reads "his" [son?]

26. 13 September 1842, *The Gladstone Diaries*, ed. M. R. D. Foot and H. C. G. Matthew 11 vols. to 1990, (Oxford: Clarendon Press, 1982), 3:224 (cited hereafter as *Diaries*).

27. Gladstone's slip or uncompleted thought.

28. 15 September 1842, *Diaries*, 3:225.

29. Monday, 19 September 1842, *Diaries*, 3:226.

30. Wednesday, 4 January 1843, *Diaries*, 3:250–51.

31. The other secret was his self-flagellation. Shannon, *Gladstone*, pp. 95, 534. Although quite innocuous in itself, a secret is important precisely *because* it is intimate and hidden—it bears shameful fantasies and painful affects, including fears of damage if it is revealed. Cf. Ralph R. Greenson, *The Technique and Practice of Psychoanalysis*, vol. 1 (New York: International Universities Press, 1967), pp. 128–33.

32. All daily entries are from *Diaries*, 6:152–224 passim.

33. An X in Gladstone's diary was his code for "rescue work done this day," meaning a morally dangerous meeting with a prostitute, connoting sexual temptation.

34. C indicates Gladstone's wife, Catherine, *née* Glynne.

35. "To lionise" was a verb in common nineteenth-century usage, meaning to view the objects of curiosity or interest in a place.

36. H. C. G. Matthew, *Gladstone, 1809–1874* (Oxford: Clarendon Press, 1986), pp. 240 n, 241 n. On Gladstone's relationship to Tennyson, see Gerhard Joseph, *Tennyson and the Text: The Weaver's Shuttle* (Cambridge: Cambridge University Press, 1992), pp. 130–140.

37. John Vincent, ed., *Disraeli, Derby and the Conservative Party: Journals and Memoirs of Edward Henry, Lord Stanley, 1849–1869* (Hassocks, Sussex: Harvester Press, 1978), p. 346.

38. Matthew, *Gladstone*, p. 240 n.

39. Matthew, *Gladstone*, pp. 90–94 passim.

40. *Fabliaux et contes des poètes françois des XI-XVe siècles, publiés par Barbazon*, 4 vols. (1808).

41. Wednesday, 19 July 1848, *Diaries*, 4:55.

42. Saturday [after Good Friday], 13 May 1848, *Diaries*, 4:35–36.

43. Monday [after Easter], 15 May 1848, *Diaries*, 4:36.

44. Thursday, 18 May 1848, *Diaries*, 4:37.

45. Sunday, 26 October 1845, *Diaries*, 3:492–93. See also Tuesday, 21 December 1847, *Diaries*, 3:677–78, where this day is marked X thrice underlined.

46. Sunday, 30 March 1851, *Diaries*, 4:319.

47. Sunday, 13 July, 1851, *Diaries*, 4:344.

48. Tuesday, 15 July 1851, *Diaries*, 4:344.

49. Friday, 20 January 1854, *Diaries*, 4:586.

50. Friday, 24 December 1830, *Diaries*, 1:334.

51. Gladstone speaking to Mrs. Humphry Ward, 8 April 1888, in Janet Penrose Trevelyan, *The Life of Mrs. Humphry Ward* (New York: Dodd, Mead, 1923), p. 59.

52. Shannon, *Gladstone*, p. 144 n. 3.

53. Gladstone, "On the Mediation of Christ" (1830), as quoted in Boyd Hilton, "Gladstone's Theological Politics," in *High and Low Politics in Modern Britain: Ten Studies*, ed. Michael Bentley and John Stevenson (Oxford: Clarendon Press, 1983), p. 35.

54. J. H. Plumb, foreword to *Gladstone: A Progress in Politics* by Peter Stansky (Boston: Little, Brown, 1979), p. xii.

55. A psychodynamic understanding of Gladstone lends itself both to a psychoanalytic structural approach and to the insights offered by object-relations theory. The two models of conceptualization are compatible and may be syntonic, applying at different levels of personality development.

56. "God's Great Statesman," *Times Literary Supplement*, 18–24 May 1990, p. 516.

6

THE MURDER AND
MYTHIFICATION OF
WALTHER RATHENAU

When Walther Rathenau, the German foreign minister, was assassinated in Berlin on 24 June 1922, he was a symbol of the Weimar Republic for both its adherents and its enemies. He became a myth that has played a role in the political imagery of Germany to the present.

Rathenau was the scion of the Jewish founder of the world's greatest electric combine, the AEG (*Allgemeine Elektricitäts Gesellschaft*).[1] He became the president of the AEG, a director of the Berliner Handels-Gesellschaft and of numerous other firms and banks, the organizer of Germany's raw-material allocation administration in World War One, a member of the Second Socialization Commission in 1919, and minister of reconstruction in 1921.

During the German Empire Rathenau idealized and craved acceptance from the dominant Junker ruling class.[2] He was crushed as a young man when he did not qualify for the elite Uhlanen guard regiment because he was Jewish. He made strenuous efforts to secure Prussian honors and royal orders. He was rewarded in 1908 with the Crown Order, Second Class, but this was not enough to satisfy his vanity. He lobbied for, and received, two Orders of the Red Eagle, Fourth Class and Second Class, in 1910.[3] In 1909 he bought Freienwalde—a royal castle near Frankfurt on the Oder, designed by Gilly (1772–1800) and formerly the property of Queen Luise of Prussia—from the Crown. He restored the castle with period furniture, tapestries, and portraits of the royal family.[4] The perceptive Viennese Stefan Zweig, who would dislike austere Prussia in any case, recalled:

> One could never really get warm in his feudal Queen Louise palace in
> Brandenburg: its order was too obvious, its arrangement too studied, its

cleanliness too clean. . . . [R]arely have I sensed the tragedy of the Jew more strongly than in his personality which, with all of its apparent superiority, was full of a deep unrest and uncertainty.[5]

To postwar Germans, Rathenau symbolized all that the Weimar Republic stood for: Jewish cosmopolitanism, bourgeois capitalism, a foreign policy of fulfillment and reparations, a domestic politics of moderation and liberalism.[6] Rathenau achieved his political positions as a function of his economic and industrial role. There was among the German elite an overestimation of the importance of Rathenau's financial and commercial relationships with the Western powers. The Rapallo Treaty he signed with the Soviet Union on 16 April 1922, thus shattering the Genoa Conference, constituted an opening to the East that included diplomatic and trade relations, economic aid, mutual cancellation of claims and reparations.[7] The treaty earned him further opprobrium and hatred in Germany.

II

Rathenau and others were aware that as foreign minister, his life was in danger. The British ambassador wrote in his diary during the Genoa Conference: "Rathenau has to face the undying hatred of the Right. . . . [H]e has often told me he is sure to be assassinated."[8] He frequently told Max Scheler that he would share Erzberger's fate.[9]

There was a public hate campaign against him, and anonymous threats came from many sides.[10] The paramilitary Freikorps in Upper Silesia sang a marching song with the chorus:

> Knallt ab den Walther Rathenau
> die gottverdammte Judensau.

> [Knock off Walther Rathenau
> the goddamned Jewish sow.][11]

It would be hard to exaggerate the vehemence of the nationalist opposition to Rathenau. *Wiking*, the organ of Organisation Consul, spewed hatred:

> The appointment of the Jew Rathenau to be German foreign minister is the height of the politically grotesque. . . . His conduct of foreign policy will not contribute to the interests of the German people. . . . [It] will be based rather upon the spirit of international finance. . . . But it will open the eyes of the German people as to who their true rulers are. . . . We will break the Jewish yoke. . . . At present we consider the Jewish question as the cardinal question and central point of our whole foreign and domestic policy.[12]

The Nazi *Völkische Beobachter* ran the headline "The Resurrected from Marx to Rathenau."[13] Another *VB* article termed Rathenau "a stock exchange and Soviet Jew" (*"Börsen- und Sowjetjuden"*). He was an adherent of "insidious creeping Bolshevism" (*"schleichenden Bolschewismus"*).[14]

A particularly significant incident, with due romantic coloring, was related by Reichschancellor Josef Wirth:

> A Catholic priest came to see me at the Reichs Chancellor's Residence and informed me simply and straightforwardly in a few words, yet with great earnestness, that the life of Minister Rathenau was threatened. For understandable reasons, I put no questions to him. The entire exchange transpired exclusively between the Catholic cleric and myself. I was well aware of the seriousness of the warning, and myself made the appropriate report to the relevant section of the Reichschancellory. Then Rathenau himself was called in. I beseeched him with forceful words to at last give up his resistance to a strong security service. In the well known manner, with which many of his friends are so familiar, he decisively refused. I thereupon disclosed the above events to him and asked him whether he understood that the step taken by the Catholic priest was a highly serious matter. My disclosure made a deep impression on Minister Rathenau. He stood before me pale and motionless for about two minutes. Neither of us dared to break the silence with a single word. Rathenau's eyes were as if gazing at a distant land. For a long time he was visibly struggling with himself. Suddenly his face and his eyes took on an expression of infinite kindness and gentleness. With a calm in his soul the like of which I had never seen in him, despite having learnt the full measure of his inner self-control in many discussions of practical and personal issues, he came close to me, laid both hands on my shoulders and said: "Dear friend, it is nothing. Who would do something to me?" Our conversation did not end with this. After a repeated emphasis of the seriousness of the disclosure and the absolute necessity of police protection, he left the Reichschancellory composed and calmly with a, to me incomprehensible, feeling of safety. Regrettably, as I heard later, Rathenau again expressly refused protection.[15]

Hellmut von Gerlach reported that he heard from a German nationalist in February 1922 of a specific murder threat against Rathenau, naming the threatening killer. Gerlach immediately rushed to Rathenau to warn him. Rathenau responded:

> The plan does not surprise me at all. . . . I know that my life is constantly threatened. But what do you want? One cannot protect oneself against it unless one is willing to become a prisoner oneself, to be locked up, or constantly watched by the police. When I took on my office I knew what I was risking. Now it means waiting to see how long the matter takes.[16]

His friend Lily Deutsch affirmed that she advised Rathenau to allow himself to be given protection, which he did briefly. But then the constant guard became a burden that he did not tolerate well, and he canceled it.[17] This was corroborated by an American, Colonel Roddie, who had been at the U.S. embassy in Berlin. He recounted that on a visit to Rathenau's Grunewald home, he had been stopped and interrogated by two plainclothes policemen. On entering the house he told Rathenau how pleased he was to see that he was now taking security measures. Rathenau became very upset, ran to the telephone, called the station, and categorically demanded that the police protection stop; he would not allow his guests to be harassed by police. Later, when Roddie left, the police guard was gone.[18] However, on at least one occasion Rathenau was concerned about intruders and reported them. They turned out to be two Foreign Ministry officials who were closing out some Swiss(!) files stored there.[19]

Secret government reports substantiate that Rathenau was under police observation. His manservant was alerted by the police. The more evident patrols in the neighborhood of his villa were instructed to become inconspicuous.[20] Democratic Party (DDP) Minister Eugen Schiffer wrote in his unpublished memoirs:

> Rathenau has great personal courage. He knows exactly how much he is hated as a man and a politician by many in the land, that they are in fact aiming for his life. But he spurns all police precautions and protective measures as shameful and goes the way that may lead to his destruction with a certain fatalism.[21]

III

On the morning of 24 June 1922, as Rathenau left his home on the Königsallee 65 in the Grunewald section of Berlin, being driven in his large, old, slow, open touring car, his murderers, who had been waiting, pulled up to the vehicle. Their leader was Erwin Kern, age twenty-four, a former first lieutenant in the navy. The others were Hermann Fischer, twenty-six, a former company commander and lieutenant, now an engineer; Ernst-Werner Techow, a twenty-one-year-old student, who drove the car; his sixteen-year-old brother, Hans-Gerd, a gymnasium student; and Ernst von Salomon, later to become a prominent Nazi writer, who was also a leading member of the conspiracy. All were members of Organisation Consul, a secret, illegal military society formed from Freikorps Ehrhardt, demobilized naval veterans who in paramilitary bands had fought Communists in Munich and Poles in Upper Silesia in the immediate postwar disorders, and had been dissolved by the government after the Kapp putsch.[22] The assassins forced Rathenau's automobile to the side, Kern shot Rathenau at close range with a submachine gun, then Fischer threw a hand grenade into the car. Rathenau was hit in five places, his spine and lower jaw were smashed; he died in his home a few minutes later, before the doctor arrived.[23]

The Republic honored Rathenau with a twenty-four-hour funeral holiday, demonstrations in all major cities, including one a million strong in Berlin. His coffin lay in state in the Reichstag, and Reich President Friedrich Ebert himself delivered the funeral oration, saying: "The despicable act struck not only the man Rathenau, it struck Germany in its totality."[24]

The government speedily secured passage of the Act for the Protection of the Republic, which amended the Weimar Constitution to make it illegal to have an association whose purpose was to kill anyone, and

established the special Court for the Protection of the Republic to en-
force the act because it was clear that the conventional judiciary would
not do so. The political vulnerability of the Weimar majority may be
traced in the fate of this law. When it came up for renewal in 1927 it was
extended for only two years and the special court was dropped. By 1929
no majority for further extension was available.[25]

IV

The circumstance of Rathenau's death raises questions of unnecessary
exposure to danger, unconscious collusion with his killers by making
himself an easy target, and the wish, or psychological need, to be mar-
tyred. In psychoanalysis, when we see that an analysand's behavior has
led to a given result, we pose the question whether the person, despite
vigorous denials to the contrary, had that intention and managed to realize it unconsciously. As various nationalist movements, including the
Palestinian, Zionist, women's, gay, and civil rights movements, have
maintained, every act of victimization implies the willingness of someone
to be the victim.

Anyone who has followed the ordeal of those, such as Salman
Rushdie, who must live under round-the-clock guard in order to forestall
assassination can only have sympathy for the desire for personal privacy.
But Rushdie is precisely the point. Rathenau ignored defensive measures
and exposed himself to danger. At a time when American bootleggers
were driving in bulletproof cars, Rathenau was driving in a vehicle so inappropriate that Weismann, the commissioner for public order and chief
of the Prussian police, warned him "that if he persisted in driving to his
office from his residence on the outskirts of Berlin in a slow open car, no
police in the world could guarantee his safety."[26] He behaved like a
person who wishes to be murdered. He was trapped between the Junker
aristocratic pattern of chivalric conduct he idealized and the need for effective action in the service of his own self-preservation.

There is, then, the unresolved problem of the victim's motivation in
Rathenau's murder. After working with Rathenau's personal archival
documents, state papers, and writings for many years, it became clear to
me that in June 1922 this tortured man exposed himself to assassination
by radical-right youth. But why?

There was in Rathenau manifest grandiosity and denial. On the
deepest level he could not accept and believe that he would be gunned
down. Self-destructiveness is the companion of self-hatred. An explanation of homoerotic submission is plausible, given Rathenau's extensive
writings and relationships glorifying blond Nordic ideals of character and
physique. Beginning with Harry Graf Kessler, Rathenau's first biogra-
pher, there is a substantial body of research asserting his homosexual
character orientation.[27]

The same data could be conceptualized in a psychoanalytical object-
relational framework as Rathenau's attraction to a needed enticing,

exciting object that is rejecting and always fails to satisfy, thus reducing him to psychological bondage to a frustrating ideal.[28] Repression—and Rathenau had an inhibited, highly controlled, repressed personality—is a defense that originates in the rejection of both the exciting and the rejecting object by the ego. Rathenau also had an exceptional degree of Jewish self-hatred.[29] In object-relational terms this is the hatred and low esteem that Rathenau felt toward himself for his humiliating dependence on an exciting and forever-rejecting object.

Now, all of this is valid in explaining Rathenau's self-exposure to murder, as far as it goes. But the melancholy tale acquires historical comprehensibility only when the full and subtle factors of class, power, and status in Wilhelmine society, which Rathenau had to deal with and was socialized to, are the setting and a part of the psychodynamic picture.

When placed in the context of the tensions of a pre–World War One German social culture in which the landed aristocratic caste had high status and a stranglehold on power at court, in the military, diplomatic, and higher administrative posts, Rathenau's self-hatred and obeisance to Junker values take on a fuller social coloration. He belonged to the stratum of Jewish high-financial and industrial bourgeoisie that had culture and economic strength but lacked the commensurate social status and political power.[30] His being a Jew, even a financially important one, in Imperial Germany barred Rathenau from becoming an officer in a Prussian guards regiment or a higher civil servant, receiving a ministerial appointment, enjoying a foreign service or judicial career, or attaining a university professorship. As an adult, Rathenau wrote the following lines loaded with social truth and depressive personal affect: "In the youth of every German Jew there is a painful moment that he remembers his whole life: when he becomes fully conscious for the first time that he has entered the world as a second class citizen, and that no degree of competence or merit can ever free him from this position."[31] It was impossible for Rathenau to be knighted (made a "Freiherr") or to be ennobled (given the title "von") regardless of his distinguished services to the German Empire. He accepted and emulated the fashions, values, and ideals of the East Elbian Junkers, behavior that with the development of ego psychology was understood by Anna Freud as "identification with the aggressor," whereby the dominant patterns are assimilated by impersonating the aggressor, assuming his attributes or imitating his conduct.[32]

Neither the intrapsychic nor the social alone is sufficient to explain psychodynamically Rathenau's self-exposure to murder. Together and in dynamic relationship they structure a strong explanation. What from the viewpoint of psychopathology may be seen as the morbidity of Rathenau had a socially syntonic element with his Jewish haute-bourgeois stratum and structural situation in German society. This was emphasized, even in the Weimar Republic, at the socioeconomic level by a press release from industrial magnate Hugo Stinnes during the Spa Conference of 1920 that referred to Rathenau, Dernburg, and Melchior as "German delegates who due [to] their alien psyches caused severe damage to German national interests" (*"aus einer fremdländischen Psyche"*).[33] Rathenau asked to talk to Stinnes on what was to be the last night of his life. He spent from ten o'clock until four in the morning trying futilely to convince Stinnes of the virtue of his policies.[34] This is the historical sociocultural setting of Rathenau's genuflection before those who hated him, and the emotional premise of his ultimate self-sacrifice.

V

The police engaged in a nationwide hunt for Rathenau's murderers. Two of the conspirators fled to the ruins of Burg Saaleck, a medieval castle in Thuringia, where Kern was shot while resisting arrest and Fischer committed suicide. Ernst-Werner Techow was sentenced to fifteen years in prison; the others served shorter terms.

The Nazi appreciation of Rathenau's racist and anti-Semitic writings began not long after his murder. *Blut und Boden* propagandist Walther Darré, who was to become Reich nutrition minister under Hitler, quotes Rathenau's *Reflexionen*[35] with approval as early as 1926.[36] A year and a half later Darré described Rathenau as an "absolute member of the master race" (*"unbedingten Herrenmenschen"*) and "conspicuously objective when confronting his racial comrades and co-religionists" (*"auffallend objektiv gegenüber seinen eigenen Glaubens-und Rassengenossen"*).[37]

With the National Socialist accession to power on 30 January 1933, the glorification of Rathenau's murderers became official government policy. The 60,000 RM cost of moving the bodies of Kern and Fischer was personally authorized by Adolf Hitler on 13 June 1933. A memorial tablet reading "Here died, fighting for Germany, July 17, 1922, our comrades Naval Lieutenant Erwin Kern and Lieutenant Herman Fischer of the Ehrhart Brigade" was dedicated at Burg Saaleck on 17 July 1933. Captain Ehrhart himself unveiled the tablet at ceremonies attended by throngs of S.A. and S.S. men and many civilians. Captain Ernst Röhm, commander of the S.A., praised the "glorious deed" of the assassins. S.S. Reichsführer Heinrich Himmler said: "Without the deed of these two, Germany today would be living under a Bolshevist regime. Let it be realized that irrespective of civil law, neither one's own nor others' blood must be spared when the Fatherland's fate is at stake."[38]

On 29 October 1933 the heroes were further honored in a ceremony at Burg Saaleck addressed by Hans-Gerd Techow, and their bodies were reburied under a gravestone reading:

> *Tu was Du Musst,*
> *Sieg oder Stirb*
> *und Lass Gott*
> *die Entscheidung*
> [Do what you must,
> Triumph or perish

and let God
make the decision][39]

Ernst von Salomon glorified the "Heroes of Saaleck" in a romantic essay in a Nazi schoolbook, writing, "Their death was beautiful" (*"ihr Sterben war schön"*).[40]

The propagandists of the Third Reich utilized the numerous portions of Rathenau's literary corpus that fitted their racist ideology.[41] To have a leading Jewish figure in public life uttering their line was too good to pass up. Writing under a pseudonym, in 1897 Rathenau had published in Maximilian Harden's *Die Zukunft* a classic piece of Jewish self-hatred, "Hear O Israel!"[42] The leading Nazi historian, Walter Frank, president of the Reich's Institute for the History of the New Germany, chose Rathenau's title for his *Studies on the Modern Jewish Question* published during the Third Reich, which included an essay on Rathenau. Frank explained, "I chose this title to express that this publication contains just as much an historical depiction as a political demand."[43] Frank quoted Rathenau's original 1897 essay with approval, calling it "a scream of hatred against himself . . . whose most striking formulations have since become the emergency stock of anti-Jewish propaganda."[44] Although Frank liked the anti-Semitism, he grotesquely caricatured Rathenau's appearance in the most racially charged terms: his head was "more Negro than European"; he had "pointed ears"; was "Moor like"; "his Lapplander nose, his Moorish mouth, his Hottentot eyes."[45] The irony in Rathenau's identification with Germanic racist values and heroic ideals is that the Nazis appreciated his racism, used him as proof of their theories, and saw him as a man who wanted to be like the master race. But he could never make the grade, despite buying a royal castle, pursuing national approval in foreign policy, and exposing himself to assassination. Neither in life nor in death would he be good enough.

VI

Immediately after World War Two a new German democracy, seeking a homegrown liberal Western tradition with which to identify, resurrected Rathenau's reputation. A plaque was dedicated at the site of his murder on the Königsallee. In 1947 the eightieth anniversary of his birth was memorialized in Berlin. Today virtually every West German city of size has a Rathenau Platz. The German Democratic Republic overlooked Rathenau's finance-capitalist background to present him as a pioneer of German-Soviet friendship and a foreign policy of coexistence.[46]

The Bonn republic found in Rathenau a German statesman who was a "good European," who worked for relations based on trust with the Western powers, and who presciently advocated the economic integration of the developed industrial sector of Europe, arguing before World War One that national economic boundaries were outmoded in an economically interdependent world. The first reissuance of

Rathenau's letters in Germany after World War Two was entitled *A Prussian European.*[47]

In the late 1960s when Willy Brandt, then the foreign minister of the Federal Republic, was pursuing a new *Ostpolitik* to open accommodations with the East bloc and the Soviet Union, he called on the heritage of Walther Rathenau's Rapallo policy. He said in 1967: "The German-Russian rapprochement was a totally natural event and was in no way intended in Rathenau's mind to initiate a sensational, one sided, orientation of German foreign policy."[48]

With his murder Rathenau became a hero for a republic that needed heroes. The nationalist Right regarded him as an international Jew whom it could blame for Germany's misfortune. The National Socialists used his life and morbid ideas for their own racist purposes. The Federal Republic found in Rathenau an exemplar of policies of reassurance toward the East, which was a precondition for unification.

NOTES

1. A. Riedler, *Emil Rathenau und das Werden der Grosswirtschaft,* (Berlin: Verlag Julius Springer, 1916); *50 Jahre AEG* (Berlin: AEG, 1956).

2. Peter Loewenberg, "Walther Rathenau and the Tensions of Wilhelmine Society," in *Jews and Germans from 1860 to 1933: The Problematic Symbiosis,* ed. David Bronsen (Heidelberg: Carl Winter Universitätsverlag, 1979), pp. 100–128.

3. Rathenau, *Tagebuch 1907–1922,* ed. and intro. Hartmut Pogge-v. Strandmann (Düsseldorf: Droste Verlag, 1967), pp. 74, 100ff., 118. The Reichschancellor, Bernhard Fürst von Bülow, was patronizing and full of condescension, writing of Rathenau: "The Order and the splendid blue ribbon by which it was worn around the neck pleased him very much, since he placed value on external symbols." *Denkwürdigkeiten,* vol. 3, *Weltkrieg und Zusammenbruch* (Berlin: Verlag Ullstein, 1931), p. 44.

4. Julius Bab, "Der Schlossherr von Freienwalde," *Das Jüdische Magazin* 1 (July 1929): 13–16.

5. Stefan Zweig, *The World of Yesterday: An Autobiography* (New York: Viking Press, 1943), p. 181.

6. Peter Loewenberg, *Walther Rathenau and Henry Kissinger: The Jew as a Modern Statesman in Two Political Cultures* (New York: Leo Baeck Institute, 1980).

7. David Felix, *Walther Rathenau and the Weimar Republic: The Politics of Reparations* (Baltimore: Johns Hopkins University Press, 1971).

8. Edgar Vincent Viscount D'Abernon, *The Diary of an Ambassador: Versailles to Rapallo, 1920–1922* (New York: Doubleday, 1929), p. 323.

9. Max Scheler, "Nachwort," in *Gespräche und Briefe Walther Rathenaus,* ed. Ernst Nordlind (Dresden: Carl Reissner Verlag, 1925), pp. 122–23. Matthias Erzberger was a Catholic Center Party leader who was assassinated by the Right on 26 August 1921 for having signed the Armistice in 1918.

10. See, for example, Karl Pottel to Rathenau, 22 February 1922, Bd. 6, #424; H. F. Simon to Regierungsrat Paul Schwartz, 21 March 1922, Bd. 8, #836; 29 March 1922, Bd. 8, #974; 4 April 1922, Bd. 9, #1041; 2 April 1922, Bd. 12, #1413; and Margarete Adam to Rathenau, 17 May 1922, Bd. 12,

#1382, in Akten betr. Persönliche Angelegenheiten des Ministers, 1 b, Political Archive, Foreign Ministry, Bonn.

11. Harry Graf Kessler, *Walther Rathenau: Sein Leben und Sein Werk* (1928; Wiesbaden: Rheinische Verlags-Anstalt, 1962), p. 356.

12. 15 February 1922, as quoted in Howard Stern, "The Organisation Consul," *Journal of Modern History* 35:1 (March 1963): 28.

13. Felix, *Rathenau and the Weimar Republic*, p. 166.

14. 22 April 1922, as quoted in Ernst Schulin, *Walther Rathenau: Repräsentant, Kritiker und Opfer seiner Zeit* (Göttingen: Musterschmidt, 1979), p. 133.

15. Kessler, *Rathenau*, pp. 355–56.

16. Hellmut von Gerlach, *Von Rechts nach Links* (Zürich: Europa Verlag, 1937), p. 259.

17. Harry Graf Kessler, *Tagebücher: 1918–1937* (Frankfurt am Main: Insel Verlag, 1961), p. 555.

18. Ibid., pp. 616–17.

19. Köhn to H. F. Simon, 22 June 1922, Akten betr. Persönliche Angelegenheiten des Ministers, 1b, Bd. 12, Political Archive, Foreign Ministry, Bonn.

20. Regierungsrat Paul Schwarz to Oberstleutnant, Berlin West, Wilhemstrasse 64, 3 February 1922, Confidential, R.M. 146, Akten betr. Persönliche Angelegenheiten des Ministers, Bd. 4, 1–11 February 1922. Political Archive, Foreign Ministry, Bonn.

21. Nachlass Eugen Schiffer, Rep. 92, Nr.1, Heft 1, p. 25. Hauptarchiv (ehem. Preuss. Geheimes Staatsarchiv), Berlin-Dahlem.

22. Stern, "Organisation Consul," p. 21.

23. *Vossische Zeitung*, 25 June 1922.

24. Kessler, *Rathenau*, p. 368.

25. Arnold Brecht, *Aus Nächster Nähe: Lebenserinnerungen, 1884–1927* (Stuttgart: Deutsche Verlags-Anstalt, 1966), pp. 390–92.

26. Harry Graf Kessler, *Walther Rathenau: His Life and Work* (New York: Harcourt, Brace, 1930), p. 355 n. 16. This note is in the English edition only.

27. Kessler, *Rathenau* (1930), p. 72:

He sometimes honored very inconsequential people with his friendship. In that case, however, they had to be blond, and of the fair-haired Siegfried type, that satisfied his romantic admiration for the Nordic race. Indeed, if they had obvious limitations, this served to strengthen their resemblance to the Nordic ideal type in his eyes. These friendships showed, almost to the point of caricature, how singularly his emotional life was a mixture of erotism and theory.

See also Loewenberg, "Walther Rathenau and the Tensions of Wilhelmine Society," in Bronsen, *Jews and Germans*, pp. 113–14, particularly nn. 69–72.

28. W. Ronald D. Fairbairn, *An Object-Relations Theory of the Personality* (New York: Basic Books, 1952), p. 115. The "object" (to say the least an infelicitous term) represents an original relationship of the child toward the mother.

29. Peter Loewenberg, "Antisemitismus und jüdischer Selbsthass: Eine sich wechselseitig verstärkende sozialpsychologische Doppelbeziehung," *Geschichte und Gesellschaft* 5:4 (1979): 455–475.

30. On the eve of World War One, Robert Michels wrote:

In Germany the Jew is not yet emancipated, or at least only on paper, but not yet in deed. While the most gifted elements among the Jews in other lands, such as France, Italy, England, often go into the administration, yes a few of them even become government ministers—I think of the Italian War Minister

Ottolenghi; of Disraeli, later Lord Beaconsfield in England; of Crémieux, Gambetta and others in France—while the most intellectual and intelligent elements among the Jews in the advanced democratic countries, such as the western European states, are absorbed by the government apparatus and the political life of the nation, the Jews in Germany see themselves completely excluded from these modes of existence; they cannot even become judges or officers, not to speak of higher civil servants.

"Zum Problem der internationalen Bourgeoisie," in *Probleme der Sozialphilosophie* (Leipzig: B. G. Teubner, 1914), pp. 175–76.

31. Walther Rathenau, "Staat und Judentum" (1911), in *Gesammelte Schriften*, 5 vols. (Berlin: S. Fischer, 1918) 1:188–89.

32. Anna Freud, *The Ego and the Mechanisms of Defence*, trans. Cecil Baines (New York: International Universities Press, 1946), p. 121.

33. Nachlass Koch-Weser, Bundesarchiv, Koblenz, Nr. 27, 20 July 1920, p. 263, and 23 July 1920, p. 271.

34. Kessler, *Rathenau*, p. 363.

35. Walther Rathenau, *Reflexionen* (Leipzig: S. Hirzel, 1908).

36. R. Walther Darré, "Walther Rathenau und das Problem des Nordischen Menschen," *Deutschlands Erneuerung*, Heft 7 (July 1926).

37. R. Walther Darré, "Walther Rathenau und die Bedeutung der Rasse in der Weltgeschichte," *Deutschlands Erneuerung*, Heft 1 (January 1928): 11–14 passim.

38. *New York Times*, 18 July 1933, as quoted in Frederick L. Schuman, *The Nazi Dictatorship: A Study in Social Pathology and the Politics of Fascism*, 2d rev. ed. (New York: Knopf, 1936), pp. 297–98.

39. Akten betreffend Ermordung des Reichsminister Rathenau, R 43/I 904, Bundesarchiv, Koblenz.

40. "Die Helden von Saaleck," in *Kampf: Lebensdokumente deutscher Jugend von 1914–1934*, ed. Bert Roth (Leipzig: Philipp Reclam jun., 1934), pp. 97–99; quotation, p. 97. A photograph of Burg Saaleck faces p. 96.

41. Loewenberg, "Antisemitismus und jüdischer Selbsthass."

42. W. Hartenau, "Höre Israel!" *Die Zukunft*, 18 (6 March 1897): 454–62. It was reprinted by Rathenau in *Impressionen* (Leipzig: S. Hirzel, 1902), pp. 1–20. Harden reran it as a spiteful obituary a week after Rathenau's murder, *Die Zukunft*, 30 (1 July 1922) 4–11. Cf. Sander L. Gilman, *Jewish Self-Hatred: Anti-Semitism and the Hidden Language of the Jews* (Baltimore: Johns Hopkins University Press, 1986), pp. 222–23.

43. Walter Frank, *Höre Israel!: Studien zur modernen Judenfrage* (Hamburg: Hanseatische Verlagsanstalt, 1939, 1942), p. 6.

44. Ibid., p. 226.

45. Ibid., p. 229.

46. Wilhelm Orth, *Walther Rathenau und der Geist von Rapallo* (Berlin: Buchverlag Der Morgen, 1962); and *Rathenau, Rapallo, Koexistenz* (Berlin: Buchverlag Der Morgen, 1982). See also David G. Williamson, "Walther Rathenau: Patron Saint of the German Liberal Establishment (1922–1972)," in *Leo Baeck Institute Yearbook*, vol. 20 (1975), p. 219.

47. Margarete von Eynern, ed. and intro., *Walther Rathenau: Ein Preussischer Europäer: Briefe* (Berlin: Käthe Vogt Verlag, 1955).

48. As quoted in Schulin, *Rathenau*, p. 130.

7

KARL RENNER AND THE
POLITICS OF ACCOMMODATION:
MODERATION VERSUS REVENGE

Revenge, at first though sweet,
Bitter ere long back on itself recoils.
                    John Milton, Paradise Lost, *Book IX, Line 171*

Karl Renner's political life transcends the history of Austria's empire and its two twentieth-century republics, making him the foremost leader of Austrian democratic politics. Renner was also the most innovative theoretician on the nationalities question that plagued the Habsburg monarchy and the twentieth-century world. He was chancellor of Austria's first republic, leader of the right-wing Social Democrats, and president of the post–World War Two second republic. A study of his life and politics offers a perspective into the origins of the moderate, adaptive, political personality and a study of the tension between ideology and accommodation to the point where it is difficult to determine what core of principle remained.

II

The world in the closing decades of the twentieth century is riven with nationalities conflicts in all quarters. In Lebanon and Israel, Cyprus, Spain's Basque provinces, Belgium, Northern Ireland, Sri Lanka, Taiwan, Eastern Indonesia, Pakistan, and on our own continent in Quebec, the West Indies, and the southwestern United States, ethnic populations are in determined combat over issues of political sovereignty and cultural control. We desperately need to draw on previous models of analysis of the violent passions of nationalism and creative solutions that have been offered by those who have grappled with these problems in the past.

The logical place to look is the Austro-Hungarian Empire in the early twentieth century, where the force of nationalism was so potent that it tore the empire apart. Here we had a group of socialist political figures, above all, Karl Renner, who were also major theorists of the nationalities question. They hammered out their theory while building a movement in the daily give-and-take of electoral and parliamentary politics. The Austromarxist models of national behavior were not merely abstract concepts, they were tempered by the experience of passionate conflict and practical politics. We may draw lessons from their failures and misguided efforts as well as from the successes, both temporary and permanent, of their ideas.

Writing under a number of pseudonyms because he was the librarian of the Austrian parliament and thus an imperial employee, Renner between 1899 and 1906 formulated and published a series of brilliant proposals on the issue of conflicting nationalities and territories in Central Europe.[1] He initiated a level of thought and public discussion among the Austromarxists that was to stimulate new and original approaches to the problem of nationalism and, by comparison, put the consensus of the German SPD to shame. The German socialists felt that all the ethnic minorities in the Reich, the Poles of Poznan, the French of Alsace, and the Danes of Schleswig, should obviously become German.[2] Nationality was not recognized as   a problem even by such a left radical as Rosa Luxemburg, a Jew from Poland. By contrast the Austrian socialists engaged in creative thinking and dialogue of the first order.

Renner's approach to the problem of rival nationalities may be summarized in the following five points:

1. The state should have multiple levels of political structures that may overlap one another because they have different legal functions. The social and economic entities would be larger than the political and ethnic units. A third level would be for administrative organization. Renner invoked the illustration of a good geographic atlas that shows the same territory in its climatic, topographic, ethnic, political, linguistic, economic, botanical, animal, mineral, and historical composition.[3] These overlap and coexist on the same territory.

2. As a socialist, Renner believed that political parties should represent economic interests in all areas rather than national interests, for he believed in the commonality of class interests in political life.

3. Perhaps Renner's greatest contribution was the elaboration of the idea of personal autonomy in national questions. He proposed that the nationality of an individual no longer be determined by birth or residence but by personal choice recorded in a national register. He called this the "personal principle" (*Personalitätsprinzip*). He sought to separate cultural autonomy entirely from territory in matters of education, culture, libraries, language, and so on.

4. He envisioned multinational states in which nationality would not be a conditioning legal factor of statehood. The state should be a supranational entity. His model was a federal state organization of equal nationalities or parts of nations. The nationalities' primary concern would

be only one area of governmental functioning, namely cultural autonomy. He used the example of a city:

> Every nation has its own private autonomous house. But between the houses lie common streets carrying commerce and traffic, common markets, factories and shops, and necessarily a common city hall with offices. The economic and political life must be carried on in common if the city wishes to exist. We Social Democrats espouse this supranational economic, social, and political intercourse with full consciousness.[4]

Five years later, in 1918, he wrote: "History demands supranational formations, states that are more than a nation. The epoch of isolated small peoples, of multiple sovereignties, is over."[5]

5. Renner rejected the idea of national proportional representation in public life, administration and bureaucracy, with the sole exception of those spheres directly concerned with cultural autonomy. Here we find a shift in his thought during World War One. Prior to 1914 he espoused the distribution of government offices on the principle of proportional national quotas.[6] By 1918 he limited proportional representation to the sphere of cultural administration, and called for a policy of "the career open to talent," with the clear understanding that equal opportunity must be provided for the social mobility of all classes.[7]

III

How is such a broadly tolerant, accommodating personality made? Renner is a contrast to such exclusivist leaders as Lenin, who see only one way. A semilegendary self-presentation, especially of origins, one shrouded in myth, tells us more about an individual's conflicts and the personal resolutions he or she has arrived at than the most formal effort at factual accuracy. In central Europe there is an "official" mode of autobiography, beginning with birth date and place, parents' and grandparents' given and maiden names, residences, occupations, religious confessions, and the like. Renner avoids such autobiographic conventions. Indeed, his memoir opens with the statement of a confused identity and allusions to dual mothering and multiple internalizations. Instead of a straightforward narrative, Renner gives us his identity and his personal myth of origin that is his view of himself in the first pages of his autobiography.

Renner tells us that he has never been sure whether he was the seventeenth or the eighteenth child his mother brought into the world. He does not know whether his name is truly Karl or Anton, the name of his twin brother. He and his brother were cared for by older sisters, Anna and Emilie, who tied red and blue ribbons on the twins to tell them apart. The infant with the red ribbon was named Karl and was cared for by Anna; Emilie was the mother-surrogate for Anton. On the baptismal day the ribbons came off and were entangled. Neither mother Renner nor the sisters were able to distinguish one twin from the other or know which had first entered the world: "Even the mother, to whom the children were handed in her delivery bed, despite careful examination, could not decide which was Karl and which was Anton, who saw the light of day earlier and who later, who was the seventeenth and who was the eighteenth child." Eventually Anna arbitrarily declared: "This one is mine, he is Karl." The distraught Emilie had to accept the other as Anton. A few weeks later Anton died. For the remainder of his life Karl felt emotionally distant from his sister Emilie and had special bonds of love to Anna. "No one could imagine," writes Renner, "that the red bow would acquire deep meaning for my whole life."[8]

What can we derive from this unusual account of personal origins? First, the assumption that a child in such a large family early learned compromise and the necessity of the give-and-take that living together in a world of scarce resources in time, attention, and material demanded. Second, his sister was a substitute mother who chose him, and in many ways she took the place of his real mother, who was a much-too-burdened farm wife. Third, we are told of an early triumph over a rival—a victory that, as Freud told us from his experience, gives a man a lifetime sense of being favored by a sure destiny that smiles on him.[9] We also know that surviving children often have an unconscious "charge" or "assignment" from the family not only to live their own lives but also to fulfill the aspirations held for the lost child. Renner indicates that he lived with the identity of Anton in himself and that he may have been Anton.

But the most important clue, I believe, to the inner impulses that shaped a lifetime of creativity devoted to wrestling with the problem of nationalism is that the Renner solution—that each person should have two national identities, a political one and a personal one—is indicated in his account of his first days of life. It is no coincidence that the formulator of the *Personalitätsprinzip*, the idea that national identity should be a matter of conscious personal choice rather than determined by territory or by language, and that an individual should carry two passports, a territorial one and an ethnic one, tells us of an early confusion in identities, of a fusion and separation, and of survival, that gave him a dual place in the family for himself and his twin, and that earned him love and antagonism in the family constellation.

Renner recalls from his childhood how his mother divided the great round bread she had baked among her children. "Anxiously the children watched the knife to see whether their piece did not come out indecently small. Frequently one of the young ones broke out in a cry: 'The other one has a much bigger piece.'" During times of field work there was no midday meal at home. Each child received a hunk of bread in the morning and had to save it for lunch. "As the youngest I often experienced to my sorrow that one or another older brother, who had already eaten his bread, took mine as well and I had to hunger through until the night meal."[10] This painful early grievance against those, larger and stronger, who took what was his was a lifelong motif of Renner's.

Peasant room (*Bauernstube*) in Karl Renner's home, Gloggnitz. *Courtesy of Siegfried Nasko and the Dr. Karl Renner Museum, Gloggnitz.*

However, there was an important compensation. Karl felt he was his father's favorite. He fondly recalls receiving warmth and intimacy in childhood when sometimes the two would steal away from the cares of the house to the wine cellar, where they shared good hours of secret comfort with bread, cheese, and wine:

> A small window lets a little light in, under the window a table and bench stand. There we relaxed after father fetched a bottle of light house wine from the cellar and set it on the table. Then we feasted and heartily smacked our lips as though we were enjoying the rarest delicacies from the Sultan's table, and question and answer flew back and forth and many a good hour passed in secret sociability.[11]

Being familiar with this passage, I was not totally surprised when, following the imperative of Marc Bloch to visit the site of the history one studies, I found in the villa Renner built in Gloggnitz south of Vienna a "Bauernstube," a peasant's room, with one colored-glass window, and under the window a table and bench just as Renner had described the setting of the happy days of his boyhood closeness to father. In adulthood Karl recreated in his home the original scene of childhood comfort and love. Here he could symbolically recapture the hours of peace and bliss as the favored son. He viewed the special hours as a just restitution for the inequities he suffered at the hands of his older brothers: "If my father treated me royally with bread and cheese during his secret excursions to the wine cellar, this was no injustice to my older siblings, it was merely the rightful reparation of the damage inflicted upon the most defenseless in the family."[12] Renner relates the experience of maternal nonrecognition and deprivation to the compensatory rewards of paternal partiality and secret indulgence. The warm relationship taught him important lessons for life that he relived in his interactions with others in adulthood. He learned to get along well with men, he learned the give-and-take of family intercourse, which, as he grew in years, became political negotiation, compromise, and settlement.

Renner did not have a bitter battle to the death with his father. It was not a situation of "give me autonomy or kill me," such as, for instance, Frederick the Great faced with his father, King Frederick William I of Prussia. Renner's relationship was in the nature of a seduction and a collusion—a fraternity of the men enjoying communion in defiance of the women. By not having a desperate struggle with his father Renner learned that accommodation is possible, people will deal, they are approachable. Others will pursue their self-interests, but they can be appealed to on grounds of the common good, of belonging to the same family if this coincides with their long-term goals.

Renner's relationship to his father was as an ally. His identification was one of love, not identification with the aggressor. Rather than an oppositional stance to his father, he learned the role of manipulative agreeableness; he acquired the skills of allowing himself to be seductively co-opted rather than the tactics of conflict and confrontation. And if the counterplayer does not agree to be the seducer and co-opter, you get your way by deception.

IV

Renner was elected to the Austrian parliament from Lower Austria in 1907, the first election after the great electoral reforms of 1905. From 1905 onward he was also active on behalf of the Vienna consumer cooperatives, and in 1911 he was elected chairman of the Austrian consumer cooperative movement. He promoted the cooperative ideas as a force in the society and economy. He was responsible for the founding of the Credit Union of Austrian Workers Societies (Kreditverband österreichischer Arbeitervereinigungen) in 1912, the forerunner of what later became the large trade union bank. Its function was to free the cooperatives from dependence on the private banks, which held union funds as deposits at 4 percent interest and extended loans to the cooperatives at 8–10 percent.[13]

Because of his prewar work with consumer cooperatives, in World War One Renner was called to be a director of the Bureau of Food Supply (Ernährungsamt). He served in this capacity until 1917, when the Socialist Party asked him to terminate his association with the bureau.

Renner supported the prowar policy of the Austrian and German Social Democratic Parties of August 1914 in contrast to the position of

Friedrich Adler. He later collected his wartime essays that had appeared in *Kampf* and in the *Arbeiter-Zeitung* in a book entitled *Marxismus, Krieg and Internationale*, which he published at the time of the Stockholm Conference in May 1917. For the second edition in 1918 he added a new foreword, which included this generous reference to his differences with his rival Otto Bauer:

> My first edition carried the dedication: "Dedicated to my friend Otto Bauer, currently a prisoner of war, in memory of many years of collaboration and as a token of loyal comradeship in struggle." Since Otto Bauer has in the meantime returned home, the apparent occasion for the dedication no longer exists. Meanwhile he had the enviable opportunity to gain for some months a wealth of stimulation and insights in the middle of the Russian revolution. These insights differ variously from the conclusions we arrived at through common work in the Austrian movement and which we espoused in the Austrian monthly Der Kampf, as well as from the conceptions of the war I developed in the meantime. Since I endorse the policies of the German majority (Socialists) without reservation, although I do not subscribe to all of the theories of the German far right, the second edition cannot carry over the dedication. I am of one mind with my friend, then as now, that only deeper and broader research on the basis of Marxism can conquer the prevailing madness. I am committed to the critical and polemical investigation of the perspectives and experiences of various countries from all of the foundations of Marxism: it is great, so rich, and lies so unexploited, that there truly is room for many workers side by side.[14]

Renner's wartime comment on the Second International was to paraphrase Lassalle:

> "What really is the International?"—Almost everything!
> What is it legally?"—Nothing![15]

Renner used simple and fitting illustrations to make the point that the world lives in international anarchy when it needs international order. If a couple of hundred peasant families live near one another and have common interests, the law permits them to meet, determine their interests, and satisfy their common needs. Yet the peoples of the world do not have such institutions, although the earth is divided into pieces just as a hamlet is divided into parcels of land. Each parcel of the hamlet has its owner who rules it; trespass on a neighbor's land is forbidden; the owner closets himself behind his boundary and maintains with zealous passion that foreign events do not concern him. He is his own lord and he recognizes no common interests, rights, and duties. We know the capitalistic fanaticism concerning private property only too well. But in the end the proud peasant understands that the town and the state must have primacy over him because in the final analysis common interests cannot be denied.

It is evident, Renner held, that the countless common interests stand over the parcels of the state—high, weighty, and, yes, for our epoch, decisive interests. And every citizen of our time must concede this. The citizen may dispute the degree of common interest but cannot contest the existence and the importance of the common interest. So the citizen must be willing to see the need for the establishment of a community of states over individual states just as a village community is established over individual pieces of land.

Renner presented his case in a rustic mode that the urban intellectuals Victor Adler and Otto Bauer never could. Although he took a position against the artificial international language Esperanto, arguing that it was more important to give workingmen basic education so they might improve themselves, he did favor supranational institutions. Renner used his legal training but presented it in the homespun metaphors of peasant village life: if the owner of the higher land drains off all the ground water, the lower land will dry up; such an outcome has to be out of the question—the community forbids it and prevents it. The arid parcel is worthless if it has no access to water, hence the community makes available the right to an easement over adjoining property.

"How is it with states?" asks Renner. The German state starves when its neighbors close their borders and blockade its ports at their own discretion. Great Britain would starve if an enemy coalition were to destroy its fleet and shut off sources of supply. What kind of a town would have no community streets but only private roads open "until further notice"? As water is to a household, raw materials are to industry. The colonial powers declare the primary-raw-materials-producing countries as their own private property. They can make the industries of other nations die of thirst; there is no right to obtain "water." And so in truth every property owner may in some way divert water from a neighbor and thus consign the neighbor's land to drought.

"The International of the facts" demonstrates that each is dependent on the other and all are dependent on every other, need one another and must live with one another. But from the legal point of view there is no guarantee that this will be possible in the long run; a village exists, but no community.

Renner called for a world organization—a new concept of the International to bind states and peoples to secure their vital interests, cultures, and relationships. In his line of reasoning Renner is a definite forerunner of the League of Nations, the United Nations, and future world organizations that we do not yet know but whose power will include some portions of the sovereignty now held by states. He anticipated the argument that internationalism is the enemy of the state. His response: just as wanting to see one's property prosper by means of access and water does not mean disowning one's land, so only the person who assures the proper conditions of a people's existence is a true and wise friend of these people—and accordingly, must be an internationalist.[16]

What can we say about Renner's ideas on nationalities today? It is clear that he underestimated the demand for national sovereignty among the new nationalisms. Although he was not a doctrinaire Marxist, he overrated the power of common social and economic institutions to overcome the deep identifications with territory and place that constitute national-ism. Institutional separation of peoples and groups rather than various consociational concepts such as bilingualism, proportional representation, multiculturalism, and cultural autonomy seems to be becoming the rule in attempts to resolve ethnic conflicts in North America, eastern Europe, and the Near East. However, many of Renner's ideas about supranational frameworks have been successfully enacted in western Europe in wide-ranging social, economic, and political arrangements.[17] Ironically, Austria, due to its neutrality, is only now becoming a part of the supranational in-stitutions of the European Union.

Renner's ideas have been most completely implemented, appropri-ately, in regard to the question of the South Tyrol, which deals with a predominantly Austrian population (approximately 65 percent) in an Alpine sector of northeastern Italy. The two states have negotiated an Austrian cultural autonomy with a recognized special status on Italian territory.[18] It includes educational and cultural institutions, schoolbooks, Austrian teacher certification, libraries, language rights, and even the right of South Tyrolians to attend Austrian institutions of higher educa-tion tuition free. The particular and unique arrangements, including a "package" with its self-enforcing operations calendar, was declared ful-filled by both parties in 1992. The solution may well be considered the child of Renner's concepts that regrettably were not given a chance half a century earlier.

V

The first Austrian elections after the war were held on 16 February 1919. The Social Democrats won seventy-two seats; Christian Socials, sixty-nine; and German Nationals, twenty-six. The National Assembly voted a Great Coalition government with Karl Renner as chancellor and his fellow Social Democrat Otto Bauer as foreign minister.

The government's first task was to negotiate a peace settlement with the Allies at Saint Germain. Considering the Allied definition of the situation—that Austria was a defeated power and coresponsible with Germany for the war, and hence subject to the claims for defensible bor-ders by Czechoslovakia on the north, Italy on the south, and Yugoslavia and Hungary on the east—the delegation led by Renner did well in se-curing Carinthia from Yugoslavia through plebiscite and the Burgenland province from Hungary.[19]

Renner was far from an inflexible Marxist. Indeed, he tells us that as a student he found *Das Kapital* too difficult and incomprehensible. In fact, his socialist consciousness was first aroused by reading Ferdinand Lassalle. Karl Kautsky, Europe's senior social democratic theorist of the early twentieth century, compared the two junior socialist leaders, Renner and Bauer, in terms of their intellectual ancestry. In Renner's thought, said Kautsky, the ideas of Lassalle prevailed, and Bauer was a Marxist. "Renner writes as a Realpolitiker, Bauer as a researcher; Renner as a lawyer, Bauer as an economist; the former's strength lies in argumentation and in practical proposals, whereas Bauer's strength is in the uncovering of intricate relationships."[20] Renner had an evolutionary concept of reducing the conflict in society by meliorating the extremes rather than sharpening them and leading toward a struggle for power through revolution. He believed that capitalism would be-come redundant through the developments it initiated and that it would be replaced by a socially oriented economy and social order. Bauer, commencing from Marxist premises, viewed the bourgeois state as an instrument of class domination and a legal form of exploitation. These contrasts constituted the political poles of the theories and daily decision making within social democracy during the First Austrian Republic.

Renner engaged in an extended public debate with Bauer in the 1920s on appropriate party tactics and the means of achieving socialism. The Social Democratic Party was dominated by Bauer, who with theoretical virtuosity promulgated a series of radical formulas that applied to the Austrian situation: that seizure of the state must precede economic change; that socialists were currently witnessing a "pause" between revolutionary epochs; that the conservative state and the economical and social order were in a posture of "contradiction" that was causing a "balance of forces"; power must be seized totally and socialism would be realized as an integral system.[21]

As the Austrian Socialist Party's leading evolutionary tactician, Renner counterpoised to the arguments of Bauer that socialism is not a closed system. He argued fully in the tradition of Bernsteinian revisionism. Experience in all countries had demonstrated that it is entirely possible to begin with "partial socialism" of single branches of industry.[22] Programs of economic self-help such as cooperatives, trade unions, and social insurance develop the social sectors in a capitalist economy; they redistribute portions of the aggregate surplus value and undermine capitalist economic autocracy. He rejected Bauer's view that seizure of the state was the "Archimedean point" on which a change in the economic system could alone be predicated.

According to Renner, the idea of the state and the economy in contradiction and the idea of seizing state power constitute a double error.[23] Socialists should work to remove obstacles to economic democracy and foster it with laws and administration. Socialism is not realizable through decree as a single act that will turn a mode of production into its opposite but, rather, as administered piecework that deals with each function of capital separately and in isolation. Renner's slogan in reply to Bauer was "General socialism is general nonsense! Integral socialism is unreal socialism!"[24]

After the socialist debacle in the general strike following the burning of the Palace of Justice in Vienna on 15 July 1927, Renner vigorously attacked the disastrous party course of the "policy of the radical phase" promulgated by Bauer. In the Parteitag of 1927 he had a major debate with Bauer in which he uttered the prescient line: "It is a danger and a contradiction to always talk of revolutions and at the same time to claim that one cannot make them."[25] He was consistently the spokesman for a coalition and participation in government. He expressed his attitude toward the principle of coalition governments as he congratulated Hermann Müller, of the German Social Democratic right wing, upon becoming chancellor of a coalition government in 1928. This is exactly the course Renner was advocating without success for the Austrian party. He wrote Müller: "Nothing would have been worse than to run from the given task. It is better to have tried and to let the others be responsible for the failure."[26]

Renner's interpersonal relations have a modulated, tempered quality when compared to the black-and-white divisiveness of his left-wing rival for party leadership, Bauer. For Bauer, all of politics was an adversarial relationship. For Renner, on the other hand, adaptation to the current political situation, coalitions, and working with the forces that be were the keynote of policy. Renner was a bridge builder, an accommodationist.

Renner's view of his and Bauer's styles is presented in a letter to Kautsky in which he discusses their differences in the party executive in the fall of 1929:

> Yesterday's Party Council meeting unfortunately did not go as I wished. I found myself in absolute opposition to Otto on an issue that has nothing to do with Right and Left, rather is merely a question of political wisdom. I am of the opinion that in this moment nothing is better than patience, in fact forbearance. Such movements as Austrian Putschism come to nothing if one does not do the gentlemen the favor of placing oneself in their line of fire. Then they will meet with the power of the state and will force the middle classes in their own interest to get rid of them. But, thanks to his prisoner of war experiences (in Russia), Otto is taken by a fatal revolutionary romanticism. Nevertheless, I hope that no disaster occurs.[27]

A beautiful example of Renner's reaching out to the opposition is his relationship to the Christian Socialist parliamentary deputy Leopold Kunschak, often his vigorous opponent. In 1931 Kunschak opposed a coalition with the Socialists that Renner favored. When the two parties were preparing for civil war in the early 1930s, Renner initiated a correspondence with Kunschak in which he invoked the past, present, and future of their relationship:

> I recall an incident out of my youthful years. It was in the year 1891, I was a law student traveling to a Social Democratic Party meeting in Purkersdorf in a third-class railway carriage. The man sitting across from me was traveling to Weidlingau. From our conversation it became apparent that the other man was a political opponent and none other than Leopold Kunschak. For the past forty years political opposition divides or, if we may say so, unites us. I do not wish to diminish in any way that which divides us;

I would however like to emphasize that the adversarial struggle still includes many common goals, above all the welfare of the working classes and the political liberation and elevation of our entire people. The great ascent of the working classes, which despite their current distress is undeniable, was achieved in the world, and was realized in the thousandfold ways through the collaboration of our two parties. If the eight-hour day became law in 1919, we must certainly thank the circumstance that your influence in the Christian Socialist Party awakened the empathy for social needs among broad middle-class strata. As pertains to the democratic foundations of our young state, the collaboration of your party and mine in the establishment of our constitution, in the reestablishment of our economy, and in the maintenance of domestic peace after the collapse and revolution is a basic and immortal part of the history of our fatherland. Your honest democratic spirit played a substantial role in the achievements of that time, just as it has thereafter often proven itself. I now fear that our immediate future will also demand tests of this commitment. I place my trust that your loyally preserved democratic spirit of more than a generation will help to guard our country from silly and ruinous adventures.[28]

We note Renner's appeal to what the two men had in common. Although recognizing that they were political opponents, Renner emphasized the political positions that would stress their bonds and provide ground for working together. He did this by invoking their youthful fights, their past joint successes such as the eight-hour day, and their consistent democratic orientation, which was by no means taken for granted in Austria in the fall of 1931. He recalled these bonds as would a good therapist looking forward to constructive work in the here and now and in the future.

A further example of Renner's skill in human interaction and the mediation of conflict is demonstrated in a letter to Josef Gruber, the Socialist mayor of Linz in the fall of 1930. The situation is revealing of Renner's temperament:

I am told that in the last bank board meeting you had a collision with Director Grossmann. Considering your overburdened state, which naturally corresponds to your state of overirritation, I would not like to give such a thing any importance. On the other hand, in view of his whole position, Director Grossmann cannot ignore the situation and has given notice that he intends to convene a party mediation court. Such a thing could certainly be avoided if you would undertake the effort to get this thing settled in good order. I am convinced that you had no intention to offend him, that in fact your temper just came through. Please write me whether you do not see a way to end this affair without a necessarily highly embarrassing investigation.[29]

Here we see Renner at work as a highly effective mediator, conciliator, and smoother of the storms of interpersonal frictions. The letter is a model of wise negotiation. First, Renner gives Mayor Gruber a self-justification: he is overstressed, tired, and irritated. Second, Renner minimizes the whole affair: it is of small moment and Director Grossmann is clearly unreasonable. Third, Renner is supportive of Gruber: he certainly had no intention to offend; his strong temper merely came through; he is basically a good man. Fourth, Renner appeals to Gruber's observing ego: look at the viewpoint of the other person; Grossmann cannot simply walk away from this insult. Fifth, Renner points to the unpleasant consequences facing Gruber, which he does not need: a highly embarrassing investigation by a party tribunal. Finally, Renner leaves the initiative up to Gruber: he will find a way out. Renner indicates the options and his own generally preferred direction but, acknowledging Gruber's maturity and competence, does not tell him what road to follow.

Adam Wandruszka summarized Renner's posture: "Even in his theoretical writings and in his position to the classics of socialism, Renner reveals himself as a pragmatist and an empiricist which he was all of his life. He always approaches all questions from the standpoint of practical experience, from the position of reality, with a predisposition for an approach from the concrete single case."[30]

VI

A major mystery in the life of Karl Renner is what happened to him after 1934. He was jailed for more than three months after the socialist rising in February. While other socialist leaders were emigrating or in concentration camps, Renner lived in his villa in Gloggnitz in Lower Austria, about one hour southwest of Vienna. Undisturbed, he traveled abroad to international conferences in Basel, Paris, and Brussels and made visits to Czechoslovakia. Various suspicions were raised that he was a collaborator or at least that he had in some way compromised himself and made his peace with the Austrofascists and the National Socialists.

Archival research shows that Renner was under constant observation by the Austrofascist government after 1934.[31] He visited the police regularly and presented statements and affidavits emphasizing the nonpolitical role he was playing and committing himself "not to engage in undertakings against the Austrian government or state as well as to prevent my presence abroad to be misused for such purposes." He further acknowledged that the Austrian government did not desire his participation at a pre-Congress meeting at the International Labor Office in Geneva and committed himself not to participate in such talks. He also committed himself to resign as president of the International Association for Social Progress (Internationale Vereinigung für sozialen Fortschritt). He agreed not to criticize the regime or to discuss Austrian politics while abroad. He affirmed that the sole purpose of his trips was to attend international conferences on the social conditions of labor.[32] We see in these positions his talent for adaptation, not necessarily in the admirable sense of the term. The German *Anpassungsfähigkeit* says it well.

Joseph Buttinger, leader of the underground Revolutionary Socialists in the 1930s, describes Renner's conduct during the years 1934 to 1937:

> Renner had exerted no influence, claimed no rights, acknowledged no
> obligations to the new movement, and had not even wanted to know what

was happening in the party. He rarely met any of the old leaders; in the few talks that he had with Danneberg in these years, the underground was hardly mentioned. Renner had been one of the first to receive permission to travel to Czechoslovakia in order to take the baths at Karlsbad, but he had always avoided the exiled leaders like the plague. Later, deigning to talk to Friedrich Adler in Paris, he expressed himself in most derogatory terms about Otto Bauer's political attitude. The whole underground business was nonsense, said Renner.[33]

Renner provided two substantial political services for Hitler in 1938. He legitimated the Anschluss with Nazi Germany by supporting Hitler's plebiscite in April. And he argued in justification of the Munich Agreement of September 1938 that set the stage for the end of the Czechoslovak state.

A few days after the Anschluss in March 1938, Renner went to Hermann Neubacher, the first Nazi lord mayor of Vienna, and offered to appeal to the Social Democrats to vote Yes in the plebiscite confirming union with Germany to be held on 10 April. Neubacher consulted Josef Burckel, the gauleiter Hitler had picked to reorganize the Austrian NSDAP and carry out the plebiscite. Burckel called Rudolf Hess in the Munich party headquarters, who decided that Renner's declaration should be published in the press as an interview. This was done in the *Neuen Wiener Tagblatt* of 3 April 1938.[34] As historian Radomir Luza wrote: "Actually, Renner and some other Austrians did not want to know, or said that they did not know, that the Anschluss for which they were voting had separated German nationalist aspirations from any humanistic tendencies."[35]

In mid-September 1938, as the Munich crisis was coming to a climax, Renner wrote an unpublished history of the peace negotiations at Saint Germain that had confirmed the dissolution of the Austro-Hungarian Empire and the creation of the succession states.[36] The purpose of his essay was to place the current diplomatic crisis of 1938 in the context of the loss of the Bohemian and Sudeten German populations to Austria in 1918 and 1919. It is also an autobiographical account of his role as president of the Austrian delegation that in 1919 signed the peace treaty formally ending World War One for Austria.

The essay is Renner's unequivocal endorsement of the transfer of the Sudeten territories to Germany. He views Hitler's demand as a permanent solution to a problem created by the peace treaty and a correction of an injustice committed in 1919. He sees the "disturbed balance of Europe" rectified by the "unexampled perseverance and energy of the German Reich."[37] Renner explains that he feels compelled to recount the events of the "fight against Czechoslovakian imperialism" and the "glaring injustice against the German people" that at last, thanks to the Munich work of appeasement, has found a bloodless, albeit for the Czechs a tragic, expiation.[38]

Renner presents the Social Democrats as historic German nationalists,[39] and justifies war to reclaim former parts of Germany that were separated by international law such as German Austria, or such as Danzig, Memel, and other borderlands that were broken off. . . . If in 1919 it was right to unify dispersed nations by war, then it must now and in the future be right that those nations which are still divided or were newly divided in 1919, should unify themselves by all means, including, in case of need, the means of war.[40]

Renner's essay communicates all of the hurt of 1919 in the national and the personal sense. He recounts how as Austrian chancellor and president of the Austrian delegation to the Peace Conference he had had to sit in the castle at Saint Germain and face not only the "big five"—Clemenceau, Wilson, Lloyd George, Salandra, and a Japanese representative—"but also well-known acquaintances and sometime friends: former members of the Austrian parliament: Czechs, Yugoslavs, Poles, Rumanians. The chancellor politely nodded to them and they embarrassedly responded. They sat at the table of the victor and Austria's chancellor sat at the poor sinner's bench of the defeated."[41]

We can feel with Renner the sense of shame, humiliation, anger, and betrayal of that hour and day, on 2 June 1919, when former parliamentary colleagues whose national and ethnic rights within the Habsburg Empire he, as a Social Democrat and theorist on the nationalities question, had steadfastly espoused over two decades now treated him as an enemy and, he felt, took advantage of "his" beaten condition. He personalized his country's situation. He was again in the position of having his bread stolen by his stronger older brothers.

There is rage and hurt in Renner's essay when he contrasts the expressed aspiration of the Western powers in 1919, to "have guaranteed the existence and interests of all the concerned peoples, including the Austrians, without bequeathing either anarchy or murderous rivalries," with the state of the world in 1938: "What naivete! What irony speaks to us today out of these words! The facts of today express their judgment of this sentence and at the same time of the entire work of the treaty."[42]

Renner depreciates the Czechs as a small people "younger in their culture" than the Germans.[43] He is enraged by the Czech claims to Bohemia dating back to 1620 and the Allied suggestion that the Sudeten Germans should remain united with, and collaborate with, the Czech majority in building the new state: "Remain united, what an exquisite euphemism for submission! The Sudeten Germans should collaborate toward the development of national unity! What unity? It can only be the national unity of the Czech people, it can thus only mean complete slavery."[44] He writes of the "Diktat von Paris 1919" and the "raped" Sudeten Germans, of how "the large and small powers, who sat at the victor's table in Saint Germain, twenty-two in number, heedlessly walked over the violated, and without pangs of conscience enriched themselves on the booty of war which fell to each of them."[45] This is the language and propaganda idioms of National Socialism.

There is a quality of self-righteous revenge in this essay that is uncharacteristic of Renner in any of his other works. Usually he is marvelously even tempered, judicious, and generous toward all claimants and points of view. He had a historical record of reaching out to the non-German ethnic communities and creatively thinking of formulas to meet their needs as well as those of the empire.

This strikingly different tone of 1938 cannot be fully explained by opportunism or a desire to get on the Nazi bandwagon. There are no explicit references to Hitler's leadership or praise of him that one would expect in a sycophantic piece of that time. The closest he comes to National Socialist rhetoric is when, in the second foreword to the piece, written on 1 November 1938, the day after Hitler's signature on Chamberlain's "piece of paper"—the Anglo-German declaration promising to settle all future questions between the two countries by consultation—Renner declares: "[The Munich agreements] open a new chapter in European history, introduce new methods to it and free the path for other, entirely new goals of which we may have presentiments, but which cannot yet be demonstrated."[46]

VII

Renner frequently used the oral imagery of being abandoned, of being denied food—and love. One place he did so was in his attack on the government in World War One. He compared unfavorably the Austrian to the German position on the political equality of workers in the war. He said that in Germany every person truly became a citizen in the war, with the result of forging a people out of the great historical experience. However, he went on to say, the working class in Austria did not achieve this. "We, how shall I put it, were not invited to the table, not invited to dessert. Now we are invited to the war's hangover (*zum Katzenjammer des Krieges*) (loud applause). Now one invites us after all that was important, by this I do not mean important ideas but powerful in effect, has already occurred."[47] His charge was that his people did not get, they did not receive, the prize of equality with the other classes of Austria. They were bidden to share the miseries of the war without the satisfactions of equality in the state.

This verbal imagery recurred in 1938 when he described his feelings as Austria's chancellor as he had sat at the Peace Conference of Saint Germain in 1919. Austria's former wartime allies and his sometime Socialist comrades of the Second International had been seated at the victor's table while he had been reduced to sitting at the pauper's bench, personally slighted, and made to feel as though he were waiting for table scraps from the victors. Note his language in describing what he perceived as a humiliation. This is the evocation of narcissistic injury, of being rejected, of not getting his due and not getting enough.

These dynamics explain Renner's mortification when he felt he was not being recognized by his former comrades at Saint Germain. The question again became, Do I exist at all in the eyes of these people? His childhood quest for recognition and wholeness crystallized politically and intellectually in the drive for the encompassing experiential unit of the nation that binds together many disparate, larger and smaller, brothers and sisters. Renner in the Nazi period was counteracting the feelings of fragmentation and enfeeblement he knew and feared from childhood. He would undo and revenge the narcissistic slights of the past including Saint Germain; he would favor the stronger, inclusive larger unit, the "German" family, which promised security, integration, and omnipotence.

In this period of European history Renner was predominantly angry and vindictive. Here he brought out and ventilated a narcissistic injury he had nursed for two decades and found the current humiliation and dismemberment of the Czechoslovak state a balm for his wounds. In the words of Addison: "We are pleased by some implicit kind of revenge to see him taken down and humbled in his reputation who had so far raised himself above us."[48] Now those statesmen and peoples, above all the Czechs, who had been his opponents in 1919 when Renner desperately attempted to marshal support for the best possible peace conditions for the new Austrian state, were in their turn humiliated, sold down the river by their erstwhile allies, and had to watch the dismemberment of their country in impotent rage.

In Renner's autobiography we see that his vivid terms of oral deprivation express not only hunger but something much more fundamental: a nonrecognition by his mother, a deep searching question of who he is. He found no empathic responsiveness from his mother. She did not know him. He does not know whether he is really the child who is alive or the one who is dead. Certainly he needed a food-providing, caretaking mother, but the need was not only for nourishment. Renner tells us that he needed the experience of being recognized, of empathically modulated food-giving. The need that remained unfulfilled was not food; it was what Heinz Kohut has termed "the broader psychological configuration—the joyful experience of being a whole, appropriately responded to self."[49] Renner did not have this. His "self" was fragmented because of a lacking empathic response from his mother. He did, however, benefit from empathic responses from his father, who, he recalls, took him along to the tavern and gave him special attention and treats. He also received loving care from his older sister, Anna, which is why he was able to integrate so many conflicts and adapt so well to the challenges of life and politics in central Europe in the first half of the twentieth century.

Renner spent the seven years of Nazi rule and World War Two in undisturbed retirement in his substantial villa. With the approach of the Red Army in the spring of 1945, the war was nearing its end. On 2 April 1945 the seventy-four-year-old Renner approached the Soviet commander in the town of Gloggnitz with an offer to form a provisional government. He was immediately passed up the chain of command to Marshal Tolbukhin of the Third Ukrainian Army, who, with the personal approval of Stalin, permitted Renner to establish the first postwar Austrian provisional government under Soviet aegis.

On 15 April Renner wrote Stalin. Once again we see his skill in accommodation with those who have power. After a lengthy prologue in which he detailed his decades of friendly contacts with the Bolsheviks, including giving fleeing Russian revolutionaries of czarist times shelter in his home and passports to Switzerland, he explains that by chance he is the first member of the Social Democratic Party executive who remained in Austria to have regained his freedom, and, happily, he was also the president of the last freely elected Parliament. Renner asked for food supplies and for help in maintaining Austria's borders against loss of territory to its neighbors. He again feared Yugoslav incursions into Carinthia. Renner declared: "The West, as demonstrated in 1919, knows too little of our situation and does not have enough interest in us to insure our conditions for self-sufficiency." After expressing admiration for the great achievements of Soviet power, Renner assured Stalin that "the trust of the Austrian working class for the Soviet Republic is boundless. Austrian Social Democrats and Communists will work together in founding the new republic. That the future belongs to socialism is unquestioned."[50]

Initially, Renner had the confidence of the Russians but not of the Western Allies. As early as April 1945 the Americans and British objected to the Communist role in the Renner provisional government.[51] In June Renner was perceived by the Americans as being under Russian influence.[52] An unusual expression of U.S. ambivalence toward Renner is the subjunctive exposition of what the authors of an OSS memorandum *wish he had said* regarding his support of the Nazis in 1938:

> One could wish that . . . Renner had been able to state, "I hated the Dollfuss-Schuschnigg system as much as anybody, and there was many a reason why I might well have taken the attitude that it wasn't worth moving a finger to preserve. But my notions of what Anschluss should be were those of Social Democrats, *viz.*, federation with a democratic German Republic. I therefore felt that my party was only too right in 1933 when it repudiated the notion of Anschluss with Nazi Germany. Moreover, from what I saw of Nazism in Austria I could not, no matter what my previous ideas and feelings about the subject, associate myself with the forceful imposition of such a system upon my country."
>
> But he did not talk in those terms, and instead the Chancellor went on, "The Nazis were there. What could I do? What could I say? The facts had to be recognized. And so I decided to declare my allegiance [*mich dazu bekennen*]." . . . He did everything, therefore, to divert the persecution of the NSDAP from his own person [*habe er alles getan, der NSDAP von sich abzulenken*].[53]

By September 1945 the Americans saw evidence of the stability and popular support of the Renner government and favored its recognition.[54] The British, however, continued to object to Renner and to mistrust him because of his past pan-German affiliations.[55] Following the November elections, Renner secured Allied cooperation for his provisional government.

Renner allowed himself to be seduced and co-opted by Hitler as well as by Stalin, just as he had been by his father. He did this for his own ends in each case: the survival of self and of Austria in a dangerous world. There is something typically Austrian in this emotional posture and in Renner's career.[56] He made his accommodation for Austria with the Nazis, and the Soviets and the Western powers, always in the service of personal survival and power. A famous and cynical Habsburg epigram went "What others have conquered by the sword, you, O Austria, have acquired by the marriage bed!" So Renner's motto could well have been: "What others achieve by conflict and confrontation, you, O Karl-Anton, have reached by being co-opted, yet bending the stronger to your own purposes!"

For five years after the war Renner once again represented a defeated, and now occupied, Austria as it attempted to reestablish its independence and economic prosperity. His primary aim was to end the foreign occupation and reunify the land. This was the period of Renner's maximum achievement under most difficult and disadvantaged circumstances. He succeeded in creating a united provisional government for Austria, so that although the country and its capital, Vienna, were divided into four zones of occupation, there were never different governments in the respective zones, as in Germany. He gave the Communists a much larger proportion of power in the provisional government than their share of the population. He led the Soviets to believe the Communist Party would do well in the general elections. When these were held in November 1945 the People's Party and the Social Democrats, in that order, emerged as the major parties; the Communists were insignificant.

Renner died in 1950, five years prior to the realization of his goal of an autonomous and democratic Austria free of foreign troops. He had laid the diplomatic basis of trust for its achievement by his successors.

The question of not only the morality but also the rationality of Renner's tendency toward accommodation is a major issue in evaluating him historically. As a peacetime national and party leader, he did very well. The problem is why he, such a well-functioning political leader, was also a craven chameleon in cases where principle, including his own theories of democracy, multiethnic tolerance, and equality, was at stake. The answer we have found is that when his narcissistic injury was touched—when he was not recognized and rival brothers took his bread and land—then the forces of reason and conciliation were overwhelmed by the power of rage and the satisfactions of revenge.

Renner's prime consideration was the welfare of the Austrian state and its people. To further that interest he was willing to deal with whoever had power and on whatever terms possible, be they domestically in his party's left wing or Austria's political right. In international politics he would accommodate to Hitler, Stalin, or the Western powers, saying and doing whatever seemed necessary to foster what he perceived to be the interests of himself, the nation, and the working people, in that order. In viewing Renner's career, we are examining a fascinating case of the immortal tension between principle and accommodation, which constitutes the essence of politics. At what point, he must have often asked, is the central core of what I stand for lost? How may my goals be achieved without paying too high a cost and sacrificing the heart of the matter? These are the timeless issues of morality and expediency in political action. In Renner's life we have one effective twentieth-century politician's answer.

NOTES

1. Synopticus (pseudonym), *Zur österreichischen Nationalitätenfrage* (Vienna, 1899); *Staat und Nation* (Vienna, 1899); Rudolf Springer (pseudonym), *Staat und Parliament* (Vienna, 1901); *Der Kampf der österreichischen Nationen um den Staat* (Vienna, 1902); *Die Krise des Dualismus und das Ende der deakistischen Episode* (Vienna, 1904); *Grundlagen und Entwicklungsziele der österreichischen-ungarischen Monarchie* (Vienna, 1906). Renner's scholarship on nationalities continued under his own name, including *Der nationale Streit um die Ämter und die Sozialdemokratie* (Vienna, 1908); *Der deutsche Arbeiter und der Nationalismus* (Vienna, 1910); *Österreich's Erneuerung: Politisch-programmatische Aufsätze*, vol. 1 (Vienna: Verlag der Wiener Volksbuchhandlung Ignaz Brand & Co., 1916); *Politische Demokratie und nationale Autonomie* (Vienna, 1917); *Das Selbstbestimmungsrecht der Nationen in besonderer Anwendung auf Österreich*, Part 1, "Nation und Staat" (Leipzig: Franz Deuticke, 1918).

2. Hans-Ulrich Wehler, *Sozialdemokratie und Nationalstaat: Nationalitätenfragen in Deutschland, 1840–1914* (Göttingen: Vandenhoeck & Ruprecht, 1971).

3. Renner, *Selbstbestimmungsrecht*, pp. 227–94.

4. Renner, *Was ist die Nationale Autonomie? Was ist Soziale Verwaltung? Einführung in die nationale Frage und Erlauterung der Grundsätze des nationalen Programms der Sozialdemokratie* (Vienna, 1913), p. 35.

5. Renner, *Österreichs Erneuerung*, pp. 27, 38–46; quotation, p. 39.

6. Renner, *Der nationale Streit um die Ämter und die Sozialdemokratie* (Vienna, 1908).

7. Renner, *Selbstbestimmungsrecht*, pp. 286–91.

8. Karl Renner, *An der Wende Zweier Zeiten: Lebenserinnerungen* (Vienna: Danubia Verlag Universitätsbuchhandlung, Wilhelm Braunmüller und Sohn, 1946), pp. 14–15. (hereafter cited as *Lebenserinnerungen*).

9. "I have found that people who know that they are preferred or favoured by their mother give evidence in their lives of a peculiar self-reliance and an unshakable optimism which often seem like heroic attributes and bring actual success to their possessors." Freud, *The Interpretation of Dreams*, in *Standard Edition of the Complete Psychological Works*, translated under the general editorship of James Strachey in collaboration with Anna Freud, assisted by Alix Strachey and Alan Tyson, 24 vols. (London: Hogarth Press, 1953–1975), 5:398 n. (hereafter cited as *S.E.*).

10. Renner, *Lebenserinnerungen*, p. 51.

11. Ibid., pp. 40–41.

12. Ibid., p. 52.

13. Jacques Hannak, *Karl Renner und Seine Zeit* (Vienna: Europa Verlag, 1965), pp. 217–18.

14. Renner, *Marxismus, Krieg und Internationale: Kritische Studien über offene Probleme des wissenschaftlichen und des praktischen Sozialismus in und nach dem Weltkrieg* (Stuttgart: Verlag von J.H.W. Dietz Nachf., 1918), p. iv.

15. Ibid., p. 184.

16. Ibid., pp. 185–87.

17. Robert A. Kann, *Renner's Beitrag zur Lösung Nationaler Konflikte im Lichte Nationaler Probleme der Gegenwart* (Vienna: Verlag der Österreichischen Akademie der Wissenschaften, 1973).

18. Heinrich Siegler, *Die österreichisch-italienische Einigung über die Regelung des Sudtirolkonflikts* (Bonn: Verlag für Zeitarchiv, 1970); *Österreichs Souveranität, Neutralität, Prosperität* (Vienna: Siegler, 1967), chap. 3, "Das Problem Sudtirol," pp. 40–70, trans. as *Austria: Problems and Achievements Since 1945* (Bonn: Siegler, 1969); Mario Toscano, *Alto Adige–South Tyrol: Italy's Frontier with the German World*, ed. George A. Carbone (Baltimore: Johns Hopkins University Press, 1975); Kurt Waldheim, *Der österreichische Weg: Aus der Isolation zur Neutralität* (Vienna: Verlag Fritz Molden, 1971), trans. as *The Austrian Example* (New York: Macmillan, 1973), see chap. 9, "Sudtirol"; Franz Huter, *Sudtirol: Eine Frage des Europäischen Gewissens* (Munich: R. Oldenbourg, 1965); Antony Evelyn Alcock, *The History of the South Tyrol Question* (Geneva: Michael Joseph, 1970).

19. Karl R. Stadler, *Austria* (London: Ernest Benn, 1971), chap. 3, pp. 82–105, is particularly good on these Austrian achievements in the peace settlement.

20. Karl R. Stadler, "Karl Renner: der Mann und sein Werk," in Renner, *Eine Bibliographie* (Vienna: 1970), p. 12.

21. Peter Loewenberg, "Austro-Marxism and Revolution: Otto Bauer, Freud's 'Dora' Case, and the Crisis of the First Austrian Republic," in *Decoding the Past: The Psychohistorical Approach* (New York: Alfred A. Knopf, 1983; Berkeley: University of California Press, 1985; New Brunswick: Transaction Publishers, 1995), pp. 161–204.

22. Renner, *Wege der Verwirklichung* (1929) Offenbach a.M.: Bollwerk Verlag Karl Drott, 1947), p. 13.

23. Ibid., pp. 96–98.

24. Ibid., p. 118.

25. Adam Wandruszka, "Österreichs Politische Struktur," in *Geschichte der Republik Österreich*, ed. Heinrich Benedikt (Vienna: Verlag für Geschichte und Politik, 1954), p. 454.

26. Renner to Hermann Müller, 9 July 1938, Renner Nachlass, II, Verwaltungsarchiv, Vienna.

27. Renner to Karl Kautsky, 3 September 1929, Kautsky Nachlass, XIX, 174, International Institute for Social History, Amsterdam.

28. Renner to Leopold Kunschak, 11 November 1931, Renner Nachlass, II, File K. Staatliches Verwaltungsarchiv, Vienna.

29. Renner to Josef Gruber, 27 November 1930, Renner Nachlass, File G., Staatliches Verwaltungsarchiv, Vienna.

30. Wandruszka, "Österreichs Politische Struktur," p. 453.

31. See, for example, the instructions to the frontier post in Feldkirch to search Renner's luggage and person most carefully on his exit and entry to Aus-

tria under the pretext of currency controls. Ministerium des Innern, BKA, Inneres, General Direktion für öffentliche Sicherheit 316:904-St.B. No. 51, 23 January 1935, Verwaltungsarchiv, Vienna.

Renner was spied on in the train from Paris to Austria in October 1935 and his conversation reported. He said in the train that he looked forward to a coalition government with Social Democratic participation and the return to a half parliamentary regime. Report of 4 October 1935 by a security police spy. The cover letter says: "You will see from this how little one may rely on the promises of old party chiefs [*alten Parteibonzen*]." Bureau of the Vice Chancellor to State Secretary Baron Hammerstein, 10 October 1935, ibid., No. 50.

32. Renner, "Niederschrift," 23 January 1935, ibid.

33. Joseph Buttinger, *In the Twilight of Socialism: A History of the Revolutionary Socialists of Austria*, trans. E. B. Ashton (New York: F. A. Praeger, 1953), pp. 422–23.

34. The entire text is reprinted in Hannak, *Renner*, pp. 650–52. In Hannak's opinion Renner committed "a far-reaching mistake" (p. 652). Hannak and Josef Hindels are exceptions among Austrian socialist historians in confronting Renner's association with Nazi policies. See Josef Hindels, "Karl Renner ohne Legende" (1981), in *Karl Renner in Dokumenten und Erinnerungen*, ed. Siegfried Nasko (Vienna: Österreichischer Bundesverlag, 1982), pp. 213–19.

35. Radomir Luza, *Austro-German Relations in the Anschluss Era* (Princeton: Princeton University Press, 1975), pp. 71–72.

36. Renner, "Die Grundung der Republik Deutschösterreich, der Anschluss und die Sudentendeutschen: Dokumente eines kampfes ums Recht" (typeset but not published; Wien, 1938), Dokumentationsarchiv des Österreichschen Widerstandes, No. 57656. This document is omitted from the otherwise complete *Renner Bibliographie* (Vienna: 1970) and from his Nachlass in the Austrian Staatsarchiv. See Anton Pelinka's historiographic critique of Renner's "beatification," which includes ignoring this document. "Karl Renner—A Man for All Seasons," *Austrian History Yearbook*, vol. 23 (1992), pp. 111–19.

37. Renner, "Die Grundung der Republik Deutschösterreich," p. 6.

38. Ibid., p. 47.

39. Ibid., p. 85.

40. Ibid., p. 53.

41. Ibid., p. 71.

42. Ibid., p. 57.

43. Ibid., p. 73.

44. Ibid., pp. 77–78.

45. Ibid., pp. 20, 50–51.

46. Ibid., p. 7.

47. Karl Seitz and Karl Renner, *Krieg und Absolutismus: Friede und Recht* (Vienna: Verlag der Wiener Volksbuchhandlung, 1917), p. 29.

48. Austin Allibone, ed., *Prose Quotations from Socrates to Macaulay* (Philadelphia: J. B. Lippincott, 1882), p. 627.

49. Heinz Kohut, *The Restoration of the Self* (New York: International Universities Press, 1977), p. 81.

50. Renner to His Excellency Marshal Stalin, Moscow, 15 April 1945, in Hannak, *Renner*, pp. 672-75. For background of their relationship, see Stalin's critique of Renner's ideas on nationalism in Stalin, *Marxism and the National*

Question (1913) (New York: International Publishers, 1942). Renner is there cited by his early pseudonym Rudolph Springer.

51. Manfred Rauchensteiner, *Der Sonderfall: Die Besatzungszeit in Österreich 1945 bis 1955* (Vienna: Heeresgeschichtlichen Museum/Militärwissenschaftliches Institut, 1985), pp. 73–74.

52. OSS Report, 6 June 1945, "Political Situation: Travel," Secret/Control, RG 226, L 57155, in Oliver Rathkolb, ed., *Gesellschaft und Politik am Beginn der Zweiten Republik: Vertrauliche Berichte der U.S. Militäradministration aus Österreich 1945 in englischer Originalfassung* (Vienna: Hermann Böhlaus Nachf., 1985), p. 110.

53. Edgar N. Johnson and Dyno Lowenstein (OSS), Conversation with Renner, 15 September 1945 (written 5 October 1945), RG 226, XL 23.818, Secret/Control (For U.S. Personnel Only), in Rathkolb, *Gesellschaft und Politik*, pp. 122–28; quotation, pp. 126–28 passim, and 128 n. k passim.

54. Edgar N. Johnson and Paul R. Sweet (OSS), "The Question of Recognizing the Renner Government," 6 September 1945, Secret/Control, Privatarchiv Sweet, in Rathkolb, *Gesellschaft und Politik*, pp. 170–73.

55. SSU, R & A, 26 September 1945, RG 226, Xl 18.806 [Secret/Control, U.S. Officials Only], "Reasons for British Failure to Recognize the Renner Government," in Rathkolb, *Gesellschaft und Politik*, pp. 185–86.

56. Anton Pelinka considers this a typical Austrian problem and Renner as the prototype for Austria's ambivalent position toward National Socialism and the model for the person and symbol of former president Kurt Waldheim in Austrian history. See *Karl Renner zur Einführung* (Hamburg: Junius Verlag, 1989), pp. 107–10.

8

THE INNER WORLD OF
VLADIMIR ZHIRINOVSKY:
THE SELF-PRESENTATION
OF A "HERO"

Rational choice theory and applications of game theory fail to contribute to foreign policy decision making when they ignore the policymaker's need for actor-specific models. In other words, the abstract model of rationality has to be supplemented or replaced by an empirically derived theory about the mind-set of a particular actor.

Alexander George (1993)

This is a psychopolitical evaluation and analysis of the autobiography of the radical-right Russian leader V. V. Zhirinovsky, *Last Dash to the South*.[1] The utilization of psychoanalysis in political policy studies has a heritage that goes back at least to the distinguished work of Harold Lasswell, Nathan Leites, and Alexander George. The most famous case was the wartime study of Hitler done for the OSS in 1943 by Walter Langer, Henry Murray, Ernst Kris, and Bertram Lewin, which was later declassified and published.[2] I view this paper as a contribution to that tradition of scholarship.

Origins and birth

Z. emphasizes the "Russian" quality of his background, particularly on his mother's side ("a typical average Russian family"), which included a soldier in the czarist army. He describes the circumstances of his birth on 25 April 1946 as primitive ("my uncle . . . helped my mother and cut the cord with a kitchen knife") and under his aggressive initiative and control ("I myself provoked it somehow. . . . I could not wait") [2-1].

Mother

Z.'s mother was married to Andrei Vasilyevich Zhirinovsy, who died of tuberculosis in August 1944, eighteen months prior to Z.'s birth.[3]

Although Z. avows "a triple love" for his mother [7-l], his account is full of resentment against her. She was a hero mother who delivered six children, yet she is described as "childbearing machinery" [2-l]. His "joyless childhood" "was deprived of the most basic family comfort and human warmth." He "never had enough to eat." His mother was always working, "never had any time," "I would not see her for days on end" [2-r]. From age two or three he was in a twenty-four-hour nursery, which he did not like; he "was practically never home. I spent six days a week in a room with 26 beds and 12 little kids" [3-r]. "The main thing was to get rid of me" [4-r]. No one saw him off to school with a hug or embraced him, demonstrations of affection other children received [5-l]. A further scarcely disguised grievance against his mother is that his birthdays as a child were never celebrated. His first celebration was at age sixteen [4-r]. What Z. implies is that no matter how poor, any mother can make a birthday special for her child.

Mother gave him plates of soup from her work "on the sly" [2-r]. Then she took a lover, and he got the food (and love) in Z's place while Z. remained hungry: "When she had to choose between us, she chose him because he was her lover" [3-l].

Father

In comparison with his mother, Z.'s father is barely mentioned. He was Volf Isakovich Eidelshtein, who was officially listed as Jewish, and who died in 1946 in a car crash [2-l, 3-l].[4] Z. describes him as "an ordinary legal advisor" [2-1]. His parents were married five months before Z. was born, possibly leaving him in doubt about who really was his father.[5] One would expect pressing questions and fantasies about his father. Who was he and what was he like? Who are his family? What kind of people are they? Are there grandparents, uncles and aunts, cousins whom I could visit, get to know? Yet Z. gives no evidence of recollecting such curiosity. Z. attributes his shyness and timidity [9-r], also his "high culture," to his father's genes [8-r]! This may well be a euphemism for his father's Jewishness.

Wife and Son

Z.'s wife and son are scarcely introduced, and then only in a dismissive manner: "I have never been deeply in love with my wife. . . . The same goes for my attitude toward my son". He views this affectual isolation as a positive asset "so I have been able to preserve my strength for politics" [16-r] In fact, Z. reenacted with his wife and son exactly what his father did to him: abandoned the boy to be alone and vulnerable with his mother.

Relationship to Bill Clinton

President Clinton is much on Z.'s mind. He is addressed both directly and indirectly in the autobiography. Z. writes: "We say to Bill Clinton:

Do not repeat the mistakes of Napoleon and Hitler. You, Bill Clinton, are my age, you and I belong to the same generation in the same world" [31-r]. More obliquely, "Today the whole world knows about me. . . . I am famous" [26-l]. "There are reports on me by various intelligence services of the world, I am mentioned . . . in reports to the presidents of the world's leading countries" [26-r].

The coincidence of the lives of both men is so striking as to be improbable. Both were born in 1946, both lost their fathers that year due to automobile accidents. Clinton's father was killed in a car accident three months before he was born. Both were placed in foster care by bereaved hardworking mothers; in Z.'s case a residential child care institution, in Clinton's case with his grandparents.[6] Both then had to deal with stepfathers as they grew up. If they should meet, Clinton would do well early on to point out to Z. these conjunctures in their lives. Such a move may ease tension and start them out on a familiar basis.

There is something bland and almost a missing element in Z.'s description of his father, who "died early as a result of a car crash" [2-l]. Children are usually obsessively curious about the circumstances of such a personal catastrophe, posing questions such as What was father doing at the moment of death? Where was he going? Who did it, and who was at fault? What was the ethnicity of the driver?

No One Can Be Trusted

Father abandoned him at birth. Mother let him down, did not protect and feed him. Aunt Mariya moved in and "grabbed the entire kitchen." She "surrounded" him with "poisonous puffs of tobacco smoke" [3-l]. His brother does not give him accurate information about admission to higher education and housing in Moscow [9-r].

Ability to Adapt and to Get Things for Himself

Z. learned from his hard knocks. He demonstrates an ability to get what he needs through persistence and connections. He got the Komsomol letter of recommendation he needed for higher education. He got an initial student grant [10-l], then got it raised [10-r].

He was rejected for assignment to Turkey, which he badly wanted [10-r]. Yet he worked at it, switched training tracks, "made the maximum effort" until he got to Turkey [11–l].

He secured scarce resources for himself, such as a large living space—a room of 26 square meters (approximately 858 square feet) in Transcaucasia—by using his connections. "I approached the members of the military council, the chief of the political directorate, and some other people" [12-l], yet in the next paragraph he complains of discrimination and being victimized ("everywhere I felt myself discriminated against" [12-r]. He became chairman of the cooperative and worked for twelve or eighteen months to the end of his strength to get a better apartment [12-r].

Affect, Ego Functions, Frustration Tolerance

Z. appears to have poor impulse control, demanding service ahead of other lawmakers in the parliament cafeteria,[7] getting into repeated fist-fights with fellow lawmakers, grabbing and breaking tape recorders of journalists.[8] He deliberately uses unmodulated affect to intimidate and control others, like a six-year-old. Through coarse, sudden, and raw expression of emotion, especially anger, he gets others to do what he wills. This is a strategy that reinforces fantasies of his omnipotent control, confirms his grandiosity, and aggressively devalues those around him, demonstrating to himself that he can dominate and control his environment.

Identify with Me in My Deprivation

Z. presents himself as a deprived victim of Soviet postwar circumstances: no father, crowded housing and toilets, hunger, no new clothes. These are experiences that many Russians lived through and with which they are invited to identify. They can feel a shared past, as if to say: "I know what he is talking about. I went through the same grim childhood. This man knows, he understands, he has been where I was."

A Loner

Z. was shy and timid. No one shared his triumph at college graduation; "I was entirely alone" [11-l]. "There was no friendship" [11-r]. No close friends, teachers, or mentors are mentioned. Z. rationalizes this absence of attachments, taking pride in it as a source of uniqueness and strength in politics, as though one precludes the other. He is an aggressive narcissist.

The picture of an emotionally isolated person who becomes a political leader fits Freud's model of leadership. Freud said such an individual is a narcissist who derives his gratification from the adulation of crowds rather than from intense interpersonal relationships:

> His ego had few libidinal ties; he loved no one but himself, or other people only in so far as they served his needs. To objects his ego gave away no more than was barely necessary. . . . The leader himself need love no one else, he may be of a masterful nature, absolutely narcissistic, self-confident and independent. We know that love puts a check upon narcissism.[9]

Pattern of Provocativeness, Then Claiming Victimization

Z. characterizes himself as a victim in early life. As a young child he ran in a school corridor, collided with another child who "for some reason . . .

began to bleed," and Z. was punished. He cites this as an "injustice . . . which hurt me badly." [4-l]. Invariably, in schools the world over children are forbidden to run in the hallways, and are punished if they do so and another child gets hurt. It is unusual for an adult to remember such an "injustice" from kindergarten with all the affect of a fresh grievance.

Z. recounts having been arrested by the militia three times, always when he just happened to be at the wrong place at the wrong time. "For some reason" the militiaman "chose to follow me" [8-l]. He never was guilty of any crime or infraction of the law.

He was head of his Komsomol group, and a Jewish woman teacher persecuted him and removed him as Komsomol organizer [5-r]. He was again a Komsomol organizer in college but "made a hard-hitting speech," which marked him as "politically unreliable" and frustrated his first effort to get to Turkey [10-r]. What was in that speech?

He was arrested in Turkey for doing nothing (except purveying communist propaganda) [11-l], when he knew that the promotion of communist ideology was at the time an offense under the Turkish Penal Code.

Russians Are Discriminated Against

In Alma-Ata in the Caucasus, the locals are privileged and Z., as a Great Russian, is victimized, is at the bottom of the heap. He experienced "ethnic oppression" under the Kazakhs: it was harder to get an apartment, to get good grades, or to advance in his studies [6-r]. In the Caucasus "everywhere I felt myself discriminated against" [12-r]. This despite Russian dominance and preference over the ethnic peoples of the Soviet Union.

Z. offers a crude sample of Slavophilism—his judgment of the negative consequences of the "too rapid Europeanization of Russia": destruction of the patriarchal Russian family, drunkenness, absenteeism, smoking [24-l].

Turkey, the Bad

Z. was a Turkologist who wanted very much to get to Turkey. He spent years working hard and planning toward that end. In 1964 he studied Turkish language and literature at the Moscow Institute of Oriental Languages, about which he says, "Thank God I got into the Turkish department" [10-r]. But in January 1968 his chance to go with a Soviet sports delegation as a translator fell through due to a bad character reference. Then he spent eight months as a student trainee working on the Turkish desk of the Radio Committee, broadcasting to foreign countries. Thereafter he switched to practical training at the State Committee for Foreign Economic Relations because "I badly wanted to travel to Turkey" [10-r]. Finally, his quest was successful.

Z. spent eight months in Turkey, arriving on 24 April 1969 with a delegation of Soviet engineers under the Turco-Soviet Cooperation Program who were to work on a proposed iron and steel plant in Iskenderun.[10] His activities were closely followed by the Turkish police. He worked on the construction of the Seydisehir aluminum plant, and on 30 June 1969 became the interpreter at the Bandirma sulfuric acid plant. On 9 July 1969 he fraternized with Turkish soldiers, praising the comparative prosperity of Red Army troops. On 30 September 1969 he distributed Soviet propaganda, consisting of Lenin pins he obtained from the visiting Russian ship *Chugev*, to Turkish youth. Zhirinovsky describes what he terms "a bit of an incident" which, it turns out resulted in his arrest, detention by Turkish security police for sixteen days, trial, and departure from Turkey, calling it "unlucky" and "a blow of fate." Under Turkish law Communist propaganda was illegal. He engaged in Soviet propaganda with Turkish troops and youth. There is no recognition that he provoked his arrest and jailing.

He was arrested by Turkish security forces on 5 October 1969 and held until 21 October, when the Soviet Embassy intervened on his behalf. He was released on bail of TL (Turkish Lira) 5,000 (approximately $550) and barred from leaving Turkey. He was acquitted for lack of evidence on 10 December and left for Moscow four days later.

Z. pictures the Turks as all bad, they have no redeeming features. Z. has no mixed feelings concerning Turks, no gray area, no differentiation reflecting that some Turks were kind to him and others may have been brutes. He totally devalues the Turks. To him, they have no culture; there would be no loss if the entire Turkish nation perished [34-r]; they should be punished [35-r]. Why this intense hatred of the Turks? His feeling are so rigid, unmodulated, and absolute that I believe they carry a grievance of a deep personal hurt or humiliation.

Savior-Hero

Z. has a grandiose view of his own broad education and wide intellectual horizons. We are asked to think of him as a Renaissance man who claims "knowledge of philosophy, history, philology, literature, sociology, jurisprudence, political science, . . . [to be] a journalist, writer, leader, and orator, . . . to know foreign languages, . . . [to have a] grasp of economic problems, ecology, child-raising, the activity of law enforcement . . . and state security. The army, young people, sports, art" [16-l]. He is glib, verbally facile, a true dilettante, knowing a little about a lot.[11]

Z. pictures himself in the aggressive-savior symbolism of a surgeon who radically cuts out pathology to save the patient (Russia) [15-r], saying, "When a sick man is lying on the operating table, you need a single doctor, not a team of consultants."[12]

He drove out all opposition from his Liberal Democratic Party and had himself made the dictator with full power over all party affairs, from finances to appointments, until 2 April 2004. Z. adopts the identity of a hero-dictator for power and adulation, a combination or merger implying dominance and admiration suggesting "mirroring" approval, which a small child needs and never receives enough of from its mother or caretaker.[13]

Deceptive Use of Language

The idea of "a dash to the south," "a small push to the south," [36-l] is fantastical wordplay that ignores both the political reality of the Turkish army (Europe's largest) and NATO, and the geographic mountain barriers of Asia Minor. The Russians had anything but a quick "dash" through Afghanistan. Z. has no sense of the connotative meaning of words, their emotional nuances. His "dash to the south" is reminiscent of Winston Churchill's chimerical verbal formula for the Balkans as "the soft underbelly of Europe."

The Jew

Z.'s handling of his half-Jewish identity is conspicuous by its absence. He writes of Jews "from the west" who "headed a long way east" to Alma-Ata where "there were a lot of Jews" [6-l], but he does not say why this migration occurred.

According to press accounts Z. applied for and received permission to change his name from Eidelshtein to Zhirinovsky in June 1964, when he was eighteen.[14] An early 1994 report is that Z. "admitted recently that his father was Jewish."[15] in 1983 he sought to emigrate to Israel, and in 1990 he was active in a Jewish cultural organization named Shalom,[16] reputed by some Russian emigres to have been a KGB front organization.[17]

There is an absence of Jewish reference when Z. says "a small people is exterminated just because it is small and unable to defend itself" [28-l], citing as examples the Ossetians and the Abkhaz.

Nationalities Problem

Each citizen of the former Soviet Union has an internal passport documenting nationality, social origin, ethnicity, and family status. The Russians were the dominant nationality in the Soviet Union and many Great Russians take chauvinistic pride in their Russian nationality. Yet Zhirinovsky is adamant that Russian internal passports must be abolished:

> Passports will not contain the section "nationality," and that section will not appear on forms [28-1]. We must take the nationalities issue off the agenda, so that nobody should ever suffer a moment's hesitation over the thought that something might violate his rights on national grounds [30-r]. Everything else is personal. Nationality, religion, family status, and so forth—that is everyone's personal business. A time will come when there will be no passports in Russia [31-1].

Z.'s opposition to internal passports for all Russian citizens is a distinctly unpopular stance in Russia. I postulate that behind this strident position, which appears to be cosmopolitan and anti-parochial, we may hear the echo of his Jewish father, his own experiences of discrimination, and Z.'s problems with his internal passport or his fears about it.

The South

The South is described as both Russia's "main problem" [12-l], the source of all Russia's grief from time immemorial, and as "the very center of the world, . . . a fragrant region" that the Turks do not deserve [34-r]. The Mediterranean is a "warm" sea [37-r]; it is Russia's hope for a soft, beneficent future. Z. would make "the whole south . . . one big zone of sanatoriums and rest homes." It could become a center of recreation, vacations, "short-sleeved open-necked shirts with no tie," and youth camps [17-r], much like the Crimea was in the Czarist and Soviet eras, only this time it would be all of the South to the Mediterranean and Indian Oceans—a warm, smiling, fragrant maternal play space. Z. has a deeply felt hatred of, and dependence on, his early mother, to whom he would like to return in a regressive fantasy of symbiotic bliss.

The South is one place in a world full of enemies where there are also brotherly friends and allies—"our eternal friend India" [33-l] and "friendly Iraq" [37-l].

Psychopathology

In his personal life Z. destroys the potential for gratifying human relationships with his wife, his son, and parliamentary colleagues. He distinctly lacks feeling for other individuals and nations. He does not see others as separate persons deserving empathic regard. He views the world as an extension of his grandiose self-representation. His personal interactions are based on calculations of power and interest rather than emotional attachments. His aggression is predatory, and his self-structure is perversely grandiose.[18] He destroys intimate communication in relationships and forfeits the possibility of learning something of value in human interactions.[19] He is filled with primitive hatred and envies those who have what he desires and who are not dominated by a similar hatred. Behind Z.'s envy is the need to spoil and destroy anything good that might come from contact with those whom he needs.[20]

Z. asserts Russian superiority and aggressive territoriality in central and eastern Europe, the Middle East, and South Asia. He idealizes the South and devalues the Turks. He expresses a vindictive ideology, a search for power, a desire to dominate and coerce submission from the Turks and those whom he views as enemies. He cruelly attacks perceived enemies in Russian politics and foreign countries and has paranoid fears of their retaliation. The human qualities of Turks and others he hates are polarized and split off so they can be loathed without guilt, fear, or shame. His hostility becomes an enjoyable, self-righteous energy that confirms his, and Russia's, freedom and autonomy.[21] It is as if the only alternative to being victimized as a Russian is to become a tyrant within his own party, in his land, and over neighboring peoples. His repeated assertions of hatred and superiority over others are his only form of survival and meaning.

Method

The following are a few concrete examples, derived from clinical psychoanalysis, of sensing and formulating latent unconscious meanings illustrated from the text of Zhirinovsky's autobiography.

1. *Affect.* Listen for and follow the affect rather than the content of a communication, although the manifest text may indicate otherwise. Emotion conveys what is really going on. This is particularly relevant in a document whose purpose is political propaganda, when the point is being made to persuade and move popular opinion.

2. *Imagery.* Metaphors, figures of speech, analogues, similes, images, allegories, allusions, are never random, but are always freighted with meaning that may be interpreted.

3. *Repetition of themes.* The longitudinal repetition of themes in structure, style, or content indicates a latent unconscious message that should be listened to and interpreted.

4. *Internal conflict.* Evidence of ambivalence—the presence of more than one feeling toward an object (love and hate, attraction and repulsion, wanting and not-wanting, leaving and staying).

5. *Absence of material.* What is not said or even referred to often communicates where the anxieties and conflict lie. Silence speaks.

6. *Action or inhibition.* The freedom and ability to act in certain circumstances and the inhibition of action in others is visible in personal behavior and the conduct of political affairs.

7. *Frustration tolerance.* Impulse control, willingness to wait, patience, as opposed to demanding immediate gratification of needs and wishes. Recourse to action in order to relieve the tension of waiting demonstrates low frustraion tolerance.

8. *Rationalization.* Constructing more or less valid reasons for a desired course of action in order to obviate the real emotional reasons.

9. *Polarization and splitting.* Dividing the world and its occupants, or individuals, into those who are wonderful, idealized "good" persons, and those who are loathed, pictured as all bad, with no redeeming features. No evidence of balanced, mixed feelings towards objects, no gray areas, no differentiation reflecting that all people have some pleasant and some obnoxious qualities. Feelings are rigid, unmodulated, and absolute.

10. *Symbolic Politics and Anxiety.* Politics creates and lives by symbols. This is equally true of times of stability and of crisis politics. D. W.

Winnicott defined the transitional object as the symbol of the mother's presence and security for the infant and small child and the space between mother and child as the arena of first symbolization and creativity.[22] The symbolic codes of politics constitute transitional objects that gave security against anxiety in a world of chaos.

11. *Trauma, Demography, and Leadership.* Massive trauma is a crucial bridge to history. Human history is the story of large scale traumas of war and its sequelae, disease and epidemics, famine, loss and migration, economic crises, earthquakes, floods, droughts and pestilence. Social anxiety and trauma are the theoretical link from individual to group, cohort to leader, population to national politics.[23]

12. *Narcissistic Rage.* Heinz Kohut defined narcissistic rage as arising from a deficit of early parental empathy. The specific distinction of narcissistic rage is the "need for revenge, for righting a wrong, for undoing a hurt by whatever means. . . ."[24] The concept of narcissistic rage is relevant to, and should appropriately be applied to, the understanding of leadership, politics and society.

A leader who addresses and captures the emotional needs of a deprived and traumatized generation can build a devoted following and a dedicated political movement.

NOTES

1. The citations to *Last Dash to the South* (1993) Foreign Broadcast Information Service, FBIS-SOV–94–022-S (2 February 1994) are to page and column left [l] or right [r]; e.g., [7-l] stands for page 7, column left. Zhirinovsky is referred to as Z. I alone am responsible for the conclusions.

2. Walter Langer, *The Mind of Adolf Hitler: The Secret Wartime Report* (New York: Basic Books, 1972).

3. Associated Press and CNN in *Los Angeles Times*, 4 April 1994, p. A4.

4. *Turkish Daily News* (Istanbul), 5 April 1994.

5. *Los Angeles Times*, 4 April 1994, p. A4.

6. Donald Young, "William Jefferson Clinton," *Encyclopedia Americana* (Danbury, Conn.: Grolier, 1993), 7:85–86.

7. *Wall Street Journal*, 25 January 1994, p. A10.

8. AP report, *San Luis Obispo Telegram-Tribune*, 8 April 1994, p. A-7.

9. Freud, "Group Psychology and Analysis of the Ego" (1921), in *Standard Edition of the Complete Psychological Works of Sigmund Freud*, translated under the general editorship of James Strachey in collaboration with Anna Freud, assisted by Alix Strachey and Alan Tyson, 24 vols. (London: Hogarth Press, 1953–1975), 18:123–24.

10. This and subsequent data on Z.'s activities in Turkey, personal communication, Turkish embassy, Washington, D.C., to author, 11 and 12 May 1994.

11. "Vladimir Zhirinovsky talking with David Frost," aired on 25 March 1994. Tape courtesy of John Floresceau, David Paradine Television, Los Angeles.

12. *New York Times International,* 5 April 1994; quotation, p. A6.

13. Heinz Kohut, *The Analysis of the Self: A Systematic Approach to the Psychoanalytic Treatment of Narcissistic Personality Disorders* (New York: International Universities Press, 1971), pp. 105–99, 270–95.

14. *Los Angeles Times,* 4 April 1994, p. A4.

15. *Near East Report* (Washington), 38:3 (17 January 1994): 12.

16. Paul Quinn-Judge, "Pantie-hero," *New Republic,* 14 February 1994, p. 24.

17. Personal communication from Boris and Eve Nestorovsky, Los Angeles, 5 May 1994.

18. J. Reid Meloy, *The Psychopathic Mind: Origins, Dynamics, and Treatment* (Northvale, N.J.: Jason Aronson, 1992).

19. Otto F. Kernberg, *Aggression in Personality Disorders and Perversions* (New Haven: Yale University Press, 1992).

20. Melanie Klein, *Envy and Gratitude* (New York: Basic Books, 1957).

21. Mardi J. Horowitz, "Clinical Phenomenology of Narcissistic Pathology," *Psychiatric Clinics of North America* 12:3 (September 1989): 531–39.

22. D. W. Winnicott, "Transitional Objects and Transitional Phenomena," "Playing: A Theoretical Statement," "Playing: Creative Activity and the Search for the Self," "Creativity and its Origins," and "The Location of Cultural Experience," in *Playing and Reality* (London: Tavistock, 1971).

23. Franz L. Neumann, *Angst und Politik,* in *Recht und Staat,* 178/179 (Tübingen: J.C.B. Mohr <Paul Siebeck>, 1954), trans. by Peter Gay as "Anxiety and Politics," in Franz Neumann, *The Democratic and Authoritian State* (New York: Free Press, 1957), pp. 270–300.

24. Heinz Kohut, "Thoughts on Narcissism and Narcissistic Rage," in Paul H. Ornstein, ed., *The Search for the Self: Selected Writings, 1950–1978,* 4 vols. (New York: International Universities Press, 1978), 2:637–38.

III

PSYCHODYNAMICS AND THE SOCIAL PROCESS

9

ANXIETY IN HISTORY

They shall sit every man under his vine and under his fig tree; and none shall make them afraid.

Micah 4:4

When the historical process breaks down and armies organize with their embossed debates the ensuing void which they can never consecrate, when necessity is associated with horror and freedom with boredom, . . . [i]n wartime, when everybody is reduced to the anxious status of a shady character or a displaced person, . . . even the most prudent become worshippers of chance.

W. H. Auden, "The Age of Anxiety" (1944–1946)

Anxiety is the most pervasive presenting complaint in the modern world,[1] but it is as ancient as the Bible. It is the most important factor in politics, both democratic and authoritarian, and yet it is the least understood component of decision making. I will examine the function of anxiety in history and politics in an effort to enhance our understanding of its process and effects.

When President Franklin D. Roosevelt, in his first inaugural address, told the depression-battered American people that "the only thing we have to fear is fear itself,—nameless, unreasoning, unjustified terror,"[2] he was assuring them that he knew the danger and its causes, and that he could master and control the panic-inducing situation. He was assuaging their anxiety by offering certainty—a sure hand at the helm of the ship of state—and hope for the future. This is the model for the crisis leader.

From its inception psychoanalysis has been a body of thought in perpetual revision. I will delineate some of the adaptations made in the theory of anxiety from Freud's first theory of 1895 to his second theory of 1926, through the more recent modifications of Donald Winnicott in the forties and fifties and Heinz Kohut in the sixties and seventies. I will attempt to show that these theories are complementary rather than mutually exclusive and that for the social scientist and humanist together they provide a rich body of theory that is useful in the perception and structuring of historical research. In demonstrating the value of comprehension of the psychodynamic theory of anxiety for historical research I will introduce examples from modern French, German, Swiss, and U.S. history.

Freud radically revised, in midcareer, the psychoanalytic understanding of anxiety. In 1895 he had carefully delineated the phenomenology of anxiety states in what is still an accurate picture: irritability, oversensitiveness to noise, anxious expectation, hyperalertness, hypochondria, moral anxiety, doubting, scrupulousness, and pedantry. Anxiety is somatically manifested by rapid or irregular heartbeat; disturbances in breathing; attacks of sweating, tremors and shivering, vertigo, congestion; waking up at night in fright (*pavor nocturnus*); phobias; gastrointestinal disturbances including nausea and vomiting, diarrhea and constipation, ravenous hunger; and tingling sensations. Freud initially attributed this clinical picture to sexual practices such as abstinence, coitus interruptus and coitus reservatus, or other unconsummated sexual excitation.

Thus in 1895 Freud had explained anxiety as transformed libido that was dammed up and expressed as a neurotic symptom. The model is a deflection of somatic sexual excitation and its manifestation is anxiety: "Where one has grounds for regarding the neurosis as an *acquired* one, upon careful examination directed to that end, one finds a series of injuries and influences from *sexual life*."[3] Freud never entirely abandoned his first theory of anxiety as dammed up libido, and it has become enshrined in the ideas of Wilhelm Reich.[4]

In 1926 Freud made a crucial change in the theory of anxiety: now anxiety was no longer transformed libido but a reaction to a signal of a danger, unconscious in the adult, of a loss of love, care, security. Anxiety is a signal of the threat of the occurrence of a traumatic situation involving the distressing experiences of helplessness, hopelessness, loss, and separation. The danger is the painful recurrence of

> the longing for the beloved and wished for person who is absent. . . . Anxiety appears as a reaction to the loss of the object. . . . If the infant demands the observed presence of the mother it is only because it already knows by experience that she satisfies all its needs without delay. The situation which it regards as a "danger" against which it wants to be protected is that of being unsatisfied, of *an increasing tension due to need*, against which it is powerless. . . . The absence of the mother is now the danger; when this occurs the infant gives the signal of anxiety, before the dreaded economic situation (of deprivation) has set in. . . . In these two perspectives, as an automatic phenomenon and as a rescuing signal, anxiety is shown to be the product of the infant's psychic helplessness which is of course the counterpart of its biological helplessness. . . . It is evident . . . that anxiety cannot be found to have any other function than as a signal for the avoidance of a danger situation.[5]

Freud makes the distinction between the loss of the object and the loss of the object's love; the latter is the critical determinant of anxiety. "The loss of love is the condition necessary for anxiety."[6]

Anxiety, says Freud, has an unmistakable relation to *expectation*; it is anxiety *about* something. He goes on to make a further differentiation between realistic anxiety and neurotic anxiety. Realistic anxiety is a response to a known danger; neurotic anxiety is anxiety over a danger that we do not know. Neurotic danger must be searched for or invented.[7]

Freud makes a vital connection to trauma experienced, recalled, and feared. Anxiety is "the admission of our helplessness" in the face of danger. He terms such an experienced situation of helplessness a *traumatic* one:

> The individual will have made an important advance in his capacity for self-preservation if he can foresee and expect a traumatic situation of this kind which entails helplessness, instead of simply waiting for it to happen. Let us call a situation which contains the determinant for such an expectation a danger-situation. It is in this situation that the signal of anxiety is given. The signal announces: "I am expecting a situation of helplessness to set in," or: "The present situation reminds me of one of the traumatic experiences I have had before. Therefore I will anticipate the trauma and behave as though it had already come, while there is yet time to turn it aside." Anxiety is therefore on the one hand an expectation of a trauma, and on the other a repetition of it in a mitigated form. Thus the two features of anxiety which we have noted have a different origin. Its connection with expectation belongs to the danger-situation, whereas its indefiniteness and lack of object belong to the traumatic situation of helplessness—the situation which is anticipated in the danger-situation.
>
> Taking this sequence, anxiety—danger—helplessness (trauma), we can now summarize what has been said. A danger-situation is a recognized, remembered, expected situation of helplessness. Anxiety is the original reaction to helplessness in the trauma and is reproduced later on in the danger-situation as a signal for help.[8]

I will illustrate the modern psychodynamic understanding of anxiety with a case vignette:

> Ida entered psychoanalytic psychotherapy in a crisis of fragmentation following the quadruple traumas of moving to a new city, her husband's having a psychotic break and leaving her, the birth of a second child, and the sudden, unanticipated death of her father, to whom she was closely attached. All of these acute events occurred within one week, leaving her with feelings of desperation and hopelessness. She was dysfunctional in the world, unable to find or hold a job, to take care of herself and her children, to build friendships and relationships in a new community. She was often tearful, anxious, and depressed. Her judgment and reality testing were impaired. Many of her reactions were those of a little girl rather than a woman of twenty-nine. She was financially dependent on her wealthy, controlling mother.

Over the ensuing eight years of psychoanalysis Ida built a life for herself. She had a series of relationships with men, each one more gratifying than the last; she is now married; her children are doing well in school and socially; she holds a professional position as a program administrator after a series of career frustrations that included being dismissed from a position following a conflict with the director of the organization.

Recently, Ida was a candidate for an administrative position that she strongly desired. It was in a prestigious institution, the salary was a substantial raise over what she had been earning, the terms of professional opportunity and scope of creative autonomy would be great. After she had been promised the job and assumed she had it, the chairman of the search committee told Ida that negative references had been received from her prior employer. Her new position was in jeopardy, and she felt it slipping through her fingers. The chairman did not call her and seemed to avoid her.

Ida panicked. She dreamed of a white shark chasing her onto land and attacking her. Her associations were to her former director. She lost control of her time schedule and commitments. She saw herself back in a position of hopeless child, as she had been eight years earlier, jobless, outcast, and helpless, and again completely dependent on her mother. She had the impulse to tell the employing administrator of her personal life, financial straits, and the problems of her last employment.

Instead, Ida reasoned that her getting the new position would depend on being able to demonstrate competence, a professional attitude, and the ability to deliver the services in an expert, reliable way. She mobilized her friends and allies in the community who thought well of her work to write letters of reference and to call the search committee chairman. She took the initiative to arrange another interview, in which she presented an alternative budget that showed her grasp of the financial realities of the project. She drafted a new survey flyer that was an improvement on the institution's previous one. She imparted the conviction that she was indeed the person for the position and she received the appointment.

Ida experienced the anxiety of the danger of being thrown back to an early situation of helplessness, of being trapped by circumstances she could not control, and of being the victim of her past and the malice of a former employer. Because of her understanding of the psychodynamics of her anxiety, she was able to bring her coping mechanisms to bear and devise rational and persuasive ways to turn the situation around to her advantage rather than regress to a state of hopeless passivity. She helped herself, acting on her own behalf. She mastered her anxiety and altered the anxiety-inducing situation in her favor.

I will argue that the Freudian perception of anxiety as a signal of the danger of helplessness and hopelessness is a political and historical category of understanding whose full implications have yet to be explored. We are now on the grounds of massive psychic trauma and its sequelae in the posttraumatic stress disorders. We have careful and detailed studies of large populations of survivors of concentration camps, Hiroshima and Nagasaki, the Buffalo Creek flood, and the Chowchilla schoolbus incident; of World War Two, Korean War, and Vietnam War veterans; and of victims of hostage taking, including U.S. embassy personnel in

Iran and passengers on a Netherlands train commandeered by Molluc-
cans. The evidence is clear: given a large enough social or collective
traumatic event, no one escapes a posttraumatic stress disorder. Its hall-
mark is fixation on the trauma but with new variations and with an
altered conception of the self and of the world. The symptoms are lifelong. Adaptive and coping capacities are enfeebled.[9]

Social trauma is the crucial bridge to history. We are no longer speaking of singular cases or a unique psychogenesis. Our history as humans is
the story of large-scale traumas of war, disease and epidemics, famine,
dislocation and migration, economic crises, droughts, and pestilence.
Trauma is the theoretical link from individual to group, cohort, population, nation, the world. And here the historian appropriately introduces
categories for understanding groups and institutions, politics, national
boundaries, educational systems, military service, youth movements,
traditions, civic culture, myth, symbol, the artifacts of popular and high
culture.[10]

II

In times of helplessness, anxiety increases inordinately. The late Hel-
lenistic and Roman period witnessed the end of the *polis civitas* when the
city of Rome was the world. The period is marked by public spectacles of
human butchery in the arenas and the rise of apocalyptic and messianic
movements.[11] Christianity with its promise of eternal bliss for the virtuous and eternal torture for the evil was a mode of dealing with anxiety.

The age of the Renaissance, approximately from 1300 to 1650, for all
its cultural creativity, was marked by famine, pestilence, and disease un-
equaled in human history. The Hundred Years War between England
and France broke out in 1338. The Hussite Wars devastated large parts
of Germany and eastern Europe. And the human race has known no
scourge comparable to the Black Plague, the bubonic infection that
arrived in Europe in 1347 and swept from Constantinople to the Atlantic
coast and up to Russia by 1350, killing one-third of Europe's people.
In some places, such as Siena, the death rate was over 50 percent.
Not anxiety but panic enveloped the continent: city people fled to the
countryside. Thus the infection was spread, not only by rat-infested ships
but by those who were taking flight. In Giovanni Boccacio's immortal
Decameron we hear the wonder and puzzlement of Florentine refugees at
the scourge, whose natural causes were not understood and therefore attributed to God:

> In the year then of our Lord 1348, there happened at Florence, the finest
> city in all Italy, a most terrible plague; which, whether owing to the influ-
> ence of the planets, or that it was sent from God as a just punishment for
> our sins, had broken out some years before in the Levant; and after pass-
> ing from place to place, and making incredible havoc all the way, had now
> reached the west; where, spite of all the means that art and human fore-

sight could suggest, as keeping the city clear from filth, and excluding all suspected persons; notwithstanding frequent consultation what else was to be done; nor omitting prayers to God, frequent processions; in the spring of the foregoing year began to show itself in a sad and wonderful manner.[12]

The Black Death recurred every few years, until by the turn of the century Europe's population was half of what it had been in 1347, and less in some areas. At the end of the fifteenth century Columbus's sailors returned from the New World with syphilis, a quid pro quo for the measles, pox, and other infectious diseases that Europe introduced into the indigenous population of the Americas.

The Protestant Reformation of the early sixteenth century was a major rupture in the stability of Western Christendom, a trauma of major proportions whose effects took centuries to work out to a new and secure equilibrium. The response of European religion, culture, and politics to these traumata was a new piety, flagellation, the widespread practice of torture, and epidemics of demonic possession, which for the first time in history seized groups in the late fifteenth century. In this period we see the emergence of the witch mania that tortured and killed thousands. In one year nine hundred were killed in Würzburg, six hundred in Bamberg, and eight hundred in Savoy during a festival. In the year 1514, three hundred were executed in the small diocese of Como.[13]

The cultural expression of these disasters was an iconography of death and destruction. During its first thousand years Christian art had developed no symbol of death; after the Black Plague, the figure of Death descends like a curse on mortals and reaps his grim harvest with a scythe. We treasure Albrecht Dürer's (1471–1528) immortal *Ritter, Tod, und Teufel* of 1513, which graphically portrays the ever-present reality of death and the devil riding with us through life. To cite one other classic, this from the Prado in Madrid, we have Pieter Bruegel's (1525–1569) *Triumph of Death* representing the artist's losses and anxieties about himself and his loved ones.

Western Christianity began to burn Jews and heretics in the eleventh century. In the previous six centuries Jew hatred had not expressed itself in frequent violence, but beginning in 1096 the Crusades meant massacres of Jews, especially in the Rhineland. In 1144 we find the first recorded accusation, in Norwich, England, that Jews had sacrificed a Christian child. In the thirteenth century Jews were charged with the desecration of the Host. Violent, persecutory anti-Semitism came into ascendancy and prevailed in Europe. The Jews were either murdered or expelled from all of western and central Europe, climaxing in the Spanish expulsion of 1492. Under the leadership, first of demagogues who roused the mobs, then of states, the simple solution to crisis was scapegoating: the formula answer to an alleged Jewish plot to poison wells and spread disease. Anxiety over contamination and death produced a projective assault on an easily identifiable, slightly but significantly different, vulnerable group that it was socially permissible and theologically necessary to hate, torture, and kill.[14] The cultural historian Johan Huizinga stressed the responses to anxiety of the early modern period on "the decay of overripe forms of civilization" such as the elaboration of protocol, a cult of death, ritualistic behavior, pessimism, and a violent tenor of life.[15]

The bicentenary of the French Revolution, invited us to view that momentous event in light of the management of anxiety. One of the outstanding works engaging with an historical manifestation of anxiety in the Revolution is George Lefebvre's *The Great Fear of 1789: Rural Panic in Revolutionary France.* The "Great Fear" refers to the general feeling of anxiety that swept areas of rural France in the second half of July and early August, 1789, at which time the countryside joined the towns in revolution.

The agrarian revolt that broke out in rural areas was momentous for France and for the Western world; it was when the peasants got land from the aristocracy, a social event that more than any other lastingly imprinted the Revolution on the political life of France and insured the rural base for republicanism in the national history. The Revolution gave the peasants their land, and on 4 August 1789 the National Assembly abolished feudal privileges and serfdom, thereby ending the practices in western Europe. Lefebvre describes the rising of the peasants against the feudal lords:

> In the woodlands of Normandy, in the Hainaut and Upper Alsace, chateaux or abbeys were attacked by those seeking to burn archives and force surrender of manorial rights. In Franche-Comte and the Maconnais peasants set fire to many chateaux, sometimes laying them waste. The bourgeoisie was not always spared: they, too, had to pay. In Alsace the Jews suffered.[16]

He analyzes the fear as a "defensive reaction" against an "aristocratic plot" that did not yet exist. The two were inseparable elements. The fear was of "brigands" in the service of aristocrats who were believed to be stalking the countryside, burning, pillaging, and raping. It was a delusion, a symbolic representation, and a projection. Says Lefebvre: "Anxiety is self-explanatory. One has everything to fear from an adversary as one imagines him to be."[17] The characteristic response of a village to the arrival of the news was panic:

> Mass hysteria would break out among the peasant women: in their imagination, it was already too late—they were raped, then murdered, their children slaughtered, their homes burnt to the ground; weeping and wailing, they fled into the woods and fields, a few provisions and bits of clothing clutched to their bosoms. Sometimes, the men followed close behind once they had buried anything of value and set the animals loose in the open country. Most often, though, whether through common decency, a genuine bravery or fear of authority, they responded to the appeal of the *syndic*, the cure or the seigneur. Preparations would be made for the defence of the village under the direction of the seigneur himself or some

old soldier. Everyone armed up at the entrance of the village or at the bridge; scouting parties were sent out. At nightfall patrols were kept up and everyone stayed on the alert. In the towns, there was a sort of general mobilization: it was like being in a city under siege. Provisions were requisitioned, gunpowder and munitions collected, the ramparts repaired and the artillery placed in position.[18]

A comparison with those areas of France that did not experience the Great Fear is instructive. Some areas, such as Brittany, were immune to it. The crucial variable is that the authorities were able to assert their authority and exercise a calming influence on the population. Local councils took competent measures to restrain both the aristocracy and the lower orders, acting in a confidence-inspiring way, thereby giving the people a sense of order and control.[19] As a social-psychological phenomenon, the Great Fear is a manifestation of the anxiety caused by loss of authority, the absence of the security of control and mastery, of not having a firm hand at the helm. After the events in Paris on 14 July 1789, the old order was perceived as gone and the peasantry, in those areas subject to the Great Fear, was adrift and therefore subject to its own unrestrained wishes and fears.

The news of the purported coming of the brigands, sometimes from all directions at once, traveled with great speed. Lefebvre documents the velocity of the rumor:

> To travel from Clermont in Beauvaisis to the Seine—a distance of about fifty kilometres—it took twelve hours of daylight; it travelled the five hundred kilometres from Ruffec to Lourdes in nine days; its speed here was lesser by a half, but it obviously moved more slowly at night. During the day, it seems to have gone at about four kilometres an hour. It moved from Livron to Arles—a hundred and fifty kilometres—in forty hours, which makes four kilometres an hour, night and day.[20]
>
> La Tour-du-Pin got its warning on the 27th at three o'clock, Bourgoin at five o'clock, Virieu, the Bievre plain and the Cote-Saint-Andre all the same time. The fear rushed down all the valleys of the Bas-Dauphine towards the Rhone valley, from Lyons to Saint-Vallier. Towards the South, it went by the Voiron road to reach the Isere at Moirans, and whilst it went up one side to reach Grenoble by eleven o'clock, it went down the other side to pass through Saint-Marcellin at midnight; it was in Romans at three in the morning on the 28th, moving from here to Tain, then Valence: it was now well established and on that same day the chateaux of the lower Dauphine began to burn.[21]

The motive of the peasants was revenge; they did not only destroy the archives. "It was," writes Lefebvre, "the desire to punish the seigneur through the goods which were so precious to him and which were the symbol and the basis of his power." Such an expression of vengeance will in turn give rise to feelings of guilt, anxiety, and fears of retaliation. As Lefebvre put it, "fear walked abroad"; there was a "general feeling of anxiety." He observed that "fear of brigands and fear of aristocrats always managed to occur simultaneously in the mind of the people." He is explicit that this fear was a delusion: "To admit that the brigands existed and might appear at any moment was one thing; to imagine that they were actually there was another."[22]

Peter Paret suggests that the Great Fear of 1789 "would not have been significantly improved by its author's comprehension of psychoanalysis."[23] Perhaps not. But I venture that a psychodynamic understanding could illuminate precisely the sudden collapse of order, the accelerating anxiety, the projection of aggressive intent, and fears of revenge and retaliation that are phenomenologically described in Lefebvre's classic account. There is an oedipal element in the peasant's overthrow of the seigniorial paternal authority and the fear of the vengeful return of that authority. The peasants feared that the aristocrats were going to do to them exactly what they had already done or were about to do to the aristocrats in late July and early August 1789.

The time specificity of the peasants' anxiety is crucial. "At the end of July," says Lefebvre, "the general feeling of insecurity was so much more frightening than it had ever been before, and on the eve of the harvest there was a truly overwhelming sensation of fear and anxiety."[24] A psychodynamic understanding of guilt, anxiety, and the defense mechanisms of projection and displacement is what is missing from Lefebvre's analysis, and this would explain why the peasants had this great fear of retribution just as they were planning to, or already had, seized the manor houses, burned the records, and abused and intimidated the lord of the manor into either fleeing or signing over his seignorial rights. The peasants feared that the "brigands" as agents of the nobility would do to them what they were about to do to the aristocrats: burn, pillage, steal, drive out, and seize for themselves.

III

In what has come to be considered a classic in socioeconomic history, Hans Rosenberg related the long-cycle depression in central Europe, 1873–1896, to widespread feelings of pessimism, cultural despair, and the rise of anti-Semitism.[25]

> The Great Depression of 1873 to 1896 was not only an economic, but also a psychic phenomenon.[26] To a high degree the period from 1873 to 1896 was a neurotic era inclined to madness. Among its major indications are the grotesque anxiety of the "Reds" and the "Revolution," the class hatred and Jew hatred, the passionate sharpening of confessional conflict, the wild agitation against "liquid capital" and "cosmopolitan" commerce, the accelerating volume of nationalistic shouting, the widely diffused tendency to radicalization, even among the conservatives, the discrediting and retreat of the moderate middle groups.[27]

A study of a particular vocational subgroup—urban master artisans in traditional handicrafts—in the precise years of Rosenberg's long-cycle depression, 1873 to 1896, found that the displaced artisans could not adjust to industrialism and became the defiant bearers of antimodern il-liberalism, which was a prelude to fascism. Their feeling of political hopelessness and a prevalent cultural pessimism gave rise to a general sense of crisis among the master artisans.[28]

Blackbourn and Eley, while critiquing the Rosenberg-Volkov focus on the economic downturn of 1873–1896 as overstated and the correla-tions between political events and economic fluctuations as unproven, question that a direct relationship can be drawn between the economic crises of the Wilhelmine era and the development of fascism decades later. I agree with them. Yet Blackbourn and Eley also point to a late-nineteenth-century instability and anxiety in Germany. To them, the cause of anxiety is the increasing concentration of capital and industry and the larger framework of major economic downturns of the business cycle in 1857, 1901–1902, and 1907–1909, as well as the long-cycle de-pression of 1873–1896.[29] Similarly, the traditional focus on the Great Depression of 1929 as the critical point of the disintegration of the democratic party system of the Weimar Republic has been revised by Thomas Childers, who places it earlier—in the aftermath of the inflation and stabilization crises of the midtwenties.[30]

IV

Adolf Hitler was a charismatic leader, not merely in the colloquial sense of having a persuasive style and a devoted following, as might be said of Franklin D. Roosevelt, John F. Kennedy, or a rock star. We can apply the term *charismatic authority* to Hitler in its precise Weberian meaning, as a personal authority who "knows only inner determination and inner restraint. The holder of charisma seizes the task that is adequate for him and demands obedience and a following by virtue of his mission."[31]

Hitler communicated power, certainty, control; he had an easy ex-planation for how Germany had arrived at its current predicament and an action-oriented program for the future. He offered security, a sense of community (*Volksgemeinschaft*), comradeship, and the promise of na-tional strength and order in place of impotence and chaos.[32] He appealed to all the psychic needs of those Germans who felt desperate hopeless-ness and futile rage at an abstract economic system and a humiliating peace. As Martin Broszat put it:

> Given the impression of resoluteness which he conveyed, Hitler knew how to articulate and, as it were, to celebrate what his listeners half consciously desired and felt. He voiced what they secretly thought and wanted, rein-forced their still unsure longings and prejudices, and thereby created for them deeply satisfying self-awareness and the feeling of being privy to a new truth and certainty. Such leadership and oratory did not require a re-fined intellectual discrimination or a calm, mature individuality and personality, but . . . a psychological and mental disposition which was itself so infected by the mood of crisis and panic of the time that it instinctively sounded the correct note.[33]

Justice Oliver Wendell Holmes, Jr., once said, "We live by symbols." This is especially true of crisis politics and the search for stability. An example of the importance of Hitler and the emotional charge of his message as a symbolic image, in distinction to its cognitive content, is the experience described by two sisters in 1934 upon hearing Hitler for the first time at a rally in Kassel. The sisters' family name was Heder; they lived in Kreis Fritzlar; their ages were nineteen and twenty-one; and their father had been killed on the Russian front in 1915.

> As the first sonorous and warm words sounded, deep silence befell the place. Never again in life did an event exert such a deep hold on us, as did this first speech of the Führer. And then the words fell, destroying, accusing, blazing and rousing, pulling along everyone including those who were doubtful. He spoke with force to the mass and yet again to each individual and he fascinated them. His fateful words engraved themselves deeply into our hearts. Again and again the enthusiasm interrupted the silence and transmitted itself to the thousands who listened outside the tent to the broadcast. Then it was over. The *Horst-Wessel* song reared to the sky. We saw flowers over flowers, but the man in the unpretentious brown uniform with a face marked by an inflexible will, with small eloquent hands wasn't there any more. We don't know how we got home. This evening we could not sleep; the experience was still too strong. Many a prayer ascended to heaven on this evening asking for the protection of the Führer.[34]

We note the sisters were so elated on their first encounter with their new savior/father/leader that they could not sleep. They prayed for him.

The imperial colors, black-white-red, the image of Bismarck and the implied continuity with his Reich and its splendid triumph over France, and the figure of the Junker Generalfeldmarshal Paul von Hindenburg as the president who called Hitler to power are positive symbolic codes or "signs" of continuity with cherished ideals, security, and success. The images of the "November Criminals" and "Dollstoss" who betrayed Germany in World War One, the "Jude" and "Sozi-Bonzen" who were Germany's "misfortune" symbolized the negative images to be obliterated and mercilessly overcome.

On 22 August 1932 five Nazi S.A. murderers received death sentences for hacking and kicking a Communist organizer to death in Potempa, Silesia. Hitler used the occasion to demonstrate to the German public his brutality, ruthlessness, and contempt for normative rules of political conduct. His telegram to the killers congratulated them and promised they would soon be released as "a question of honor." He assured them he was linked to them in "boundless loyalty" "in the face of this monstrous, bloodthirsty sentence."[35] Further examples of his trampling upon the normative values or "social cement" of German and Western conduct and culture were the festive burning of books and the banning of "degenerate" art. He projected an image of barbaric, irresistible power and an extraordinary capacity for aggressive violence independent of traditional moral norms. The message was that opposition was pointless and hopeless. Resistance was futile.

Hitler promised decisive action, certainty, power, and mastery of the world. These are the best antidotes to feelings of helplessness, bewilderment, weakness, passivity, humiliation, and vulnerability. Hitler and Nazism were Germany's answer to collective historical narcissistic injury. He gave an integrated, simple explanation of the past, the crisis of 1929–1933, and a vision of a glorious future. He appeared to contain anxiety and threats of hopelessness. He posed as the representative of order, morality, and power. He restored an active sense of purpose so the German people could experience society as stable, vital, disciplined, supportive, and dependable. Hitler posited a regime of unity at home, a new respect in the world, dynamic energy, and the end of disorder in the streets and the government.[36]

A dramatic yet little known case of the use of a highly emotive national symbol as an antidote to realistic anxiety is the Swiss crisis of the summer of 1940. With the capitulation of France on 17 June 1940, Switzerland was surrounded on all sides by Axis powers. Hitler's ground forces were not engaged in either the East or West; hence it was a time of extreme danger for Switzerland. The president of Switzerland, Marcel Pilet-Golaz, gave a Petainist radio address on 25 June, suggesting that Europe was under a new order, that Switzerland must adapt to the New Europe, and "that the people should follow the government as a sure and devoted leader [*Führer* in the simultaneous German translation], who will not always be able to explain, elaborate, and give the reasons for his decisions."[37] The army was to be partially demobilized, as though the threat to Switzerland had been from France. Pilet-Golaz said not a word about resisting aggression.

Not all Swiss were in concord with a mood of collaboration with Hitler. A group of army officers were resolved not to surrender to Nazism and to fight it out to the end. General Henri Guisan called a secret meeting of all commanding officers, from corps commanders down to battalion commanders, a total of 650, on 25 July. They boarded a steamer on the Lake of the Four Cantons and were taken to the meadow of Rütli, a site shrouded in myth and sentiment in Swiss culture, a place hallowed by history and tradition and known to all schoolchildren. There in 1291 the three forest cantons had sworn to one another an oath of perpetual mutual defense, out of which modern Switzerland was born. The term *Eidgenossenschaft* is the Swiss-German expression for the federal union and is synonymous with *Switzerland* in official usage, and Rütli is synonymous with Swiss patriotism and freedom.

At the Rütli meadow General Guisan gave a short informal speech from penciled notes, evoking the theme of centuries-old Swiss independence and pledging "that it will be respected to the end." He urged the assemblage not to listen to those who spread despair and defeatism, and stressed the need for the army to be at its post rather than demobilize. He was ordering the army to new fortified positions, the Alpine *reduit na-*

tionale, on 1 August, the national holiday commemorating the oath at Rütli. According to an official handout, Guisan said:

> In 1939 the Federal Council entrusted the army with the task of protecting our centuries-old independence. This independence has been respected, until now, by our neighbors, and we will see to it that it will be respected to the end. As long as in Europe millions stand under arms, and as long as important forces are able to attack us at any time, the army has to remain at its post.
>
> Come what may, the fortifications you have built preserve all their value. Our efforts have not been in vain, since we still hold our destiny in our own hands. Don't listen to those who, out of ignorance or evil intention, spread negative news and doubt. Let us trust not only in our right but also in our strength, which enables us, if everybody is possessed of an iron will, to defend ourselves successfully.
>
> On August 1 you will fully realize that the new positions that I have ordered you to occupy are those in which your arms and your courage in the new situation will be most effective for the defense and the good of the country.[38]

An extract of Guisan's speech was handed out as an order of the day to be read to the troops. It was also in the press and on the radio. The effect was electrifying on Swiss morale. Guisan could not have chosen a more evocative place to issue his call to the Swiss people that the army should not demobilize but remain intact to resist Axis aggression. In what was a paradigm case of symbolic politics, Guisan effectively drew on associations of the stubborn defense of liberty at a time of equivocation and grave crisis.

V

Two major episodes of anxiety in history occurred in our own country, on the West Coast, during World War Two: the relocation of Japanese Americans in camps in 1942 and the anti-Latino zoot-suit riots of 1943. The Japanese relocation was not founded in reality, was irrational on its face, and was illegal.[39] It was not founded in reality because there was not a single demonstrated case of espionage by a Japanese American. It was irrational because the relatively large Japanese Nisei and Sansei populations of the exposed Hawaiian Islands were not interned. And, as one who watched the relocation as a boy of eight in San Francisco, it is personally gratifying that Congress has recognized the injustice of this impulsive act of anxiety and is now making symbolic restitution for the gross violation of the civil liberties of Americans.

The war in the Pacific was not going well in 1942 and early 1943. The United States had suffered a series of setbacks and defeats at the hands of the Japanese, who showed themselves to be a courageous and determined enemy. The Japanese tide of conquest was at its height in mid-1943.

The zoot suit riots in Los Angeles in the first ten days of June 1943 were attacks on young Latino males who wore distinctive black suits with long jackets and pegged pants, apparel often accessorized with a floppy hat and chains. Service men from all over the country were stationed in southern California for basic training and had their heads shaved and their civilian clothes replaced by "government issue." The GIs and navy recruits, aware that they were given perfunctory combat training in boot camp before being rushed out to the Pacific Theater to meet a determined and lethal brown-skinned foe, rioted and victimized local Latino youths.

In June 1943, a Los Angeles newspaper published directions on how to "de-zoot" a boy: "Grab a zooter. Take off his pants and frock coat and tear them up or burn them. Trim the 'Argentine duckstail' that goes with the screwy costume."[40] In chasing, capturing, and degrading "pachucos," in unmanning them by taking off their clothes and cutting off their "duck-butt" hair, the GIs turned the passive boot-camp experience of humiliation and identity loss into the active experience of beating local Latino youngsters, shaving their heads, and taking away their clothes. The moves against an available brown-skinned "enemy" assuaged their anxiety over the more remote and dangerous enemy awaiting them in the Pacific.

The politics of anxiety frequently produces an unreasoning impulse to find a quick solution, sometimes by legal means, often by illegal violence, that soothes the immediate anxiety but fails to solve the long-term problem. The results are often deleterious, although they rarely approach the historic magnitude and evil of Nazism.

The psychohistorical understanding of anxiety is that it is a response to a sense of powerlessness, a loss of mooring or centering. The experiences of an epidemic, a lost war, an old order destroyed, family savings and security wiped out, and strife in previously safe streets are the social equivalents of the death of a parent or loved one, divorce, loss of a job, or a catastrophic diagnosis. Such crises are the "danger point" creating anxiety, and the overpowering urge is to do something, to act aggressively and violently in ways that seem at the moment to meliorate the painful anxiety. The danger is the regressive need to find and follow the leader who gives reassurance with simplistic, often projective and xenophobic formulas that promise stability, order, reckonability, power, mastery, and false security.

NOTES

1. *The Diagnostic and Statistical Manual of Mental Disorders*, 4th ed., rev. (Washington, D.C.: American Psychiatric Association, 1994), has fourteen subcategories of anxiety disorders, pp. 393–444.

2. F. D. Roosevelt's first inaugural address, 4 March 1933, *Documents of American History*, vol. 2 since 1898, 9th ed., ed. Henry Steele Commager (Englewood Cliffs, N.J.: Prentice-Hall, 1973), p. 240.

3. Freud, "On the Grounds for Detaching a Particular Syndrome from Neurasthenia under the Description 'Anxiety Neurosis,'" in *Standard Edition of the Complete Psychological Works of Sigmund Freud*, translated under the general editorship of James Strachey in collaboration with Anna Freud, assisted by Alix Strachey and Alan Tyson, 24 vols. (London: Hogarth Press, 1953–1974), 3:99 (hereafter cited as *S.E.*).

4. Wilhelm Reich, *The Mass Psychology of Fascism* (New York: Farrar, Straus & Giroux, 1970).

5. Freud, "Inhibitions, Symptoms and Anxiety," in *S.E.*, 20:136–38.

6. Ibid., p. 143.

7. Ibid., p. 165.

8. Ibid., pp. 166–67.

9. Arnold M. Cooper, "Toward a Limited Definition of Psychic Trauma," in *The Reconstruction of Trauma*, ed. Arnold Rothstein (Madison, Conn.: International Universities Press, 1986), pp. 41–56.

10. I appreciate in this connection Walter P. Metzger, "Generalizations about National Character: An Analytic Essay," in *Generalization in the Writing of History*, ed. Louis Gottschalk (Chicago: University of Chicago Press, 1963), pp. 77–102, particularly pp. 96–97.

11. E. R. Dodds, *Pagan and Christian in an Age of Anxiety* (New York: Norton, 1965).

12. *The Decameron* (London: Chatto and Windus, 1920), pp. xix–xx.

13. In his 1957 presidential address to the American Historical Association, William L. Langer used the late Middle Ages, especially the Black Death of 1347–1350 and the ensuing period of devastating disease to demonstrate the importance of depth psychology for historical research: "The Next Assignment," *American Historical Review* 63:2 (1958): 283–304. Lynn White, Jr., interprets the Renaissance, 1300 to 1650, as a period of abnormal anxiety due to rapid velocity of cultural change: "Death and the Devil," in *The Darker Vision of the Renaissance*, ed. Robert Kinsman (Berkeley: University of California Press, 1974), pp. 25–46. William J. Bouwsma stresses the growth of urbanization in "Anxiety and the Formation of Early Modern Culture," in *After the Reformation: Essays in Honor of J. H. Hexter*, ed. Barbara C. Malament (Philadelphia: University of Pennsylvania Press, 1980), pp. 215–46.

14. Peter Loewenberg, "Die Psychodynamik des Antijudentums," *Jahrbuch des Instituts für Deutsche Geschichte*, vol. 1 (Tel Aviv: Nateev, 1972), 145–58. Norman Cohn lifts out the element of demagogic leadership of revolutionary messianism in the late medieval period in *The Pursuit of the Millennium: Revolutionary Messianism in Medieval and Reformation Europe and Its Bearing on Modern Totalitarian Movements* (New York: Harper & Brothers, 1961); and *Europe's Inner Demons: An Enquiry Inspired by the Great Witch-Hunt* (New York: Basic Books, 1975); see also Joshua Trachtenberg, *The Devil and the Jews: The Medieval Conception of the Jew and Its Relation to Modern Antisemitism* (New Haven: Yale University Press, 1943).

15. Johan Huizinga, *The Waning of the Middle Ages* (1924; New York: Doubleday, 1956).

16. Georges Lefebvre, "The Outbreak of the Revolution, 1787–1789," in *The French Revolution: Conflicting Interpretations*, ed. Franz A. Kafker (New York: Random House, 1976), p. 26.

17. Georges Lefebvre, "Revolutionary Crowds," in *New Perspectives on the French Revolution*, ed. Jeffry Kaplow (New York: Wiley, 1965), p. 184.

18. Georges Lefebvre, *The Great Fear of 1789: Rural Panic in Revolutionary France* (1932), trans. Joan White (Princeton: Princeton University Press, 1973), pp. 156–57.

19. Ibid., pp. 154–55.

20. Ibid., p. 155.

21. Ibid., p. 181.

22. Ibid., pp. 17, 15, 133, 140. Lefebvre, "Revolutionary Crowds," p. 185.

23. Peter Paret, "Commentary on 'Psychoanalysis in History,'" in *Psychology and Historical Interpretation*, ed. William M. Runyan (New York: Oxford University Press, 1988), p. 124.

24. Lefebvre, *Great Fear*, p. 147.

25. For cultural interpretations of anti-Semitism, see Fritz Stern, *The Politics of Cultural Despair: A Study in the Rise of the Germanic Ideology* (Berkeley: University of California Press, 1961); and George L. Mosse, *The Crisis of Germanic Ideology* (New York: Grosset & Dunlap, 1964).

26. Hans Rosenberg, *Grosse Depression und Bismarckzeit: Wirtschaftsablauf, Gesellschaft und Politik in Mitteleuropa* (Berlin: Walter de Gruyter, 1967), p. 51.

27. Ibid., pp. 56–57.

28. Shulamit Volkov, *The Rise of Popular Antimodernism in Germany: The Urban Master Artisans, 1873–1896* (Princeton: Princeton University Press, 1978), p. 294.

29. David Blackbourn and Geoff Eley, *The Peculiarities of German History: Bourgeois Society and Politics in Nineteenth-Century Germany* (New York: Oxford University Press, 1984), pp. 206–11. See also Geoff Eley, *From Unification to Nazism: Reinterpreting the German Past* (Boston: Allen & Unwin, 1986), pp. 34–41.

30. Thomas Childers, "Inflation, Stabilization, and Political Realignment in Germany, 1924 to 1928," in *The German Inflation/Die Deutsche Inflation*, ed. Gerald P. Feldman, Carl Ludwig Holtfrenich, Gerhard A. Ritter, and Peter-Christian Witt (Berlin: Walter de Gruyter, 1982), pp. 409–31.

31. Max Weber, "The Sociology of Charismatic Authority," in *From Max Weber: Essays in Sociology*, ed. Gerth and Mills (New York: Oxford University Press, 1958), p. 246.

32. Fred Weinstein, *The Dynamics of Nazism: Leadership, Ideology, and the Holocaust* (New York: Academic Press, 1980), is particularly good on the emotional appeals of Nazi imagery.

33. As quoted in Eberhard Kolb, *The Weimar Republic* (London: Unwin Hyman, 1988), pp. 98–99.

34. Cases No. 41 and 42, Abel File, Hoover Institution on War, Revolution and Peace, Archives, Stanford, California.

35. Joachim C. Fest, *Hitler*, trans. Richard and Clara Winston (New York: Harcourt Brace Jovanovich, 1973), p. 342.

36. For the first and still very credible integration of psychoanalytic object relations with the understanding of the needs of individuals for social stability, see Talcott Parsons, *Social Structure and Personality* (Glencoe, Ill.: Free Press, 1964), including the chapters "The Superego and the Theory of Social Systems," "The Father Symbol: An Appraisal in the Light of Psychoanalytic and Sociological Theory," and "Social Structure and the Development of Personality: Freud's Contribution to the Integration of Psychology and Sociology."

37. Hans Ulrich Bost, "Bedrohung und Enge (1914–1945)," *Geschichte der Schweiz und der Schweizer*, vol. 3 (Basel: Helbing & Lichtenhahn, 1983), pp. 173–74.

38. Urs Schwarz, *The Eye of the Hurricane: Switzerland in World War Two* (Boulder, Colo.: Westview Press, 1980), pp. 53–54; see also Christopher Hughes, *Switzerland* (London: Ernest Benn, 1975), pp. 121–24; and Sigmund Widmer, *Illustrierte Geschichte der Schweiz* (Zurich: Verlag Ex Libris, 1973), pp. 432–46.

39. Jacobius Ten Broek, Edward N. Barnhart, and Floyd W. Matson, *Prejudice, War, and the Constitution* (Berkeley: University of California Press, 1954); Roger Daniels, *Concentration Camps USA: Japanese Americans and World War II* (New York: Holt, Rinehart & Winston, 1971); Daniel S. Davis, *Behind Barbed Wire: The Imprisonment of Japanese-Americans during World War II* (New York: Dutton, 1982).

40. Mauricio Mazon, *The Zoot-Suit Riots: The Psychology of Symbolic Annihilation* (Austin: University of Texas Press, 1984), p. 76.

10

RACISM IN COMPARATIVE HISTORICAL PERSPECTIVE

Why do you complain about enemies?
Could they ever become friends,
to whom the very essence of your
being is eternally a silent reproach?

        Goethe, *"Buch der Spruche,"* West-Östlicher Divan

Two major schools of interpretation of racial hatred exist in the social sciences: the cognitive and the psychodynamic.[1] The *cognitive* understanding of race prejudice is that it is a failure of socially organized learning consisting of erroneous beliefs about other groups. The *psychodynamic* approach focuses on the irrationality and rigidity of racism and the function it serves in the development and coherence of personality and social process.

    The cognitive psychologist begins with the assumption that racism is fundamentally a learned behavior.[2] No one is born with prejudice. People acquire anti-Semitism by perceiving and imitating the beliefs and conduct of significant others in their environment.[3] Racism is explained by social modeling: people respond to the punishments and rewards of conformity with group norms and social approval or sanctions.[4] The cognitive theory of prejudice is the product of American social science and is accordingly optimistic. If racism is a matter of faulty learning, then appropriate social reorganization of conditioning is the solution for racial hatred.[5] To the idea that prejudice is the consequence of faulty cognitive training in the humanities and social sciences, those familiar with modern history would point to Germany's high level of education and humanistic culture, which was no antidote to Nazism. Clearly there were other forces at work.

    The psychodynamic view of racism is rooted in intensive clinical work with individuals in psychoanalysis.[6] Psychoanalytic ego psychology studies the character-defense mechanisms whose function is to protect the self from thoughts, feelings, impulses, and fantasies that are conflictual, shameful, or otherwise unacceptable. The main defenses of interest to the understanding of anti-Semitism are displacement, projection, and introjection.[7] Psychoanalytic object relations explores how the inner world of goodness and badness, intimacy and strangeness, security and fear is structured.[8]

The problem with applying individual psychology to large groups and political movements is that no single psychodynamic pattern correlates to all cases of racism or explains the institutional and ideological structures that promote it. There is a distinction between the content of an expression of racial hatred and the states of mind of the various people who may express it. Racist fantasy or an anti-Semitic action that performs a psychic function for one person at one time will fill another psychic or social need for another person at the same or another time and place. However, the psychoanalytic understanding of anxiety as a response to feelings of hopelessness and helplessness is a concept explaining a number of time-specific emergences of racism and demagogic politics.[9]

A comparison of these two social science schools of interpreting prejudice presents a fascinating study in the sociology of knowledge. American social scientists studied primarily prejudice against Afro-Americans and found the "normality" of prejudice under prevailing social contexts, especially but not exclusively in the South.[10] The research on anti-Semitism was initiated by European social scientists with psychoanalytic training against the political background of the Nazi ascendancy in the 1930s. They focused on the counterfactual, phobic, obsessive, and delusional qualities of anti-Semitism.[11]

Both groups of social scientists have studied racism only synchronically or statically. They examined contemporary societies in which racial prejudice is deeply rooted in the social culture. What is now needed is a comparative and diachronic historical approach in which the expression of racism shifts with changes in the scientific and social ideologies and the psychological content of the hatred is expressed in current forms at specific political and economic junctures.

II

Anti-Judaism is a topic of immense import to all humans. No hatred has been more enduring and no attitudes have been as revealing of tensions in the general culture as the persistent hatred of Jews in the post-Classical world.[12] No subject has deeper roots in the traditions of Western civilization, or in human personality and group process. No discourse takes us into more hidden areas of the unconscious or encounters more intractable resistances than the emotions released by anti-Judaism.

As both historians and psychoanalysts know from their work, human events are overdetermined.[13] The precise timing and the form of outbreaks of Jew hatred are the problem of historians in various periods as they study the multiplicity of factors conditioning events. However, the consistency with which certain patterns and fantasies have reappeared and been acted out, from the Middle Ages to the present, cannot fail to impress the historian. It is these repeated manifestations of unconscious fears and longings and the dynamics that underlie them that is the subject of this chapter. Thus, when I address the depth psychology of anti-Judaism, I am dealing with only one element, albeit an essential one, of the constituents of anti-Judaism.

For the past thousand years the Jews have been persecuted under a complex of specific and apparently timeless accusations that are totally irrational and have no objective basis in fact. The accusations include deicide—that the Jews killed Christ; desecration of the Host—that they pierce communion wafers in churches and make them bleed; and ritual murder—that Jews steal and ritually kill Christian children at Easter in order to use their blood in the ceremonial Passover meal. Millions of Jews have died because of these fictitious fantasies.

When charges such as these continue to live despite having been disproved *ad nauseam* and when no amount of rational discourse can succeed in laying the myths to rest, then, we conclude, they must have some powerful psychological truth behind them. There must be a hidden latent meaning behind these fantasies that will not die. The psychoanalytical approach to such material is to treat it as evidence of unconscious fantasies that have a symbolic significance. They are rationalizations that stand for something else. We must strip the facade from the accusations and seek their unconscious meaning, just as we would with dreams, slips, daydreams, and other irrational fantasies.

The unconscious motives manifested by hatred of the Jews is a neglected and particularly relevant aspect of the problem because they place the focus on the irrational core of anti-Judaism. Historians have tended to overlook the role of unconscious forces in Jew hatred because this would direct attention to the emotional aspects of the problem rather than to the "rational" and "objective" factors with which historians are at home.

III

Sigmund Freud treated the problem of anti-Judaism in his writings throughout his life. His most explicit statement about it was just prior to his death, as he sought refuge from the Nazis in England. From exile he surveyed the madness of Jew hatred terrorizing his central European homeland:

> A phenomenon of such intensity and permanence as the people's hatred of the Jews must of course have more than one ground. It is possible to find a whole number of grounds, some of them clearly derived from reality, which call for no interpretation, and others, lying deeper and derived from hidden sources, which might be regarded as specific reasons. . . . The

deeper motives for hatred of the Jews are rooted in the remotest past ages; they operate from the unconscious of the peoples, and I am prepared to find that at first they will not seem credible.[14]

Freud dismissed the "reality" reasons that are sometimes proffered to explain anti-Judaism, such as the alleged "alien" status of Jews, or the fact that they everywhere constitute a minority, as not worthy of serious consideration. He looked instead to the unconscious motives. The formulator of the Oedipus complex saw the unresolved murderous wishes of sons against their fathers as the deepest root of anti-Judaism. Freud held that the Christian charge of deicide—"You killed our God!"—is a projection and displacement of universal death wishes against the father. Christianity put the son in place of the father, and by admitting complicity in his death, Christians have been absolved of guilt for it. By loving and deifying Jesus, Christians are relieved of guilt feelings arising from death wishes against the father that are common to all humans. The Jews, in not acknowledging the divinity of Jesus, are thus cast in the role of unrepentant parricides and made the victims of guilty rage.

Freud also considered three other unconscious reasons for anti-Jewish feelings. Sibling rivalry—the jealousy of Jews who denoted themselves the "chosen" people of God the Father, the favored among his children—is a motive whose strength is as persistent as the murderous wishes of brother against brother. Freud saw as another motive the Jewish rite of infant circumcision, with its unconscious meaning of castration and all of the dread and anxiety it arouses. "The castration complex," said Freud in the "Little Hans" case, "is the deepest unconscious root of anti-Semitism; for even in the nursery little boys hear that a Jew has something cut off his penis— a piece of his penis, they think—and this gives them a right to despise Jews."[15] In a 1919 emendation to his "Leonardo da Vinci," Freud wrote:

> The conclusion strikes me as inescapable that here we may also trace one of the roots of the anti-Semitism which appears with such elemental force and finds such irrational expression among the nations of the West. Circumcision is unconsciously equated with castration. If we venture to carry our conjectures back to the primaeval days of the human race we can surmise that originally circumcision must have been a milder substitute, designed to take the place of castration.[16]

The final consideration Freud raises to explain anti-Judaism is displaced anti-Christian hatred. The demanding super-ego of Christianity is so difficult to live with that resentment can easily be directed to the source whence it came: the Jews. In these five unconscious motives presented by Freud—deicide, parricide, sibling rivalry, castration fears, and anti-Christianity—we have the basic depth-psychological perceptions for an analysis of anti-Judaism through the ages.

Freud made an explicit reference to medieval anti-Judaism in the most stoic terms when he discussed humankind's instinct toward aggression and aggression's role in social group formation:

The advantage which a comparatively small cultural group offers of allowing this instinct an outlet in the form of hostility against intruders is not to
be despised. It is always possible to bind together a considerable number
of people in love, so long as there are other people left over to receive the
manifestations of their aggressiveness. . . . In this respect the Jewish
people, scattered everywhere, have rendered most useful services to the
civilizations of the countries that have been their hosts; but unfortunately
all the massacres of the Jews in the Middle Ages did not suffice to make
that period more peaceful and secure for their Christian fellows.[17]

IV

The relationship between Judaism and Christianity has historically been
characterized by ambivalence.[18] It has been a mixture of attachment and
revolt as befits the relationship of parent and offspring. The child regards
the father with awe and gratitude, yet also views the father as a resented
rival from whom to seek emancipation. The religion of the Son and
Mother sought to supplant the faith of God the Father.

The close relationship between the Jews and Jesus Christ is undeniable. He was of the Jewish people; they knew him; they witnessed his
death and resurrection. The Jews and Christ can under no stretch of
imagination be disassociated. This is why the Christian religion has both
a special tolerance for, and a violent hatred of, Judaism, attitudes that
exist side by side. On the one hand, Judaism was protected under canon
law and continued to survive. The Jews were never regarded as heretics.
They were a non-Christian faith tolerated among Christians. The existence of Jews was essential for Christianity, for they were the witnesses
of the Gospels and their conversion would signal the second coming of
Christ.

Yet, nonmonotheistic, non-Western religions have never persecuted
Jews as brutally and relentlessly as the Christian world. A partial explanation for this is the fact of monotheism, whose one and only God is a
jealous father who does not tolerate any ambivalence toward himself
("For I the Lord thy God am a jealous God, visiting the iniquity of the
fathers upon the children unto the third and fourth generation of them
that hate me" Exodus 20:5). These intolerant demands are projections
onto God of the superego, the power of the father, and ambivalence
toward him by the son. The believers' hatred of the infidel is therefore
the measure of their own unconscious struggle to repress ambivalent
feelings toward their God. When Christians persecute Jews, they are destroying their own inner enemy, that part of themselves that doubts and
questions Christ but that cannot be admitted to consciousness.

Thus anti-Judaism is often camouflaged anti-Christianity. It is a
revolt against the power of the Christian superego and morality. As such,
hatred of the Jews is a displacement and projection of unconscious revolt
against Christ. This serves a particularly valuable function because, by
condemning Jews as those who do not believe in Jesus, the Jew hater can

maintain a love for Christ untarnished on a conscious level. A pogrom that martyrs Jews imposes the destiny of Jesus on the Jews: it sacrifices them in an effort to expiate the Christian's guilt and remorse for unconscious sins. The Jew is also made the scapegoat for repressed desires, both voluptuous and sadistic.

Accusations that are made without foundation are always indications of the projection of guilt. This means that as a mental defense mechanism, thoughts, emotions, and behavior that induce guilt are attributed to someone else instead of to the subject. In this way guilt feelings are relieved, reality is denied, and unacceptable thoughts remain unrecognized. What we witness in the blood accusations against Jews is the projection of subjective aggressions onto Jews, thereby diverting the perception of guilt from the self.

The God of the Jews is the deification of the superego. He is perhaps the most rigorous of all paternal images of conscience. He demands the control of instincts of love and aggression. The Jew as a person is felt by many Gentiles to be the embodiment of these strong restrictions, is seen as the representative of a powerful superego and its derivatives of achievement, perfection, guilt, anxiety, and depression. The Jew is a source of fear and paternal restriction. To the unconscious, the Jew symbolizes the guilt-inducing principle "Thou shalt not . . . ." Thus, the Jew represents the archaic authorities of the unconscious who are seen as lusting for vengeance, mutilation, and slaughter.

The fact that Jews are circumcised arouses intense unconscious fear of castration and mutilation as punishment for forbidden incestuous and murderous feelings. Jewish male circumcision and its association of mutilated genitals stirs up superstitious horror of castration in guilt-laden psyches. The Jew is regarded with a mixture of fear and hate as a dangerous, mysterious, and demonic person. Of Jewish infant circumcision, Bruno Bettelheim said: "It can only symbolize castration in a society where severe punishment, particularly in regard to sexual behavior, is part of the individual's frame of reference."[19] There can be little doubt that the frustration of sexual wishes and guilt over them has been a governing theme of Western Judeo-Christian morality.

Jews symbolize libidinous desires that are inadmissible to consciousness. The unconscious instincts, which have been repressed, have thereby gained a bloody, dirty, dreadful, murderous character. One way of keeping these impulses from consciousness is to see them in Jews, who then become low, debauched antisocial creatures with unbridled sexual lives. These instinctual projections are then excised and detested as "Jewish" sensuality.

The three medieval accusations against Jews of killing Christ, desecration of the Host, and ritual murder have several things in common that suggest their unconscious relationship to one another.[20] They all relate hatred of Jews to the Christian religion. They are all independent of any real contemporary historical situation. They all contain the delusion of the Jew as a persecutor. These charges have always been able to induce murderous violence.

Indeed, what makes Jew hatred such an incomprehensible phenomenon is that its functional fantasies are entirely beyond the dominance of reason and the evidence of reality. In attempts at historical explanation of events such as wars and revolutions there is always a reality admixture with which one must reckon; for example, there was, in fact, a British High Seas Fleet between 1898 and 1914, whether it posed a reality threat to Germany or not.[21] But when we view Judeophobia in the form of blood libels, we are dealing with total fantasies that demand historical treatment in appropriate terms: the language and symbols of the unconscious. These demonic fantasies are distinguishable from distortions based on reality in that they are delusions entirely sprung from the unconscious and not accessible to reason, and therefore are incurable.

Perhaps the most uncanny and mystifying accusations made against Jews are the apparently immortal charges of desecration of the Host and ritual child murder. The first recorded case of the blood-murder accusation was in Norwich, England, in 1144. *The Anglo-Saxon Chronicle*, a contemporary account based on the statement of a Jewish convert, described the event:

> In his (King Stephen's) time, the Jews of Norwich brought a Christian child before Easter and tortured him with all the torture that our Lord was tortured with; and on Good Friday hanged him on a cross on account of our Lord, and then buried him. They expected it would be concealed, but our Lord made it plain that he was a holy martyr, and the monks took him and buried him with ceremony in the monastery, and through our Lord he works wonderful and varied miracles, and he is called St. William.[22]

No Jews were tried nor punished for this putative "ritual murder," for there was no evidence that a murder had been committed. What is most interesting from a psychoanalytical perspective is the manifest identification of the child William with the martyrdom and crucifixion of Jesus on Good Friday. Thus the passion, death, and resurrection of Christ were reenacted, with Norwich's Jews as the available evildoers and targets for their persecutors' ambivalence about, on the most immediate level, dead children, and on the religious level, Christianity itself.

Identical charges were brought against the Jews at Gloucester in 1168. Then the ritual-murder charge spread to France (Blois, 1171), Germany (Tauberbischofsheim, 1235), Spain (Sepulveda, 1468), and Italy (Trento, 1475), to name only the initial instance in each land. In all cases the pattern took the same general outline. First a demagogic fanatic, often an itinerant monk, came and incited the people against the Jews with dire forebodings of evil events. Then the dead body of a Christian child was found near the home of a Jew. The Jews of the community were accused, usually with the cooperation of a Jewish convert to Christianity, of murdering the child and using its blood in baking the Passover matzos. The Jewish elders were arrested and tortured on the rack until they died or confessed the crime.[23] Then all Jews who did not accept baptism were burned at the stake.

The accusation and its consequences in the murder of Jews spread to Poland (Sochaczer, 1556), Lithuania (Bielsk, 1564), and Russia (Sandomir, 1692). In the mid-eighteenth century ritual trials were an annual occurrence in Poland, and ritual-murder accusations have existed until modern times. A blood libel in Damascus in 1840 caused the decimation of that city's Jewish community. Other famous trials were in Xanten, Germany (1891); Polna, Bohemia (1899); Konitz, Prussia (1900); and Kiev, Russia (1910–1913). The "ritual-murder" libel lives in the minds of Jew haters even until today. Accusations of the kidnap and murder of Christian children at Passover were made against the Jewish remnant in post–World War Two Europe.[24]

Because these accusations have no shred of objective truth in them, we must look for some other, unconscious, validity behind these fantasies. What is the sin that is held against the Jews with such vehemence? The accusations of Host desecration and child murder have a common unconscious content. It is the denial of Christ. This denial must be conceived of symbolically as a repetition of Christ's murder. Jew-hating Christians accuse the Jew of a crime that they themselves commit by ambivalence and doubt over the divinity of Jesus. It is those who make the accusation who have an unconscious wish of murder and desecration. Because this guilt has been projected onto Jews, they must be killed.

Occasionally, the secular authority, such as Emperor Frederick II after the Fulda massacre of 1235, or Emperor Frederick III after the Endingen trial and execution in Baden in 1470, or the Polish King Stephen Bathory in 1576, issued a decree forbidding ritual-murder proceedings against Jews. More commonly, an investigation by the papacy was followed by a finding that the whole affair was a fabrication and a tissue of lies. The various papal bulls condemning the blood libel, such as that of Innocent IV on 5 July 1247 or of Sixtus IV on 10 October 1475, had no effect in halting the spread of the delusion. The most famous and exhaustive Vatican investigation of ritual murder charges was that undertaken at the direction of Pope Benedict XIV by Cardinal Ganganelli. His report was the basis of a Vatican message to the government of Poland in 1763, declaring that "the Holy See, having latterly examined all the foundations upon which the opinion rests that the Jews use human blood in the preparation of their unleavened bread and for that reason are guilty of the slaughter of Christian children, has concluded that there is no evidence whatsoever to substantiate this prejudice."[25]

No amount of rational disproof has sufficed. When Jews are accused of piercing the holy wafer and making it bleed, of flogging, stabbing, and pulverizing the Host, they are charged with repeating the torture and killing of Christ. The belief in the bleeding of the holy wafer expresses the Jew hater's unconscious wish of hatefully devouring and incorporating

God. The accusation of desecration of the Host is a projection onto Jews of guilt for fantasies of deicide and parricide. The guilt is displaced to the Jews, who must die for the crime unconsciously committed by their persecutors.

The accusation of ritual murder, that Jews steal Christian children at Passover—which falls close to Easter, the time of the Resurrection— and slaughter them for consumption at the ritual Seder meal, is similar in structure to the allegation of Host desecration. The child who is eaten in anti-Jewish fantasy is Jesus, the lamb of innocence, the bearer of humankind's guilt. It is noteworthy that tales of desecration of the communion wafer, many times included stories of the Christ child's appearing in the midst of the tortured Host, dripping blood and screaming.[26] When Jew haters accuse the Jews of consuming the blood of Christian children at Passover, they unconsciously identify these children with the resurrected Christ. The persecutors have transformed the ritual meal of Passover, with its roasted lamb shank on the table, into a devouring fantasy from their unconscious: the consuming of the "lamb Jesus," the child of God.

V

Perhaps the most difficult motif for adults who are not in psychoanalysis to recognize in themselves is the filicidal emotions that are rarely admitted to consciousness. They are, however, evidenced in our myths and defended against in the ritual-murder accusation against Jews.

The psychological fact of feeling aggression against one's own children is generally denied in our culture. We tend to emphasize the sweetness, love, and nurturant drives in the parent-child relationship. Consider, for example, the strength of the Madonna and Child theme in Western iconography, a motif that demonstrates the greatest resistance to hostile impulses by its very insistence on idealizing the internalized mother.

As anyone who has psychoanalyzed a parent knows, the most loved infant can also be experienced in the unconscious as an attacker. Let us recall that the great myth of Oedipus Rex is also Sophocles' drama of parental aggression by King Laius and Queen Jocasta toward their child.[27] The other side, or latent content, of the Oedipus myth, which Freud saw as manifestly a tale of the desire of the adolescent to kill his father and sexually to possess his mother, is the story of the hostility of Jocasta and Laius toward their baby. Let us rehearse the plot. The infant Oedipus is abandoned on a mountainside with his feet pierced and bound so he cannot crawl away. The dread secret as revealed to the adult Oedipus by the shepherd is presented thus by Sophocles:

> *Herdsman*: Ah me—I am on the dreaded brink of speech.
> *Oedipus*: And I of hearing; yet I must hear.
> *Herdsman*: You must know, then, that it was said to be his own child—but your lady within could best say how these things are.

Oedipus: How? She gave it to you?
Herdsman: Yes, O King.
Oedipus: For what end?
Herdsman: That I should make away with it.
Oedipus: Her own child, the wretch?[28]

We see that the awful truth is not incest but the mother's wish to kill her child.[29]

The infanticidal act is scarcely concealed in the myths of Abraham and Isaac, Moses in the bullrushes, the death of the Egyptian firstborn, and Jesus, the intended victim of an infanticidal edict of King Herod. We see these sadistic impulses in ourselves; in our analysands; and in our culture in the rite of circumcision, in much elective surgery performed on children and orthopedic devices placed on their bodies, and in the rationalization of child abuse, punishment, and battery as being in the service of education.[30] We may also see filicidal aggression most poignantly in the ambivalent feelings about the committing to combat of young men in war.

VI

The most primitive fear of Jews is that they are poisoners and, as a group, are literally themselves a poison. The fear of orally introjecting the dangerous foul substance that causes pain and death inside is a paranoid fear of internal persecution. To attack and destroy others for internal suffering is an attempt to use sadistic manic control to master anxiety and pain within.[31] This fear of Jewish contamination has also been expressed culturally, sociopolitically, and in the past century, genetically, as the fear of pollution of the "racial" germ plasm.

The persecution of Jews in France and Spain coincided with the coming of the Black Death in 1348–1349. Charges were made against Jews that they poisoned wells and water supplies and thus caused the plague.[32] This kind of scapegoating accusation is another case of displacement. The unaccountable suffering is attributed to a defenseless and available object, in this case the Jews, who are then made the targets of projected guilt and pent-up rage.

The tendency toward projection and displacement onto strangers is accelerated in times of social and political stress, the threat of epidemic, invasion, or war. The response of anxiety, panic, and impulsive action that appears to meliorate the stress and give a feeling of control and mastery may be understood in light of Freud's structural theory of anxiety, which views anxiety as a signal of the threat of insecurity and helplessness.[33]

The greatest of modern lyric poets, Heinrich Heine, earned his living as an exile in Paris as the correspondent of the leading German newspaper of the day, the Augsburg *Allgemeine Zeitung*. Heine had a keen perception of the eroticism of mob violence and the workings of projection and scapegoating. He vividly described how the accused perpetrators of lethal introjected badness are targeted and joyfully killed in bloody violence. His report on the Paris cholera epidemic of 19 April 1832 reads:

> On the Rue Vaugirard, where two persons who had a white powder on their persons were murdered, I saw one of these unfortunates as he was still in his death rattle. The old women pulled their wooden shoes off their feet and beat him on the head until he was dead. He was quite naked, beaten bloody, and crushed; not only his clothes but also the hair, the genitals, the lips and the nose were torn from him. A wild man tied a cord around the feet of the corpse and dragged it through the street continually screaming: "Viola le Cholera—moribus!" A beautiful woman, pale with rage, with bared breasts and blood-spattered hands, stood by and gave the corpse another kick with her foot as he came near her. She laughed and asked me to reward her tender handiwork with some francs, so that she might buy a black mourning dress because her mother had died of poison a few hours ago. On the following day the Paris newspapers carried clarifying articles explaining that the suspect powder contained no poison and that the many people who died in Paris succumbed not to a Satanic evil but to the epidemic.[34]

I will further demonstrate the defense of projection and displacement in dire adversity, not against Jews, blacks, or Latinos, not in Europe or the Americas, but in the pre–World War Two Far East. During the great 1923 earthquake that devastated Tokyo, killing over 140,000 people, rumors spread that ethnic Koreans were lighting fires and poisoning the water, and that they had caused the earthquake itself. Japanese mobs hunted down and beat to death an estimated six thousand Koreans.[35]

In 1937 Japanese imperial military and naval forces invaded China, occupying the Chinese coast, threatening the European treaty ports of Shanghai and Hong Kong and fostering insecurity and panic among the Chinese—who were divided by ideology, region, and linguistic dialect. The accusations of treason and poisoning, and the murderous pogrom-like violence within the Chinese community were so similar in structure and content to the medieval and modern charges against Jews in Europe as to leave no doubt that we are in the presence of transcultural unconscious mental processes. This historical evidence is particularly valuable because the culture of the foreign treaty ports in China, with their foreign press and extraterritorial courts and police, happily no longer exists. The newspaper files of over half a century ago are also casualties of history.

The *Shanghai Times* of 18 August 1937 captioned "Traitors Are Beaten to Death by Crowds":

> A check-up last night revealed that least three people had lost their lives through attacks by mobs, on the accusation that they were traitors. The allegation was that these men had been caught trying to throw poisonous powder into drinking water stands provided by philanthropic bodies and

also into the water used by boiled water shops from which many Chinese obtain their daily drinking water supply.

Two men were killed in Rue Pailikao at about 10 o'clock yesterday morning, while an hour later another Chinese was killed at the corner of Rue Wagner and Avenue Edward VII. Another alleged traitor was caught by a crowd on Bubbling Well Road and handed over to the police, while at 2:25 P.M. a man was most severely beaten in Avenue Edward VII near Kiangse Road. He was shielded by three Chinese police of the French force and eventually taken into the shelter of Poste Mallet.

Chinese reports state that several traitors have been caught in Chinese controlled areas and executed after confessions had been made.

Case in Court

One man, named Chien Hung-shi was brought up in the First Special District Court yesterday on suspicion of having thrown poisonous powder into drinking water jars in Yu Ya Ching Road, Mr. Paul Ru told the judge that two bottles containing white powder had been found on the accused. This was now being examined and should it be found poisonous a charge would be laid. Chien was arrested on Monday afternoon with three alleged accomplices who are now in hospital because of the beating they received from a crowd.[36]

Paranoid suspiciousness of strangers, particularly those who looked Chinese but spoke and acted differently, could occasion lethal consequences. The charge of internal subversion—poisioning—was ubiquitous on both sides, Chinese and Japanese. The multiple dialects of China provided an example of what Freud during World War One for the first time termed "the narcissism of minor differences," by which he meant: "It is precisely the minor differences in people who are otherwise alike that form the basis of feelings of strangeness and hostility between them."[37]

The following report from Hong Kong was captioned "Villager's Mistake."

Two northern Chinese, mistaken for Japanese by the villagers of the Sek Tong Village, were set upon yesterday and assaulted. They were walking through the village, where they were employed in the military laundry, when one of the villagers, overhearing their northern dialect, mistook them and shouted that they were spreading poison.

Other villagers quickly gathered on the scene and the two northerners were assaulted. One was tied with rope. The police arrived and set the men free. They were taken to the hospital where one was detained for observation. Both bore cuts and bruises.[38]

Another Hong Kong case that highlights the social marginality of the initiators of civil disorder and the socially stabilizing effect of an intact, powerful system of civil control, justice, and law enforcement is captioned:

"Hooligan Gaoled; Instigator of Attack on Man from Peiping; Thought to be Japanese":

Said to have been the instigator of one of the anti-Japanese riots in Yaumati and Mongkok on September 2, Wong Yau, 18, unemployed, was
charged before Mr. E. Himsworth at the Kowloon Magistracy yesterday
with assaulting a Peiping man, together with other members of a mob
which took the man to be a Japanese.

Chief Inspector K. W. Andrew prosecuted and asked for the heaviest
possible penalty to be inflicted on Wong.

The Peiping man, Lau Hon-san, 26, medicine hawker, said that on
September 2 he had been walking along Shanghai Street, dressed in European clothing, when Wong accosted him and called him a "Yat Poon
Tsai," (Japanese boy). Unable to speak the local dialect, Lau endeavoured
to write down the fact that he was a Chinese, but Wong, peering into his
inside jacket pockets, accused him of bearing Japanese documents. When
Lau showed that it was not so, Wong declared that he had something up
his sleeve.

A crowd was collecting, and Wong spoke to them, saying that Lau was
a Japanese. When Lau refused to give up a ring he had on his finger, Wong
struck him on the head with a brick which he was carrying and the mob
joined in. Lau managed to hold onto Wong until he was rescued by an
Indian policeman. Lau said he had just come out of hospital that morning.

Passing sentence of six months' hard labour on Wong, his Worship
said, "I am very pleased that you have been arrested because it seems you
are the prime instigator of the riot which took place on this occasion."

"It's people like you who lead astray silly and credulous fools and incite
them to acts of violence."

The matter did not close with the court case, however, for outside the
Magistracy, Wong's womenfolk began to heap abuse on Lau. Chief Inspector Andrew, driving by in his car, stopped and arrested two of the
noisiest women, taking them to Yaumati Police Station.[39]

The accusations of well poisoning were not confined to one side of
the Sino-Japanese War. The Japanese press carried the following story:

A report from Shanghai says that the Chinese drop bacteria into wells as
they retreat. It may be a very effective method of taking the lives of Japanese soldiers who occupy that district. Yet it is a most cowardly and inhuman
act. The cruelty of the Chinese people is [known] to all the world, but it is
surprising that they will resort to methods causing suffering not only to
Japanese soldiers, but also to innocent non-combatants of all races.[40]

A Reuter report conveys the Japanese charge and the Chinese denial:

Shanghai, Sept. 11, 1937
Japanese announce 80 cases of cholera, of which 20 have proved fatal
among the Japanese troops in the Paoshan district. They attribute the epidemic to the spreading of cholera bacteria by the Chinese.

The Chinese indignantly deny this.—*Reuter.*

Childish Propaganda
Shanghai, Sept. 11, 1937
The Japanese charges that the 80 cases of cholera, of which 20 have
proved fatal among the Japanese troops in the Paoshan district have been

caused by the spreading of cholera bacteria by the Chinese, is branded by Chinese military authorities here as "childish propaganda."

While declaring that cholera cases have been discovered in Hongkong and Nanking and also among the refugees in the Shanghai International Settlement, the Chinese officials state that the Japanese are spreading such malicious reports to "cover up their own atrocities" committed on non-combatants in this country.—*Central News*.[41]

We see in these examples from two non-Western cultures in a time of crisis how the hostile persecutor is projected to a stranger then orally introjected to become a sadistic, lethal danger inside the body. The issue of distance is crucial. The fear that wells and water are poisoned by proximate strangers takes the destructive weapons of attack from within and places them optimally outside, but close, where the stranger may be engaged, controlled, and beaten up or killed, thus providing relief from internal fears. The visible and available persecutors, the source of poison and danger, can be annihilated.

Lucien Febvre, the distinguished historian of *mentalité*, told us how to study mass phenomena in the past by using the psychological evidence of the present: "And what about the anonymous masses? They of course will be amenable to group psychology which will have to be founded on observation of the present-day masses available for study; the findings can then easily (at least we suppose so) be extended to take in the masses of the past."[42]

I was nevertheless surprised when my research into fears of mass poisoning in times of social stress suddenly came into my home and life in the late spring of 1992. Following the Los Angeles civil disorders, which included the breakdown of police control on 29 April 1992, there was high public anxiety for several days. The city had a siege mentality, with National Guard troops, a civilian curfew, uncontrolled mobs, beatings and shootings, looted businesses (largely Korean shops serving the central city), and more than three thousand fires.

On 7 May my wife, who works in a West Los Angeles firm, came home saying we could not drink the water in West Los Angeles because it had been poisoned by gangs of blacks from South Central Los Angeles, where the riots were taking place. A member of our family said, "Why didn't anyone tell me? I have been drinking the water all day." We viewed the rumor as a paranoid fantasy and did, in fact, drink tap water that evening. The source of the information was Charlene, a colleague at my wife's place of work. A call to Charlene, a young mother, led to her friend Sally, who also had a baby and who had warned her not to expose the child to city water. When I asked Sally where she had heard of the poisoned water, she directed me to her husband, Cedrick, who works in a prominent West Los Angeles law firm. Cedrick affirmed that he had heard that the gangs had taken responsibility for poisoning the water supply and this had been carried on a local television channel. He also said that a member of staff who worked as a volunteer with South

Central youth gangs reported she had heard the gangs threaten to poison the city water supply in revenge for police brutality.

On the same day, 7 May 1992, at 6:00 A.M., a hydraulically operated pilot valve in the Lower Hollywood Reservoir malfunctioned, releasing superchlorinated water into the system in the Hollywood area.[43] The local media carried the story. The superchlorination was a major planned operation by the Department of Water and Power in response to a rise in bacteria count and had been delayed a week because of the riots. Trucks carrying sixteen tons of chlorine and a portable chlorination machine were brought in. The situation was discovered at 9:00 A.M. and was corrected immediately. Flushing continued until three o'clock, when most of the chlorine was gone. Water systems in the Hollywood area were flushed for seven more hours, and the "all clear" was given at ten that same evening. Chlorine has a distinctive pungent odor; it can be clearly smelled and tasted. At no time was there a threat to anyone's health. The one hundred telephone operators of the Los Angeles Department of Water and Power received more than twenty-two thousand calls from throughout the city that day and well into the night (Nine thousand calls is normal for a Thursday and the department assumes there were many more calls that did not get through). Operators were instructed to tell the public that the amount of chlorine in the water system was not deemed to be harmful. Hollywood is not West Los Angeles.

In a western city in 1992, during a situation of high social tension and racial violence, a germ of fact: superchlorination of water in one district, was turned into a projective fantasy of rioters' "revenge" by mass poisoning of the community. Evil, hate-filled, destructive wishes are projected from the self to the disorder in the city and then reintrojected as poison into the body.

VII

A great deal of behavioral science research, on mass reactions to human and natural disaster has been done in recent years, some of which is directly applicable to the emotions displaced onto Jews. The 1942 Coconut Grove fire in Boston, which killed 498 persons, was the subject of a psychiatric survey of disaster victims by the Harvard Medical School and Massachusetts General Hospital. The findings among survivors included an overflowing hostility that spread out to all relationships but was manifested as furious hostility against the doctors and hospital personnel.[44] The surgeons were bitterly accused of neglect of duty and foul play. Some patients, in attempting to hide their ill will became wooden and formal, with affectivity that resembled that of schizophrenics.[45]

The professional staff of the Menninger Foundation gathered psychological reactions to a disastrous flood of the Kansas River in July 1951. Scapegoating and dependency longings were found to be common after the crisis. "Unjustified reproaches," wrote William Menninger, "were most often directed toward the city officials and the Red Cross for inconsiderateness, failure to take care of refugees, provide funds and homes, and similar complaints. An amazing degree of dependency developed in fairly large numbers of refugees."[46] The dependency longings Menninger described are indicative of the dynamics motivating persons who seek and follow demagogic leaders in times of helpless anxiety and social crisis.

In a review of disaster literature sociologists Thomas Drabeck and Enrico Quarantelli conclude that attribution of blame following disaster is typical, and that it is motivated by unconscious guilt for not having died themselves in individuals who survive disaster.[47] The result is scapegoating, in which innocent persons are selected and blamed on the basis of latent hostilities from a guilt-ridden populace. As the psychoanalyst Martha Wolfenstein formulated it: "Probably the more latent hostility there is present in an individual the greater will be his need to blame either himself or others for destructive happenings."[48]

Adolf Leschnitzer has drawn the relationship of anti-Judaism to the witch-hunting of the early modern period. He offers the intriguing thesis that the violent late medieval persecution of the Jews, which abated with the enlightenment of the sixteenth and seventeenth centuries, was displaced onto the burning of witches. The persecution of witches constituted the dark underside of the rational age of scientific advances. In the century and a quarter between 1575 and 1700 at least a million "witches" were burned at the stake in Europe. Leschnitzer points to the structural and emotional parallels between this witchcraft mania and modern anti-Judaism: a background of economic and social dislocation; displacement of antisocial impulses onto a defenseless minority group; viewing the object of hate as an ally of the Devil; cruelty and torture to extort confession; the confiscation of possessions and property of the victims; and, finally, the crushing of all opposition to persecution by the charge of guilt by association as if to say: "He who defends witches is an agent of the Devil; he who protects Jews becomes a Jew."[49]

VIII

With the triumph of rationalism and the decline in religious demonology of the nineteenth and twentieth centuries, witch burning was secularized and the targets of demonologcal projection again became the Jews. The ritual-murder libel did not die. In the teachings of National Socialism it became transmuted to an ideology of the Jew as rapist and contaminator of blood purity. Medieval libels of well poisoning and ritual murder became compounded with sexuality and copulation in Adolf Hitler's thought. We need only to read *Mein Kampf* to see how not only children but whole peoples are allegedly bastardized and thus destroyed by the poisoning of the blood through sexual intercourse:

> The black-haired boy lurks for hours, satanic joy in his face, waiting for the unsuspecting girl, whom he defiles with his blood and thereby robs from

her people. He tries by every means to destroy the racial foundations of the peoples he plans to conquer. . . . So he tries systematically to lower the racial level by a continuous poisoning of individuals.[50]

The ideational content of these accusations, both medieval and modern, is a delusion of persecution. The delusional position of Jew-haters is that they must persecute the Jews because they themselves are persecuted by the Jews. Because of the projective quality of the fantasies of persecution, the Jews are always demagogically accused of the very crimes that are about to be committed against them. They are charged with robbery, murder, rape, and the destruction of Christian ritual symbols just before their persecutors commence to plunder, to desecrate houses of worship, to mutilate and kill. Those who martyr and kill Jews actually are expunging the asocial, antireligious, ambivalent parts of themselves. Jews are thus made to bear the burden of hate and destructive aggression that has never been absorbed in Western civilization.

NOTES

1. By *psychodynamics* I mean the mental processes that relate prior emotional events to subsequent responses, with the assumption that the earlier psychic events influence the later ones. I use *anti-Judaism* to mean hatred or persecution of Jews as adherents of a religion as distinguished from anti-Semitism, which connotes a specific nineteenth- and twentieth-century ideology basing Jew hatred on "racial" theories.

2. Gordon W. Allport, *The Nature of Prejudice* (Cambridge, Mass.: Addison-Wesley, 1954), p. 9.

3. Milton Rokeach, *The Open and Closed Mind* (New York: Basic Books, 1960), p. 135.

4. Gertrude J. Selznick and Stephen Steinberg, *The Tenacity of Prejudice: Anti-Semitism in Contemporary America* (New York: Harper and Row, 1969); Gunnar Myrdal, *An American Dilemma: The Negro Problem and Modern Democracy,* (New York: Harper and Brothers, 1944).

5. Morton Deutsch and M. E. Collins, *Interracial Housing: A Psychological Evaluation of a Social Experiment* (Minneapolis: University of Minnesota Press, 1951). Cf. Jim Sidanius: "[E]xtreme attitudes (at least extremely negative attitudes) tend to be associated with low levels of cognitive functioning." in "Political Sophistication and Political Deviance: A Structural Equation Examination of Context Theory," *Journal of Personality and Social Psychology* 55:1 (1988): 37–51; quotation, p. 46.

6. Ernst Simmel, ed., *Anti-Semitism: A Social Disease* (New York: International Universities Press, 1946); Rudolph M. Loewenstein, *Christians and Jews: A Psychoanalytic Study* (New York: International Universities Press, 1952).

7. John Dollard et al., *Frustration and Aggression* (New Haven: Yale University Press, 1939).

8. Peter Loewenberg, "The Unsuccessful Adolescence of Heinrich Himmler," in *Decoding the Past: The Psychohistorical Approach* (New York: Knopf, 1983; Berkeley: University of California Press, 1985; New Brunswick: Transaction Publishers, 1995), 209–39.

9. Loewenberg, "The Psychohistorical Origins of the Nazi Youth Cohort," in *Decoding the Past*, pp. 240–83.

10. John Dollard, *Caste and Class in a Southern Town* (New Haven: Yale University Press, 1937).

11. T. W. Adorno et al., *The Authoritarian Personality* (New York: Harper, 1950); Nathan W. Ackerman and Marie Jahoda, *Anti-Semitism and Emotional Disorder: A Psychoanalytic Interpretation* (New York: Harper, 1950); Bruno Bettelheim and Morris Janowitz, *Social Change and Prejudice, Including Dynamics of Prejudice* (New York: Free Press, 1964).

12. See Gavin I. Langmuir, *History, Religion, and Antisemitism* (Berkeley: University of California Press, 1990), and *Toward a Definition of Antisemitism* (Berkeley: University of California Press, 1990).

13. John Klauber, "On the Dual Use of Historical and Scientific Method in Psychoanalysis," *International Journal of Psychoanalysis* 49:1 (1968): 80–88. See also Otto Fenichel's recognition of the centrality of the historical dimension:

The instinctual structure of the average man in Germany was no different in 1935 from what it was in 1925. The psychological mass basis for anti-Semitism, whatever it may be, existed in 1925 too, but anti-Semitism was not a political force then. If an understanding of its origin and development in that ten-year period in Germany is sought, then the investigation must be focused on what happened there in those years, and not on the comparatively unaltered unconscious.

"Elements of a Psychoanalytic Theory of Anti-Semitism," in Simmel, *Anti-Semitism*, p. 12.

14. Freud, "Moses and Monotheism: Three Essays" (1939), *The Standard Edition of the Complete Psychological Works of Sigmund Freud*, translated under the general editorship of James Strachey in collaboration with Anna Freud, assisted by Alix Strachey and Alan Tyson, 24 vols. (London: Hogarth Press, 1953–1974), 23:90–91 (hereafter cited as *S.E.*).

15. "Analysis of a Phobia in a Five-Year Old Boy" (1909), in *S.E.*, 10:36 n.

16. Freud, "Leonardo da Vinci and a Memory of his Childhood" (1910), in *S.E.*, 11:95–96 n. For circumcision as symbolic castration, see also Bruno Bettelheim, *Symbolic Wounds: Puberty Rites and the Envious Male*, rev. ed. (New York: Collier, 1962), pp. 152–60; and Herman Nunberg, *Problems of Bisexuality as Reflected in Circumcision* (London: Imago, 1949).

17. Freud, "Civilization and Its Discontents" (1930), in *S.E.*, 21:114.

18. For the psychoanalytic conceptualizations of the relationship of Judaism to Christianity, I am indebted to Loewenstein, *Christians and Jews*, pp. 95–106.

19. Bettelheim, *Symbolic Wounds*, p. 160.

20. I am indebted to Simmel, "Anti-Semitism and Mass Psychopathology," in *Anti-Semitism*, pp. 54–61, for insights into the unconscious psychodynamics of medieval accusations against Jews.

21. Jonathan Steinberg, "The Copenhagen Complex," *Journal of Contemporary History* 1:3 (1966): 23–46.

22. As quoted in Langmuir, *Definition of Antisemitism*, p. 210; See also Joshua Trachtenberg, *The Devil and the Jews: The Medieval Conception of the Jew and Its Relation to Modern Antisemitism* (New Haven: Yale University Press, 1943; Cleveland: World Publishing, 1961), p. 130.

23. R. Po-Chia Hsia, *The Myth of Ritual Murder: Jews and Magic in Reformation Germany* (New Haven: Yale University Press, 1988), pp. 17–36. Hsia locates the case of William of Norwich in 1148, p. 9.

24. For post–World War Two blood libels against Jews in Poland, including the bishop of Lublin and the Kielce pogrom of 1946, in which forty-one Jews were killed, see Paul Meyer, Bernard D. Weinryb, Eugene Duschinsky, and Nicolas Sylvain, *The Jews in the Soviet Satellites* (Syracuse: Syracuse University Press, 1953), pp. 250–53. For the Soviet Union in the postrevolutionary era, see Solomon Schwarz, *The Jews in the Soviet Union* (Syracuse: Syracuse University Press, 1951), pp. 254–57.

25. As quoted in Max L. Margolis and Alexander Marx, *A History of the Jewish People* (Philadelphia: Jewish Publication Society of America, 1941), p. 581.

26. Norman Cohn, *The Pursuit of the Millennium: Revolutionary Messianism in Medieval and Reformation Europe and Its Bearing on Modern Totalitarian Movements*, 2d ed. (New York: Harper & Brothers, 1961), pp. 72–73.

27. Norman B. Atkins, "The Oedipus Myth, Adolescence, and the Succession of Generations," *Journal of the American Psychoanalytic Association* 18 (1970): 860–75.

28. Sophocles, *Oedipus the King*, trans. R. C. Jebb, in *Greek Drama*, ed. Moses Hadas (New York: Bantam Books, 1965), p. 141.

29. See the evocative chapter "The Parent as Sphinx," in Leonard Shengold, *Soul Murder: The Effects of Childhood Abuse and Deprivation* (New Haven: Yale University Press, 1989), pp. 41–68.

30. Harold P. Blum, "Punitive Parenthood and Childhood Trauma," in *The Psychoanalytic Core*, ed. Harold P. Blum, Edward M. Weinshel, and F. Robert Rodman (Madison, Conn.: International Universities Press, 1989), pp. 167–85.

31. Melanie Klein, "A Contribution to the Psychogenesis of Manic-Depressive States" (1935), in *Contributions to Psychoanalysis: 1921–1945* (New York: McGraw-Hill, 1964), pp. 304–5.

32. Langmuir, *Definition of Antisemitism*, pp. 61–62, 308; Cohn, *Pursuit of the Millennium*, pp. 73–74, 138.

33. "Anxiety in History," chapter 9 in this volume.

34. As quoted in Kurt Baschwitz, *Du und die Masse: Studien zu einer Exakten Massenpsychologie* (Leiden: E. J. Brill, 1951), pp. 162–163; the translation is mine.

35. *New York Times*, 22 January 1995, p. A6.

36. *Shanghai Times*, 18 August 1937; in the possession of the author.

37. Freud, "The Taboo of Virginity" (1917), in *S.E.*, 11:199. Freud returns to this idea in "Group Psychology and Analysis of the Ego" (1921), in *S.E.*, 18:101 n. 4; "Civilization and Its Discontents" (1930), in *S.E.*, 21:114; and "Moses and Monotheism" (1939), in *S.E.*, 23:91.

38. *South China Morning Post*, 14 September 1937; in the possession of the author.

39. Ibid., 12 September 1937; in the possession of the author.

40. *Japanese Advertiser*, 19 September 1937; in the possession of the author.

41. *South China Morning Post*, 12 September 1937; in the possession of the author.

42. Lucien Febvre, "Histoire et Psychologie," in *Combats pour l'histoire* (Paris: Colin, 1959), p. 208; translated by K. Folca in *A New Kind of History and Other Essays*, ed. Peter Burke (New York: Harper & Row, 1973), p. 2.

43. For this and the following data I am indebted to Robert Yoshimura, assistant director of water quality; Myra Lopez, supervisor of Call Center operations; Lucia Alvelais, Erna Bridges, and Edward Friedenberg, Office of Public Affairs; all of the Los Angeles Department of Water and Power, personal communications, 8 May and 25 June 1992.

44. Stanley Cobb and Erich Lindemann, "Neuropsychiatric Observations," *Annals of Surgery* 117:6 (June 1943): 814–24.

45. Erich Lindemann, "Symptomatology and Management of Acute Grief," *American Journal of Psychiatry* 101:2 (September 1944): 141–48.

46. W. C. Menninger, "Psychological Reactions in an Emergency (Flood)," *American Journal of Psychiatry* 109:2 (August 1952): 130.

47. Thomas E. Drabeck and Enrico L. Quarantelli, "Scapegoats, Villains, and Disasters," *Reflections* 3:1 (1968): 11–21. I am indebted to William Clark for bringing this article to my attention.

48. Ibid., pp. 13–14.

49. Adolf Leschnitzer, *The Magic Background of Modern Anti-Semitism: An Analysis of the German-Jewish Relationship* (New York: International Universities Press, 1956), pp. 97–99.

50. Adolf Hitler, *Mein Kampf* (Munich: Zentralverlag der NSDAP, 1927), p. 357; the translation is mine.

11

THE PSYCHODYNAMICS
OF NATIONALISM

*The deepest hatred grows out of broken love. Here, however, not only the
sense of discrimination is probably decisive but also denial of one's own
past. . . . Here separation does not follow from conflict, but, on the contrary, conflict from separation.*

Georg Simmel, Conflict

Nationalism constitutes the most powerful historical force as an agent of
change in the twentieth century. No movement has succeeded against it;
no movement has achieved anything without it. Nationalism's ability to
inspire dedicated action in history has been equaled in earlier times only
by religion.

The emotional freighting of exclusion and inclusion, of grievance and
entitlement; the problematic politicolegal definition of *nation,* which may
mean whatever one wishes it to mean; and the complexity in distinguishing *nation* from *ethnicity, peoplehood,* and *race* were immortalized in a
mythical dialogue in a Dublin bar in the late afternoon of 16 June 1904:

—But do you know what a nation means? says John Wyse.
—Yes, says Bloom.
—What is it? says John Wyse.
—A nation? says Bloom. A nation is the same people living in the same
place.
—By God, then, says Ned, laughing, if that's so I'm a nation for I'm
living in the same place for the past five years.
So of course everyone had a laugh at Bloom and says he, trying to
muck out of it:
—Or also living in different places.
—That covers my case, says Joe.
—What is your nation if I may ask, says the citizen.
—Ireland, says Bloom. I was born here. Ireland. . . .
—And I belong to a race too, says Bloom, that is hated and persecuted.
Also now. This very moment. This very instant. . . .

—Robbed, says he. Plundered. Insulted. Persecuted. Taking what belongs to us by right. At this very moment, says he, putting up his fist, sold
by auction off in Morocco like slaves or cattles.

—Are you talking about the New Jerusalem? says the citizen.

—I'm talking about injustice, says Bloom.

—Right, says John Wyse. Stand up to it then with force like men.[1]

"Nothing," said Joyce's friend Frank Budgen, "brings people nearer
to one another than community in fearing, loving and hating."[2] Joyce's
modern Odysseus, "Everyman or Noman,"[3] the lonely exile Irish Jew
Leopold Bloom, articulates the tensions and ambiguities of the rise of the
militant twentieth-century nationalism that continue to torment and tear
asunder both his country and his people. Nationalism, observed Isaiah
Berlin more than two decades ago,

> is one of the most powerful, in some regions the most powerful, single
> movement at work in the world today. . . . [F]ew movements or revolu-
> tions would have any chance of success unless they came arm-in-arm with
> it. . . . [N]o political movement today . . . seems likely to succeed unless
> it allies itself to national sentiment.[4]

If this analysis was true in 1972, we may affirm with conviction that it is
even more so today, when we find the world, including important parts
of Asia, Africa, Europe, and North America, being rent and fragmented
by passionate nationalistic conflicts.

Today a psychological dialectic is at work in the world. At the very
moment when the structures for supranational regional economic and
governmental institutions are being put into place, the centrifugal forces
of ethnicity, tribalism, and xenophobia have commanded anti-European
Union majorities in Denmark; fragmented nation-states such as the
former Soviet Union, Yugoslavia, and Czechoslovakia; threatened the
stability of Greece and Turkey; and strengthened antiforeign political
movements such as those of Zhirinovsky in Russia, the Republicans in
Germany, Le Pen in France, Fascists and the northern Ligas in Italy,
and Haider in Austria. Now it is painfully apparent just how thin and
superficial was the "antifascist" reeducation in the former German
Democratic Republic, how artificial and transient were the efforts of
more than three generations to build pluralistic multiethnic states in the
Soviet Union (1917–1989), Czechoslovakia (1919–1992), and Yugoslavia (1918–1992).[5]

I shall delineate what the best social science and historical research
has shown of the operative mechanisms in nation building, using Indonesia as an example of an artificial nation that was constructed from
fantasies. The cauldron of conflicted militant nationalism in modern
times was the summer in which Europe went to war in 1914. We will
look at the agony of ambivalence that the international socialist and pacifist movement experienced in that wrenching intrapsychic conflict
of whether to be a patriot or an internationalist. We will see what the

clinical and theoretical field of psychoanalysis contributes to our knowledge of the sources of ethnicity and nationalism; what Sigmund Freud's intrapsychic experience of World War One demonstrates as a particularly rich illustration of these psychodynamics; and survey the contribution of the ideas of Heinz Kohut to the understanding of nationalism. Finally, in an effort to close on a positive note, I will direct attention to two modern historical cases, the South Tyrol and Switzerland, where the most virulent national, ethnic, and linguistic conflict has been contained and detoxified by political socialization, institutions, and diplomatic structures, and I will contrast these with contemporary former Yugoslavia where the structural identifications that constitute the preconditions of moderation are absent.

II

There are two main social science schools of interpreting nationalism: the cognitive socialization model of Ernst Gellner, and the family-communication model of Karl Deutsch. Gellner stresses the role of school-transmitted culture, which he terms "exosocialization" or "education proper," as distinguished from family childhood socialization:

> The employability, dignity, security and self-respect of individuals, typically, and for the majority of men now hinges on their *education*; and the limits of culture within which they were educated are also the limits of the world within which they can, morally and professionally, breathe. A man's education is by far his most precious investment, and in effect confers his identity on him. Modern man is not loyal to a monarch or a land or a faith, whatever he may say, but to a culture. . . . That is what nationalism is about, and why we live in an age of nationalism.[6]

The historical development that Gellner sees is the nation as a culture/polity based on an educational machine from grade school to university.[7]

Not all scholars of nationalism have use for the psychological dimensions of the problem. Gellner, for instance, holds that

> contrary to popular and even scholarly belief, nationalism does not have any very deep roots in the human psyche. The human psyche can be assumed to have persisted unchanged through the many millennia of the existence of the human race, and not to have become either better or worse during the relatively brief and very recent age of nationalism.[8]

Gellner subscribes to the idea of an unaltered unconscious instinctual structure in historical humankind. He rightly calls for a culture-specific explanation of nationalism, which should place him in the province of ego psychology. Our focus must, indeed, be on how political institutions and individual people adapt to the pressures and exigencies of historical forces.

Karl Deutsch, in a seminal work, developed a demographic model of reserves of an underlying peasant folk culture that becomes socially mobilized and urbanized to secure national political, economic, and eventually bureaucratic dominance. He offers empirical case studies of Finland, Bohemia, India, and Scotland. Deutsch, himself a son of the German-speaking Jewish community of Prague, is most persuasive in his empirical study of the nationality conflict in Bohemia. The Czech underlying population, the rural peasantry and those in forestry, was mobilized to modernization and urbanization in the period 1900 to 1921 to inundate the German culture and to make Prague a Czech city.[9]

Deutsch draws on the concept developed by the Austromarxist Otto Bauer, that a nation is a community shaped by shared experiences. Bauer specified a common history, "a community of fate" that "tied together" the members of a nation into a "community of character." A "community of culture" remains entirely dependent on a preceding "community of fate" (*Schicksalsgemeinschaft*).[10] For both Bauer and Deutsch, "the fate of the community" included being subjected to common anti-Semitic persecution. It was this common fate that determined the Jewish identity of most assimilated central European Jews, including Theodor Herzl, Sigmund Freud, Franz Kafka, and Albert Einstein.[11]

A compelling feature of Deutsch's model is his emphasis on the intimate family-socialization process as the essential building block of nationalism. Deutsch distinguishes between two kinds of communication: bureaucratic and social. The bureaucratic, or what Talcott Parsons termed the "instrumental," communication connotes business, professional, and official transactions. Deutsch differentiates

> the narrow vocational complementarity which exists among members of the same profession, such as doctors or mathematicians, or members of the same vocational group, such as farmers or intellectuals. Efficient communication among engineers, artists, or stamp collectors is limited to a relatively narrow segment of their total range of activities.

The other field of communication, which Deutsch signifies as "social communication," denotes areas of

> childhood memories, in courtship, marriage, and parenthood, in their standards of beauty, their habits of food and drink, in games and recreation, they are far closer to mutual communication and understanding with their countrymen than with their fellow specialists in other countries.[12]

This is what Parsons termed the "affectual" as opposed to the "instrumental" functions, and it corresponds to the distinction Ferdinand Tönnies made between community (*Gemeinschaft*) and society (*Gesellschaft*). For Deutsch, there is a fundamental connection between a people and a community of mutual understanding: "Membership in a people essentially consists in wide complementarity of social communication. It consists in the ability to communicate more effectively, and over a wider range of subjects, with members of one large group than with outsiders."[13]

Deutsch's clear evocation of the most intimate interpersonal psychodynamic field and his relation of that field to ethnic and national conflict makes his model of nationalism richer, more complex, and superior to Hobsbawm's[14] or Gellner's structural models of nationalism. Deutsch sees nationalism as based on a common social culture, which is a highly family- and home-oriented, learned pattern of life: "We found *culture* based on the community of communication, consisting of socially stereo-typed patterns of behavior, including habits of language and thought, and carried on through various forms of social learning, particularly through methods of child rearing standardized in this culture."[15] He directly invokes the feeling of comfort and security in knowing that others understand one in the personal areas of taste, play, family and sexual life, referring to "the widespread preferences for things or persons of 'one's own kind' (that is, associated with one's particular communication group) in such matters as buying and selling, work, food and recreation, courtship and marriage."[16]

> At every step we find social communication bound up indissolubly with the ends and means of life, with men's values and the patterns of their team-work, with employment and promotion, with marriage and inheritance, with the preferences of buyers and sellers, and with economic security or distress—with all the psychological, political, social, and economic re-lationships that influence the security and happiness of individuals. Nationality, culture, and communication are not the only factors that affect all these, but they are always present to affect them.[17]

Deutsch integrates psychoanalytic developmental findings with social science communication theory to build an integrated, dynamic, historical-narrative explanation of how nationalism and nation building function in individuals and groups.

Deutsch accurately located the phenomenology of nationalism in the family, but he did not explain the dynamics of how these nationalist messages are communicated, transferred, inculcated, and internalized from caretakers to children in each case in the intimate family ambiance. This is the province of psychoanalytic research on the internalization of trust and fear.

III

Both the power and the feigned quality of nationalism are apparent when we look at such synthetic nations as the United States, Brazil, Indonesia, and Israel. These are invented nations, each with an assertive, self-worshipping, and aggrandizing nationalism, and each worthy of special attention, study, and interest.

Indonesia has been described as the most diverse nation on earth.[18] The concept of "Indonesia" is a twentieth-century creation. Consisting of fourteen thousand islands stretched over three thousand miles; religiously, ethnically, and linguistically multicultural, with Muslims, Christians, Hindus, Buddhists, and animists speaking more than one hundred distinct language groups; and with boundaries initially coterminous with the Dutch East Indian colonial empire, the twentieth-century state Indonesia does not derive from any precolonial polity. Benedict Anderson points out:

> Some of the peoples on the eastern coast of Sumatra are not only physically close, across the narrow Straits of Malacca, to the populations of the western littoral of the Malay Peninsula, but they are ethnically related, understand each other's speech, have a common religion, and so forth. These same Sumatrans share neither mother-tongue, ethnicity, nor religion with the Ambonese, located on islands thousands of miles away to the east. Yet during this century they have come to understand the Ambonese as fellow-Indonesians, the Malays as foreigners.[19]

The national tongue, *bahasa Indonesia,* is a Malay trading language adopted by young Indonesia as a national language in 1928. As Anderson explains:

> The extraordinary character of modern "political" Indonesian . . . derives from the fact that it is inevitably the heir of three separate languages and two separate linguistic-cultural traditions. The languages are Dutch, Javanese, and "revolutionary-Malay"—the traditions are Dutch-Western and Javanese. The enterprise of modern Indonesian is therefore the synthesis of a new political-cultural intelligence and perspective out of the fragmentation of the colonial and early post-colonial period.[20]

The Swiss historian and journalist Herbert Luethy describes Indonesian as a "synthetic" language that has borrowed "copiously and indiscriminately from all the technical terminologies and ideological abstractions of the modern world," and notes that it is "scarcely intelligible, in its newer parts to the average Indonesian, who listens to the official speeches all the more admiringly for being able to make nothing of them."[21] Anderson points out that "Indonesian is by no means the everyday language of more than a tiny segment of the population. One can say with some confidence that in only two cities [Medan and Jakarta] in all Indonesia is Indonesian the normal medium of communication outside official channels."[22]

The nation builder and "father" of Indonesia, Sukarno (1901–1970), described his childhood education in early-twentieth-century Java:

> There was no cohesive Indonesian language yet. Through third grade everybody spoke our regional Javanese dialect. From fourth to fifth the teachers switched to Melayu, the basic Malay language which infiltrated many parts of the Indies and subsequently became the foundation for our national language, *Bahasa Indonesia.* Twice a week we were taught Dutch.[23]

His proclamation of *bahasa Indonesia* had not only a nationalist but also a consciously equalitarian, socially cohesive purpose:

> It must be that the Marhaen[24] and the aristocrat may converse in the same tongue. It must be that a man from one island may be able to communicate with his brother on another island. If we who multiply like rabbits are

to be one society, one nation, we must have one unified language—the language of the new Indonesia. . . . When I proclaimed *Bahasa Indonesia,* we required a whole new set of appellations that could be used interchangeably between the old and young, rich and poor, President and peasant.[25]

The rich multiplicity of historical, ethnic, and religious roots requires acts of mental invention of a mythic common past, usually glorious but sometimes persecutory, and the suppression of the diversity of sectarian, clan, tribal, dynastic, and polyglot origins of the peoples who constitute the nation. In contemporary Israel, perhaps the most artificial of nations, the stress is on what Jews from varied social and geographic settings as Vilna, Fez, Amsterdam, San'a, and Addis Ababa have in common, which is not much more than what Otto Bauer termed a "community of fate," and on building of these diverse peoples a new national identity that transcends their differences. Anderson cogently applies the metaphor of childhood memory amnesia in the creation of a national identity:

> All profound changes of consciousness, by their very nature, bring with them characteristic amnesias. Out of such oblivions, in specific historical circumstances, spring narratives. After experiencing the physiological and emotional changes produced by puberty, it is impossible to "remember" the consciousness of childhood. . . . As with modern persons, so it is with nations. Awareness of being imbedded in secular, serial time, with all its implications of continuity, yet of "forgetting" the experience of this continuity . . . engenders the need for a narrative of "identity."[26]

IV

Nationalism begins in the family and the home. There is a common folk saying in the Middle East: "I fight my brother, my brother and I are against our cousins, we and our cousins against the other clans, our people versus other peoples, our nation against the world." This maxim conveys the family socialization process that begins early and that views outsiders and strangers as a cause for anxiety as well as curiosity and wonderment.[27]

The phase-specific distinctions between "us" and "them" that children experience as they grow up can give us a grasp of the roots of ethnic hatreds. By the second half of the first year of life the generalized smiling response is reserved for the mother and other special caretaking persons. This preferential smile to the mother is the crucial proof that a bond to another specific person has been established that distinguishes that loved person from all others in the world.[28] The decisive variable is the level of basic trust and confidence based on a consistent, close, warm, and pleasurable interaction with the mother or other primary caretakers.[29] This potential for a positive response to strangers constitutes a ground for optimism that projection and splitting may be integrated in adult life and that we need not always and forever be under the dominance of such primitive mechanisms of assuaging anxiety. It is not necessary for use of the concept splitting to place it at the earliest phases of infancy at the breast as did Melanie Klein and her followers, including Otto Kernberg.[30]

The recent theories and infant observations of Daniel N. Stern remind us that the infant has four to six feeding experiences a day, each one differing slightly with regard to pleasurableness. It is an ontogenetic distortion to attribute "goodness" and "badness," implying standards, intentions, and morality to these putatively pleasurable and unpleasurable experiences. The leap from unpleasure to "bad" and from pleasurable to "good" is an issue for later cognitive ego development, including verbalization and symbol formation. Stern offers the concept of affectively toned clusters of interactive experiences between infant and mother that constitute "working models" of mother for the child. At a later date these are reintegrated by the older child or adult into higher-order categorization of "good" and "bad."[31] The important point for us is that "splitting" exists in adult attitudes toward conflict in personal, group, and international settings, and that the analysis and understanding of this pervasive mechanism is relevant for coming to grips with nationalism, ethnocentrism, and racism.[32]

Projection, casting away from the self, and introjection, taking in, incorporating into the self, are among the most "primitive" defenses. Their roots are in the earliest "oral" phase of life. As Freud put it:

> Expressed in the language of the oldest—the oral—instinctual impulses, the judgement is: "I should like to eat this" or "I should like to spit it out"; and put more generally: "I should like to take this into myself and keep that out." That is to say: "It shall be inside me" or "it shall be outside me." As I have shown elsewhere, the original pleasure-ego wants to introject into itself everything that is good and to eject from itself everything that is bad. What is bad, what is alien to the ego and what is external are, to begin with, identical.[33]

A child who has distinguished between internal and external, between self and nonself, may then use what Anna Freud categorized as the defense mechanisms of projection and introjection:

> It is then able to project its prohibited impulses outwards. Its tolerance of other people is prior to its severity towards itself. It learns what is regarded as blameworthy but protects itself by means of this defence-mechanism from unpleasant self-criticism. Vehement indignation at someone else's wrong-doing is the precursor of and substitute for guilty feelings on its own account.[34]

V

The historian of *mentalité*, Lucien Febvre, told us how to study mass phenomena in the past using the psychological evidence of the present: "And what about the anonymous masses? They of course will be amenable to group psychology which will have to be founded on observation of the present-day masses available for study; the findings can then easily (at least we suppose so) be extended to take in the masses of the past."[35] We may also study the shattering mass phenomena of the past for the light they may cast on our present need for orientation to the forces of nationalism.

The war crisis of late summer 1914, known to historians as "the reversal of August," revealed to shocked Europeans the hubris of rationalism, the tragedy of peoples impelled to catastrophe by forces both within and without themselves beyond their cognitive control or ends-means calculation, and the unappreciated latent power of nationalism. It is as though at one historical moment the entire fabric of belief systems was torn open by underlying forces of envy, aggression, and violence. This "reversal of August" may be viewed in retrospect as no reversal at all but as a crisis clearly presaged by indicators, possibly even predictors: first within "the little International" of the Austromarxist movement, then in the Second Socialist International, and finally in the late days of July 1914. The pacifist, antimilitarist, socialist, and international movements were at their historic all-time peak of strength and influence in the prewar decade. The international labor and socialist movements were the beneficiaries of decades of discourse, planning, and ideological preparation for a war crisis.

On the issue of practical cooperation between the members of different nationalities, the socialist dream of international unity was shattered first in the polyglot multinational Austro-Hungarian Social Democratic Party. The test case and flash point was predictably the socialist movement of the Austro-Hungarian Empire, where Victor Adler had created a comprehensive Social Democratic Party (*Gesamptpartei*), which was proudly called the "little International," constituted of "brother parties" (*Bruderparteien*) of the various peoples who made up the multinational empire. The breach in unity came from Bohemia, the most advanced of the regional economies with the most developed working class. The Czech socialists split in 1911 to organize a specifically Czech Socialist Party. Adler put to the Czechs the critical problem: "The question is: Do the Czech Social Democrats today feel themselves to be the Czech group of the International or are they the Social Democratic group within the Czech parties?"[36] The despairing Adler said, "It is a uniquely Austrian disease that one considers the question of the signs on railway stations an issue of principle of the highest rank."[37]

VI

The International Socialist Congress at Stuttgart (1907) passed a famous antimilitarism and antiwar resolution that had been drafted by an illustrious committee of leading figures of both the left and right wings of the Second International such as August Bebel, Georg von Vollmar, Jean Jaurès, Jules Guesde, Victor Adler, and Rosa Luxemburg. The resolution invoked "the solidarity of nations" and expressed faith that the "democratic organization of the army" was "an essential guarantee for the prevention of aggressive wars, and for facilitating the removal of differences between nations." They testified "to the growing strength of the proletariat and to its power to ensure peace through decisive intervention . . . to do everything to prevent the outbreak of war by whatever means seem to them most effective." With touching faith the Socialists reiterated the age-old dream of reallocating resources from implements of aggression to the enhancement of life, of what much earlier and later ages termed turning "swords into plowshares," saying, "This would make it possible to use the enormous expenditure of money and strength which is swallowed by military armaments and war, for cultural purposes."[38] The International Socialist Congress at Copenhagen (1910) reaffirmed the Stuttgart resolution, and in the great cathedral of Basel (1912) the congress struck a religious note as the organ played Bach and the socialists sang: "All the peoples wish for peace / Peace in every human heart!"[39]

The proclamation of the German Social Democratic Party of 25 July 1914 had a clear foreign policy vision of the implications of Serb nationalism and the consequences of the Austro-Hungarian ultimatum to Serbia. With the benefit of hindsight and the perspective of eight decades we can only marvel at the clarity of vision of the German Socialist executive:

> Although we condemn the drive of the Greater Serbian nationalists, the frivolous war provocation of the Austro-Hungarian government calls for the sharpest protest. The conditions of this government are more brutal than have ever in the history of the world been demanded of a sovereign state, and can only be calculated to provoke a war.[40]

Some of the Socialists had a sense that in the war crisis they were dealing with powerful irrational forces in themselves as well as in the world. While the war enthusiasm was still high in the fall of 1914 the Swiss Socialist Fritz Brupbacher wrote: "From a pedagogical point of view, it would be interesting to analyse psychologically to what extent the difference between the ideas held before the war and those which exist now were already subconsciously there before the war."[41] The Dutch left Socialist Henriette Roland Holst concurred in 1915:

> The present world war has shown not only that internationalism was not anchored as deeply in the proletariat as we thought ten or twelve years ago but above all that like every other principle this one is helpless in the face of sentiments, trends, inclinations, and emotions that surge up irresistibly from the subconscious even if the principle is clearly worth supporting.[42]

As historian Georges Haupt put it: "The diffuse internationalism of the workers' movement could not combat the upsurge from deeper strata of sensibility, as, for instance, Jacobin patriotism or 'visceral' Russo-phobia."[43]

The intense level of internal conflict within many European Social-ists may be portrayed by citing one particularly introspective German left Socialist and one poignant Belgian pacifist poet. A self-reflective description of his intrapsychic conflict is given by Konrad Haenisch, one of the most radical on the party's left, a member of the Prussian House of Delegates who during the Weimar Republic would become the Prussian minister of culture. Haenisch pointed to "a parallelism of occurrences, . . . especially in the French and in the German Social Democracy certain psychological and the respectively political pro-cesses."[44] In Germany the inner struggle often was cast in the Goethean romantic idiom of "two souls in one breast [*zweier Seelen in der einen Brust*]":

> The conflict of two souls in one breast was probably easy for none of us. May the author try to overcome a certain inner embarrassment and speak for a moment of himself? . . . Well, then I'd like to say: not for everything in the world would I like to live through those days of inner struggle again! [On the one hand] this driving, burning desire to throw oneself into the powerful current of the general national tide, and, on the other, the terri-ble spiritual fear of following that desire fully, of surrendering oneself to the mood which roared about one and which, if one looked deep into one's heart, had long since taken possession of the soul. This fear: will you not also betray yourself and your cause? Can you not feel as your heart feels? [Thus it was] until suddenly—I shall never forget the day and hour—the terrible tension was resolved; until one dared to be what one was; until—despite all principles and wooden theories—one could, for the first time in almost a quarter century, join with a full heart, a clean con-science and without a sense of treason in the sweeping, stormy song: "*Deutschland, Deutschland über alles.*"[45]

"Fear," said Carl Schorske, is "the worst enemy of logically con-ducted politics."[46] It also cracks open the ambivalences in seemingly smooth, unconflicted surfaces of love and harmony. The psychoanalytic principle of ambivalence of feeling—that intense love and intense hatred coexist in us all and are often directed at the same object—is of prime im-portance in our understanding of the emotional dynamics of war. My example is the pacifist poet of the Belgian Left, Émile Verhaeren, who was born in a Flemish village near Antwerp and educated in the medieval university city of Louvain. Now he viewed himself as split into two per-sons, one who loved and admired Germany and one who was filled with hatred for it. In April 1915 Verhaeren published *La Belgique sanglante* [Bleeding Belgium], dedicating the book to his other, former, self:

> He who wrote this book, where hatred has not been hidden at all, was for-merly a fervent pacifist. He beheld the peoples of the world with wonder; he loved some of them. The Germans were among those he loved.

Was she not creative, productive, enterprising, audacious, and organized better than any other nation? Did she not convey the impression of security in strength to those who were her visitors? Did she not see the future with ever the sharpest and most intense eyes?

The war intervened.

Germany immediately changed. Her strength became unjust, villainous, ferocious. She had no more pride than that of a methodical tyranny. She became the scourge from which it was necessary to defend oneself so that the good life would not perish from the Earth.

For the author of this book no other disillusionment was as great or more sudden. It struck him so violently that he no longer believed himself to be the same man.

However, since in this state of hatred in which he finds himself his conscience seems to him to be diminished, he dedicates these pages with emotion, to the man he once was.[47]

Of course, neither Verhaeren nor Germany had changed. The gentle poet's civilized pacifist defense broke down in the face of the fear, anxiety, destruction, and pain of war in his Flanders home. This moving dedication is recognition of the split he experienced between his international idealism and his wartime rage and hatred.

VII

The historical comprehension of nationalism may benefit from a central insight of the Freudian canon: the intimate intrapsychic object relationship between enemies, between lovers, and between persecutor and victim. The deepest part of Sigmund Freud's self-analysis—the part that deals with his envy of and hostility and aggression toward his own children and family—took place in World War One. This piece of psychoanalytic work of the year 1915 provides an entry portal to the psychodynamic understanding of war, depression, mourning, and the parental side of the Oedipus conflict, and is the starting point for the theoretical comprehension and clinical techniques for treating such pervasive problems as child abuse and marital estrangement and discord.

As the war began, Freud participated in the patriotic nationalism that inflamed the populace, including the Left and the intellectuals, of all the belligerent countries. In the euphoric last days of July 1914 he wrote to Karl Abraham in Berlin: "For the first time in thirty years I feel myself to be an Austrian and feel like giving this not very hopeful Empire another chance. Morale everywhere is excellent. Also the liberating effect of courageous action and the secure prop of Germany contribute a great deal to this."[48] Three days later, ever the skeptic, Freud asked Abraham: "Can you perhaps tell me whether in a fortnight's time we shall be thinking half ashamedly of the excitement of these days?"[49] This early enthusiasm did not last through the fall. By December 1914 he was writing to van Eeden in Holland of his disillusionment at the atmosphere, brought by the war, of pervasive lying propagated by governments:

> Just look at what is happening in this wartime, at the cruelties and injustices for which the most civilized nations are responsible, at the different way in which they judge of their own lies, their own wrong-doings, and those of their enemies, at the general loss of clear insight; then you must confess that psychoanalysis has been right.[50]

In Freud's great seminal paper on the psychodynamics of depression, also written in 1915, he explained melancholia as due to the conflict between love and hate toward the same close and intimate object: "The loss of a love-object is an excellent opportunity for the ambivalence in love-relationships to make itself effective and come into the open." His insight, still most valuable to the clinician, not only in cases of depression and suicide but also in marital and family therapy, was that depression is

> a satisfaction of trends of sadism and hate which relate to an object, and which have been turned round upon the subject's own self. . . . [T]he patients usually still succeed, by the circuitous path of self-punishment, in taking revenge on the original object and in tormenting their loved one through their illness, having resorted to it in order to avoid the need to express their hostility to him openly. After all, the person who has occasioned the patient's emotional disorder, and on whom his illness is centered, is usually to be found in his immediate environment. . . . In melancholia the relation to the object is no simple one; it is complicated by the conflict due to ambivalence. . . . Countless separate struggles are carried on over the object, in which hate and love contend with each other.[51]

In the midst of World War One, Freud exposed the "law of ambivalence of feelings which even today governs our emotional relations to those whom we love most."[52] When two of his sons and his son-in-law were at the front in the uniform of Austria-Hungary, Freud dealt with the threat of death to his sons and the ambivalent feelings he discovered within himself about their fantasied death. In fact, Freud's son-in-law, Max Halberstadt, was wounded in France in 1916, and Martin Freud was wounded in the arm on the Russian front and also had a Russian bullet pierce his cap when he raised his head over the top of his trench.[53]

Freud's corpus was during his lifetime a living text, subject to changes, deletions, rewritings, and emendations as events, theory, and clinical insight altered his views. In 1919 he inserted a wartime dream into *The Interpretation of Dreams*. It reads:

> Indistinct beginning. *I said to my wife that I had a piece of news for her, something quite special. She was alarmed and refused to listen. I assured her that on the contrary it was something that she would be very glad to hear, and began to tell her that our son's officer's mess had sent a sum of money (5000 Kronen?) . . . something about distinction . . . distribution. . . . Meanwhile I had gone with her into a small room, like a store-room, to look for something. Suddenly I saw my son appear. He was not in uniform but in tight-fitting sport*

clothes (like a seal?), with a little cap. He climbed up on to a basket that was standing beside a cupboard, as though he wanted to put something on the cupboard. I called out to him: no reply. It seemed to me that his face or forehead was bandaged. He was adjusting something in his mouth, pushing something into it. And his hair was flecked with grey. I thought: "Could he be as exhausted as all that. And has he got false teeth?" Before I could call out again I woke up, feeling no anxiety but with my heart beating rapidly. My bedside clock showed that it was two thirty.

Freud's associations turned to the day residue:

Distressing anticipations from the previous day were what gave rise to the dream: we had once more [been] without news of our son at the front for over a week. It is easy to see that the content of the dream expressed a conviction that he had been wounded or killed.[54]

Freud told us that with self-analytical work he was now aware of his filicidal impulses and that his psychodynamics were generational: "Deeper analysis at last enabled me to discover what the concealed impulse was which might have found satisfaction in the dreaded accident to my son: it was the envy which is felt for the young by those who have grown old, but which they believe they have completely stifled."[55]

Freud also treated this dream and associations in his postwar essay on "Dreams and Telepathy" (1922), where he used the theme of dreaming of his son's death in the war to dismiss the idea of premonitory dreams.[56]

Freud became conscious of his filicidal wishes during the war. However, his knowledge of intrapsychic murder in himself was compatible with being an exceptionally loving, protective parent. Freud had a well-functioning ego. His enterprising efforts to help his son who was a wounded prisoner of war are touching. In December 1915 he wrote to Ludwig Binswanger in Switzerland:

My two sons were in heavy battles for a time, but they are both still alive, unscathed, decorated, currently in the foothills of the high mountains. The oldest [Martin, born 1889] spent a 10-day leave with us last month and made us happy by his good appearance and mood. My Hamburg son in law [Max Halberstadt] is now training in the artillery. My middle son, the engineer [Oliver, born 1891], works in a strategically vital tunnel construction.[57]

In the final days of the war Freud's son Martin was wounded and taken prisoner in Italy. We can feel the level of concern in the usually stoic Freud: "In the agitation and worries of the catastrophe, the overthrow of all relationships, in the fear for a lost son, of whom we at last learned that he is a prisoner in a hospital in the Abruzzi."[58] Freud asked for, and received from Binswanger in neutral Switzerland, speedy aid for his boy, who had lost his belongings in enemy captivity. He acknowledged his appreciation and began to make preparations for repayment to Binswanger:

Please accept my heartfelt thanks for your speedy aid. My son was taken prisoner in the last days of October with his entire Corps, among 300,000 whom the Austrian authorities claim were cut off after the conclusion of the Armistice. It took a very long time until we received word from him, learned where he was held, and only yesterday did he acknowledge receipt of our first letter. His last letter also asked for money, as Genoa is very expensive. He lost all of his pack and possessions while taken prisoner. Now, francs or lire are absolutely not to be had here. Even the banks make great difficulties and transmittal from Vienna appears to be as difficult as it is unsafe. Therefore, I decided to ask you to take care of this. It is very likely that Dr. Rank will travel to Switzerland in the next weeks to further the business of our publishing house. There he will have a franc credit at his disposal from which he can adjust my debt to you. Should this trip be delayed contrary to expectations, I know that you will give me further credit.[59]

We know from Martin how much his father's largess was appreciated. He was able to maintain a minor but decisively better standard of living than his fellow prisoners of war in the camp: "Through father's generosity and his international connections, I was well provided with money and was one of the very few prisoners able and willing to buy drinks for a friend."[60]

Apparently the Rank visit did not take place because we know that the obligation to Binswanger was not acquitted in 1919. On Christmas Day 1919 Freud wrote Binswanger of another attempt to settle his debt, this time via England:

My prisoner, whom I could supply with money through your help, is back, and in the comfort of imprisonment committed himself to a marriage of love. It seems to be successful.

Meanwhile I have acquired a deposit of money in London and can have you paid from there, if you would be so kind and let me know how many Swiss francs you came up with at that time. 500 lire are of course not the same now as a year ago and we also cannot await the rise of the Austrian kroner.[61]

The London funds were also not used to discharge the debt to Binswanger. So, exercising an option that gives an insight to his international caseload of patients, Freud in March 1920 turned to his funds in the Netherlands: "Since it makes no sense to wait for a bettering of the rate of exchange of the kroner, I have given a firm in Amsterdam instructions to settle my debt to you. All postal correspondence is so slow these days. This should have happened long ago."[62]

It is against this setting of parental concern and efforts to meliorate the situation of his sons in war that we must consider Freud's 1915 composition of thoughts on attitudes toward death: specifically the death of loved ones, which, in addition to the pain, loss, and grief, was also positively greeted because in each beloved person a hostile alien also resides.[63] He referred to our most intimate relationships:

The death, or the risk of death, of someone we love, a parent or a partner in marriage, a brother or sister, a child or a dear friend. These loved ones are on the one hand an inner possession, components of our own ego; but on the other hand they are partly strangers, even enemies. With the exception of only a very few situations, there adheres to the tenderest and most intimate of our love-relations a small portion of hostility which can excite an unconscious death-wish.[64]

Freud's subjective focus on the ambivalence within us, within all people, must be supplemented with an object-relational understanding of the splitting of good and bad internal objects. The good is what is me and mine: my family, village, clan, and people. The bad is outside: the others, them, the aliens, foreigners, the strangers. The strangers are uncanny because they contain parts of the self that are unacceptable, asocial, dirty, foul, lascivious, and cruel, and therefore these parts are projected onto outsiders.

VIII

Heinz Kohut has given us an understanding of how the nation may be used as a self-object, by which Kohut meant "a part of the self or as merged with the self or as standing in the service of the self, i.e., as utilized for the maintenance of the stability and cohesion of the self."[65] Kohut did not limit his concept to individuals; he related the effects of narcissistic injury to collectivities such as peoples, states, and nations:

In the setting of history, thwarted narcissistic aspirations, hurts to one's pride, injuries to one's prestige needs, interferences with conscious pre-conscious, or unconscious fantasies concerning one's greatness, power, and specialness, or concerning the greatness, power, and specialness of the group that one identifies with are important motivations for group behavior.[66]

Students of German history have sought to relate the events of World War One and its sequelae to the rise of Adolf Hitler and the Nazi policy of conquest in the Third Reich.[67] It is Kohut's conceptual contribution to historiographic theory to place this relationship in the emotional framework of an empathic understanding of the narcissistic injury of German defeat in World War One. The sequelae of the lost war such as the "humiliation" of the Treaty of Versailles of 1919 including the "war guilt" clause, reparations payments, and the loss of German territories; the 1923 Ruhr occupation; and the treaty limitations on German sovereignty may all be interpreted as stimuli to narcissistic rage and the need to have it rectified and assuaged. Similarly, Anwar Sadat's 1977 Jerusalem peace initiative and the ensuing 1979 Egyptian-Israeli Peace Treaty were predicated on his and Egypt's narcissistic "victory" in the Suez Canal crossing of 1973.

A further narcissistic aspect of nationalism is that the idealized people or nation comforts and supplies grandeur to those who feel personally inadequate and flawed. They may not feel worth much personally, but as members of a glorious, brave national group they acquire self-esteem, importance, and virtue. In the Kohutian sense the nation is an idealizing, transference-symbolizing, global narcissistic perfection and power.[68]

IX

The institutions of government, such as military service, education, fiscal policy, marital and family law, the establishment of religion, and building restrictions, have a direct effect on the formation of character and national identity. For example, the Swiss and German territories north of the Rhine around Schaffhausen are so intertwined that on 1 April 1944 U.S. bombers could not perceive the border and mistakenly bombed the Swiss city, causing 150 casualties and destroying 50 buildings. In February 1945, Rafz and Stein, two other Swiss cities north of the Rhine, were also mistakenly bombed and strafed, causing 44 casualties.[69] Yet governmental and historical institutions have created different German-speaking national characters and civic cultures on the two sides of this German-Swiss border because of the character-forming agency of the respective states and historical experiences. The educational socialization (exosocialization) of Gellner is here relevant, not for the dynamics of nationalism but in the building of its content. As Metzger points out:

> With respect to character-formation there is nothing "simple" about government, nothing moderate about its "jurisdiction". . . . Even the most limited democratic governments take part in the forming of character (for example, by training military conscripts) or do so indirectly by regulating private agencies (for example, by separating public school and church, by maintaining a censorship apparatus, by exempting institutions from taxation). In a larger sense, hardly anything such governments do fails to have some effect on character.[70]

There are a few conflicts in Europe where the principles of *consociationalism*[71] have effected a transcending of the most virulent forms of nationalism. The first of two cases I wish to take up has its roots in wrestling with forces of nationalism in the final three decades of the Austro-Hungarian Empire, a multinational, polyglot, multiethnic, and religious dynastic monarchy. The most creative thinkers on nationalities questions were the Austromarxists, especially Karl Renner (1870–1950) and Otto Bauer (1881–1938). The essence of their proposals is the personality principle (*Personalitätsprinzip*): to detach national identity from territory. Nationality should not be determined by birth or residence but by personal choice, which would be recorded in a national register. Cultural and educational life, including taxation to support these, would be determined by the various autonomous groups who could thus occupy the same territory and share economic, governmental, and transport facilities.[72]

Karl Renner was the president of Austria (1945 to 1950) when Alcide de Gasperi of Italy and Karl Gruber of Austria negotiated the Paris

Agreement of 5 September 1946, which set the outline for a long-term settlement of the ethnolinguistic issues in the South Tyrol.[73] In essence the agreement provides for Italian sovereignty and cultural autonomy for the German-speaking majority. A noteworthy feature of Austro-Italian diplomacy over the past fifty years is a gradualistic structure, including a "package" of 137 sections negotiated in 1969 and a "calendar of operations" for their implementation. These measures include the use of the German language in judicial, police, and other administrative procedures; in matters having to do with regional finances, water courses, forestry, education, textbooks, and teacher credentialing, and in agreements worked out in bilateral commissions.[74] Happily, in the year 1992 all 137 sections of the Austro-Italian Autonomy Package for the South Tyrol were declared fulfilled.[75] The point for international conflict resolution is that not all issues can be settled in one adjudication. There are many disputes where the process itself over time constitutes a healing function.

The second case I want to discuss is the Swiss "cellular" formula for resolving historical, ethnic, religious, and linguistic problems. Here the "territorial principle" rather than the "personality principle" is the governing paradigm. The territorial principle, which is as old as the Peace of Augsburg of 1555 and the Peace of Westphalia of 1648, is that ethno-religious identity follows the prince or the jurisdiction of the territory.

The grievances of the French Catholic population of the northern Jura in the canton of Bern propelled the creation of a new canton of Jura in 1978, which provides a model worth studying and considering in other areas of national conflict.[76] The Swiss model is to circumscribe conflict by precisely focusing and satisfying smaller and smaller geographic units by plebiscite. The political mode of handling the conflict was to hold a series of referenda, in the entire Swiss federation, in the canton of Bern, and repeatedly in the districts involved, to give full and precise expression to the popular will right down to the local village level.[77] The Swiss system is so finely tuned that one German-speaking Catholic district, Laufen, voted for and realized a solution to being neither Bernese nor Jurassien—they joined the German-speaking canton Basel-Land.

The Swiss national identity is grounded in the value of preserving the smallest ethnic, linguistic, and cultural units. The aim of childhood family and school socialization process is to inculcate the attitude that although people from another canton may have another culture, religion, or language, "they are Swiss." As a demonstration of this willingness to allow those who wish a separate politicocultural unit to have it, we may look at the results of the national referendum of 24 September 1978 to amend the Federal Constitution to add the canton of Jura: 82 percent of the voters in the federation voted to accept the new canton. In no single canton was the positive vote to create the new Jurassien canton less than 69 percent.[78] The Swiss civic culture allows for a toleration of ethnic, linguistic, confessional, and cultural pluralism in the definition of a national identity of what it means to be a Swiss. As Jonathan Steinberg felicitously put it about the Swiss, the most important characteristic of Swissness is "the equality of all human communities before the bar of history."[79] This is not a bad formula for the world as we enter the twenty-first century.

X

Individuals are made up of many different psychodynamic introjects, identifications, partial identifications, and inner objects that may be in conflict. This knowledge becomes crucial for understanding the role of various group and regional identifications in national conflict or the equally complex problem of national cohesion.

What importantly distinguishes the Austro-Italian and the Swiss cases from the tragedy of national conflict and "ethnic cleansing" in the former Yugoslavia or in the Caucasus is the presence of religious and social-class *crosscutting*[80] in cases where a national identity is maintained and its absence where wars of ethnic expulsion or extermination take place.

By class division, I refer to the correlation of ethnicity, language, religion, and occupational status, as in a common observation in dining establishments in my own part of the country, the Southwest: "English in the restaurant, Spanish in the kitchen." This fissure between owner and client on the one hand, and culinary employees on the other, is likely to include citizenship as well as religion, culture, social class, and ethnicity.

Religion and language are especially important cleavages. The situation in Yugoslavia, the Caucasus, Cyprus, and Quebec, to name just a few of the world's current national clashes, is distinguished in not being subject to crosscutting. All categories of ethno-linguistic-religious cleavage are congruent and therefore bipolar and subject to intolerant total black-and-white judgments. All Quebecois are Francophone and Roman Catholic; Anglophone Canadians are overwhelmingly Protestant. All culturally Turkish Cypriots speak Turkish and are Moslem; all Greek Cypriots speak the Hellenic tongue and are Greek Orthodox. All Armenians speak Armenian and are Christians; all Azerbaijanis speak Azeri and are Moslems. In the former Yugoslavia all Croats are Roman Catholic and all Serbs are Serbian Orthodox. During the Partisan War of 1941–1945 and in the current fighting in Bosnia, it sufficed to ask a child how she or he makes the sign of the cross to distinguish a Croat from a Serb and to decide to kill or let live.[81] By contrast, in Switzerland the core cantons of "Inner Switzerland" are German-speaking and Roman Catholic; other important German-speaking areas such as Zurich, Basel, and Bern are Protestant; and the Francophone area also has both Catholic and Protestant cantons. Thus in Switzerland the religious division, instead of being congruent with cultural-linguistic divisions, cuts across them. In the Italian Alto Adige–South Tyrol, both the Germanic and the Italian populations are Roman Catholic. Because any individual is subject to cross-pressures of various identifications and allegiances, crosscutting encourages conciliation. Moderate attitudes and actions are fostered and often prevail by mobilizing like introjects and common inner objects.

Hostility and aggression in the politicosocial world are created through murderous rage, persecutions, and foulness, in the conscious and unconscious inner fantasies of the perpetrators. A moment's reflection will convince us that we are able to postulate a characteristic or trait in another only because it has been to some degree known to us in fantasy. Peoples and nations find in their minorities and in their neighbors an available and vulnerable target on whom to project their bad internal objects—their hatred and urge to kill as well as their depreciated sense of inferiority, of being despised as slovenly parasites, cheats, and unscrupulous characters. In the passion of nationalism the enemy within becomes the enemy without.

NOTES

1. James Joyce, *Ulysses* (Paris: Shakespeare and Company, 1922; New York: Random House, 1961), pp. 331–33. I am indebted to the thoughtful analysis of James J. Sheehan, "Zukünftige Vergangenheit: Das deutsche Geschichtsbild in den neunziger Jahren," in *Das historische Museum, Labor, Schaubühne, Identitätsfabrik*, ed. Gottfried Korff and Martin Roth (Frankfurt: Campus, 1990), pp. 277–86; and "National History and National Identity in the New Germany," *German Studies Review*, Special Issue: German Identity, vol. 15 (Winter 1992), 163–74.

2. Frank Budgen, *James Joyce and the Making of Ulysses* (Bloomington: Indiana University Press, 1960), p. 274.

3. Joyce, *Ulysses*, p. 727.

4. Isaiah Berlin, "The Bent Twig: A Note on Nationalism," *Foreign Affairs* 51 (1972): 11–30. This essay was reprinted as "Nationalism: Past Neglect and Present Power," in *Partisan Review* 45 (1979), and versions of it are reprinted in *The Crooked Timber of Humanity* (New York: Vintage Books, 1992), and in *Against the Current: Essays in the History of Ideas* (New York: Viking Books, 1980; Harmondsworth, Middlesex: Penguin Press, 1982). The quotation is from the Penguin edition, p. 337.

5. Michael Ignatieff, *Blood and Belonging: Journeys into the New Nationalism* (New York: Farrar, Straus & Giroux, 1993).

6. Ernest Gellner, *Nations and Nationalism* (Oxford: Basil Blackwell, 1983), pp. 36–38 passim.

7. See Liah Greenfield, *Nationalism: Five Roads to Modernity* (Cambridge: Harvard University Press, 1992), for a historical approach that compares paths to national identity in the West, i.e., England, France, Russia, Germany, and the United States.

8. Gellner, *Nations and Nationalism*, pp. 34–35.

9. Karl W. Deutsch, *Nationalism and Social Communication: An Inquiry into the Foundations of Nationality*, 2d ed. (Cambridge: MIT Press, 1966), pp. 209–22.

10. Ibid., pp. 19–20 passim. Otto Bauer, *Die Nationalitätenfrage und die Sozialdemokratie* (1907), in *Werkausgabe*, 9 vols. (Vienna: Europaverlag, 1975),

1:172, 192. Cf. Peter Loewenberg "Austro-Marxism and Revolution: Otto Bauer, Freud's 'Dora' Case, and the Crisis of the First Austrian Republic," in *Decoding the Past: The Psychohistorical Approach* (Berkeley: University of California Press, 1985; New Brunswick: Transaction Publishers, 1995), pp. 161–204.

11. Peter Loewenberg, "Theodor Herzl: Nationalism and Politics," in *Decoding the Past*, pp. 101–35; "Sigmund Freud as a Jew: A Study in Ambivalence and Courage," *Journal of the History of the Behavioral Sciences* 7:4 (October 1971): 363–69; Ernst Pawel, *The Nightmare of Reason: A Life of Franz Kafka* (New York: Schocken Books, 1984); Peter Loewenberg, "Einstein in His Youth," *Science* 239 (29 January 1988): 510–12; and Fritz Stern, "Einstein's Germany," in *Dreams and Delusions: The Drama of German History* (New York: Knopf, 1987), pp. 25–50.

12. Deutsch, *Nationalism and Social Communication*, p. 98.

13. Ibid., p. 97.

14. Eric Hobsbawm doubts "the strength and dominance of nationalism," holding that it "will decline with the decline of the nation-state"; "the phenomenon is past its peak." E. J. Hobsbawm, *Nations and Nationalism since 1780: Programme, Myth, Reality* (Cambridge: Cambridge University Press, 1990), pp. 182–83 and n. 22 passim. This analysis prompted the *New York Times* to comment that Hobsbawm's "survey, conducted with the traditional Marxist loathing for anything so backward-looking, merely reveals nationalism's faults rather than proves that its emotions have lost their pulling power," 28 July 1990, p. 15. Two decades ago Hobsbawm argued for nationalism as "a historic phenomenon, the product of the fairly recent past, and unlikely to persist indefinitely," in "Some Reflections on Nationalism," in *Imagination and Precision in the Social Sciences*, ed. T. J. Nossiter, A. H. Hanson, and Stein Rokkan (London: Faber & Faber, 1972), p. 406.

15. Deutsch, *Nationalism and Social Communication*, p. 37.

16. Ibid., p. 101.

17. Ibid., p. 106.

18. See George Monbiot, "Unifying by Terror," *Times Literary Supplement*, 8 May 1992, p. 11.

19. Benedict Anderson, *Imagined Communities: Reflections on the Origin and Spread of Nationalism* (London: Verso, 1991), pp. 120–21.

20. Benedict R. O'G. Anderson, *Language and Power: Exploring Political Cultures in Indonesia* (Ithaca: Cornell University Press, 1990), p. 124. The chapter "The Languages of Indonesian Politics," pp. 123–51, is a brilliant exposition of the integration of multiple traditions and functions in the new language.

21. "Indonesia Confronted," parts 1 and 2, in *Encounter* 25 (December 1965): 80–89, and 26 (January 1966): 75–83, as quoted in Anderson, *Language and Power*, p. 123.

22. Anderson, *Language and Power*, p. 141.

23. Sukarno, *An Autobiography*, as told to Cindy Adams (Indianapolis: Bobbs-Merrill, 1965), p. 28.

24. A term coined by Sukarno for the nationalist masses: the lower classes, the poor, peasants, workers and laborers, including the student activists of the Young Indonesia movement.

25. Sukarno, *Autobiography*, p. 73.

26. Anderson, *Imagined Communities*, pp. 204–5 passim.

27. Mahler et al. stress the variety of reactions to strangers, of which anxiety, is only one. They regard "stranger anxiety" as a "one-sided" and "incomplete"

(p. 56) description, preferring the term *stranger reactions*: "In addition to anxiety, the stranger evokes mild or even compellingly strong curiosity. That is why we have emphasized throughout this book that *curiosity* and *interest* in the new and the unfamiliar are as much a part of stranger reactions as are anxiety and wariness." Margaret S. Mahler, Fred Pine, and Anni Bergman, *The Psychological Birth of the Human Infant* (New York: Basic Books, 1975), p. 209.

28. John Bowlby, "The Nature of the Child's Tie to His Mother," *International Journal of Psychoanalysis* 39 (1958): 350–73.

29. Erik H. Erikson refers to the conflict between "basic trust versus basic mistrust" as "the nuclear conflict" and "the first task of the ego." *Childhood and Society*, 2d ed. (New York: Norton, 1963), pp. 247–51; quotation, p. 249.

30. Melanie Klein, *The Psycho-Analysis of Children* (London: Hogarth Press, 1932); *Contributions to Psycho-Analysis, 1921–1945* (London: Hogarth Press, 1948); and *Envy and Gratitude and Other Works, 1946–1963* (London: Hogarth Press, 1975). See Otto Kernberg, *Borderline Conditions and Pathological Narcissism* (New York: Jason Aronson, 1975), on splitting: "This mechanism is normally used only in an early stage of ego development during the first year of life," p. 25.

31. Daniel N. Stern, *The Interpersonal World of the Infant: A View from Psychoanalysis and Developmental Psychology* (New York: Basic Books, 1985), pp. 252–53.

32. Vamik D. Volkan, *The Need to Have Enemies and Allies: From Clinical Practice to International Relationships* (Northvale, N.J.: Jason Aronson, 1988), pp. 28–29. See the excellent work by Kurt R. and Kati Spillmann, *Feindbilder: Entstehung, Funktion und Möglichkeiten ihres Abbaus, Zürcher Beiträge zur Sicherheitspolitik und Konfliktforschung*, Nr. 12 (Zurich: ETH, 1989): Also, Group for the Advancement of Psychiatry, *Us and Them: The Psychology of Ethnocentrism* (New York: Brunner-Mazel, 1987).

33. Sigmund Freud, "Die Verneinung" (1925), in *Studienausgabe*, ed. Alexander Mitscherlich, Angela Richards, and James Strachey (Frankfurt am Main: S. Fischer Verlag, 1975), 3:374; "Negation," in *Standard Edition of the Complete Psychological Works of Sigmund Freud*, translated under the general editorship of James Strachey in collaboration with Anna Freud, assisted by Alix Strachey and Alan Tyson, 24 vols. (London: Hogarth Press, 1953–1974), 19:237 (hereafter cited as *S.E.*)

34. Anna Freud, *The Ego and the Mechanisms of Defence* (1936), trans. Cecil Baines (New York: International Universities Press, 1946), p. 128.

35. Lucien Febvre, "Histoire et Psychologie," in *Combats pour l'histoire* (Paris: Colin, 1959), p. 208; translated by K. Folca in *A New Kind of History and Other Essays*, ed. Peter Burke (New York: Harper & Row, 1973), p. 2.

36. Victor Adler, "Das Verhältnis zu den Bruderparteien in Österreich" (1911), in *Aufsätze, Reden und Briefe*, ed. Gustav Pollatschek, 11 vols. (Vienna: Verlag der Wiener Volksbuchhandlung, 1922–1929), 8:88 (hereafter cited as *Aufsätze*.

37. Adler, *Aufsätze*, 8:90.

38. "The Stuttgart Resolution," in James Joll, *The Second International, 1889–1914* (New York: Harper & Row, 1966), pp. 196–98.

39. Joll, *Second International*, p. 155.

40. "Aufruf," *Vorwärts* (Berlin), Extraausgabe, 25 July 1914, as reprinted in Carl Grünberg, *Die Internationale und der Weltkrieg* (Leipzig: Verlag C. L. Hirschfeld, 1916), p. 51.

41. F. Brupbacher to P. Monatte, 14 October 1914, Archives Monatte, 34, as quoted in Georges Haupt, *Socialism and the Great War: The Collapse of the Second International* (London: Oxford University Press, 1972), p. 229 n. 33.

42. Haupt, *Socialism and the Great War*, p. 230.

43. Ibid.

44. Konrad Haenisch, *Die deutsche Sozialdemokratie in und nach dem Weltkriege* (Berlin: C. A. Schwetschke & Sohn Verlagsbuchhandlung, 1916), p. 6.

45. Haenisch, *Die deutsche Sozialdemokratie*, pp. 114–15.

46. Carl E. Schorske, *German Social Democracy, 1905–1917: The Development of the Great Schism* (Cambridge: Harvard University Press, 1955), p. 288.

47. Émile Verhaeren, "Dédicace," *La Beligique Sanglante*, 14th ed. (Paris: Nouvelle Revue Française, 1915), pp. 9–10. The translation is mine.

48. Freud to Abraham, 26 July 1914, in Hilda C. Abraham and Ernst L. Freud, eds., *A Psycho-Analytic Dialogue: The Letters of Sigmund Freud and Karl Abraham* (New York: Basic Books, 1965), p. 186.

49. Freud to Abraham, 29 July 1914, ibid.

50. Freud to van Eeden, 28 December 1914, in Ernest Jones, *The Life and Work of Sigmund Freud*, vol. 2, *Years of Maturity, 1901–1919* (New York: Basic Books, 1955), pp. 368–69.

51. Freud, "Mourning and Melancholia" (1917), in *S.E.*, 14:250–51, 256.

52. Freud, "Thoughts for the Times on War and Death" (1915), in *S.E.*, 14:293 (hereafter cited as "War and Death"); "Zeitgemässes über Krieg und Tod" (1915), in *Studienausgabe*, ed. Alexander Mitscherlich, Angela Richards, and James Strachey (Frankfurt am Main: S. Fischer Verlag, 1974), 9:53 (hereafter cited as "Krieg und Tod").

53. Max Schur, *Freud: Living and Dying* (New York: International Universities Press, 1972), pp. 297–98; Peter Gay, *Freud: A Life for Our Time* (New York: Norton, 1988), p. 354.

54. Freud, *The Interpretation of Dreams*, in *S.E.*, 5:558–59.

55. Ibid., p. 560.

56. Freud, "Dreams and Telepathy" (1922), in *S.E.*, 18:197–98.

57. Freud to Ludwig Binswanger, 17 December 1915, Freud Collection, B4, Manuscript Division, Library of Congress, Washington, D.C. (hereafter referred to as Freud Collection).

58. Freud to Binswanger, 2 January 1919, Freud Collection, B4.

59. Freud to Binswanger, 16 February 1919, ibid. See Ludwig Binswanger, *Erinnerungen an Sigmund Freud* (Bern: A. Francke AG Verlag, 1956), pp. 74–75, 79–80.

60. Martin Freud, *Sigmund Freud: Man and Father* (New York: Jason Aronson, 1983), p. 166.

61. Freud to Binswanger, 25 December 1919, Freud Collection, B 4.

62. Freud to Binswanger, 14 March 1920, ibid.

63. Freud, "Krieg und Tod"; p. 53; "War and Death," p. 293.

64. Freud, "War and Death," p. 298; "Krieg und Tod," p. 58. Norman B. Atkins writes: "The universal theme of parental aggression toward the child, which is self evident in the unashamed authoritarian world and is consciously utilized by rulers and manipulators of power, is minimized and to a considerable extent denied by psychoanalytic thinkers and writers, with a few notable exceptions." In "The Oedipus Myth, Adolescence, and the Succession of Generations," *Journal of the American Psychoanalytic Association* 18 (1970): 863.

65. Heinz Kohut, "Narcissism as a Resistance and as a Driving Force in Psychoanalysis" (1970), in *The Search for the Self: Selected Writings of Heinz Kohut: 1950–1978*, ed. Paul H. Ornstein, 4 vols. (New York: International Universities Press, 1978), 2:554.

66. Kohut, "The Self in History" (1974), in Ornstein, *Search for the Self*, 2:773.

67. Peter Loewenberg, "The Psychohistorical Origins of the Nazi Youth Cohort," in *Decoding the Past: The Psychohistorical Approach* (Berkeley: University of California Press, 1985), pp. 240–83.

68. Kohut, "The Psychoanalytic Treatment of Narcissistic Personality Disorders" (1968), in Ornstein, *Search for the Self*, 1:479.

69. Urs Schwarz, *The Eye of the Hurricane: Switzerland in World War Two* (Boulder, Colo.: Westview Press, 1980), pp. 34–35.

70. Walter P. Metzger, "Generalizations about National Character: An Analytical Essay," in *Generalization in the Writing of History*, ed. Louis Gottschalk (Chicago: University of Chicago Press, 1963), pp. 96–97.

71. *Consociational* was defined by David E. Apter in 1961 as "a joining of constituent units which do not lose their identity when merging in some form of union." Apter, *The Political Kingdom in Uganda: A Study in Bureaucratic Nationalism* (Princeton: Princeton University Press, 1961), pp. 24–25. Another distinguished Africanist, M. G. Smith, defined *consociation* as an association of "separately constituted corporate collectivities as equal and internally autonomous partners in a common society." Smith, "Pluralism in Precolonial African Societies," and "Some Developments in the Analytic Framework of Pluralism," in *Pluralism in Africa*, ed. Leo Kuper and M. G. Smith (Berkeley: University of California Press, 1969), pp. 94, 439. For application to European democracies, I propose a more precise definition: a system in which the various interests in society, be they religious, ideological, linguistic, regional, cultural, or ethnic, are guaranteed proportionality in representation at every level of political decision making, including civil service appointments and the allocation of public funds. I am influenced by the leading scholar of consociational democracy, Arend Lijphart, *Democracy in Plural Societies: A Comparative Exploration* (New Haven: Yale University Press, 1977).

72. Renner, writing under a pseudonym because he was a Habsburg state employee, developed the personality principle at the turn of the century. Synopticus (pseudonym), *Zur österreichischen Nationalitätenfrage* (Vienna, 1899); *Staat und Nation* (Vienna, 1899); *Der Kampf der österreichischen Nationen um den Staat* (Vienna, 1902). See "Karl Renner and the Politics of Accommodation: Moderation Versus Revenge," chapter 7 in this volume.

73. For an anthropological perspective on the cultural differences and conflicts between these two peoples, see John W. Cole and Eric R. Wolf, *The Hidden Frontier: Ecology and Ethnicity in an Alpine Valley* (New York: Academic Press, 1974); and Eric R. Wolf, "Cultural Dissonance in the Italian Alps," *Comparative Studies in Society and History: An International Quarterly* (The Hague, Mouton) 5 (1962–1963): 1–14.

74. See bibliographic references in chapter 7, n. 18.

75. Declaration of the Federal Foreign Minister to the Austrian Nationalrat, Vienna, 5 June 1992.

76. Kurt and Kati Spillmann disagree with this interpretation and have presented their views in "The Jura Problem Is Not Resolved: Political and Psy-

chological Aspects of Switzerland's Ethnic Conflict," *Proceedings of the Conference on European Nationalism: Toward 1992* (Oxford: Pergamon Press, 1992).

77. Heinz K. Meier, "The Jura Conflict: A Test Case for the Swiss Federal System" (paper presented to the 102nd Annual American Historical Association Meeting, Washington, D.C., 27–30 December 1987).

78. Carol L. Schmid, *Conflict and Consensus in Switzerland* (Berkeley: University of California Press, 1981), pp. 125–36. The table of cantonal votes is on p. 133. Schmid is especially good on the educational policies in creating a civic culture of accommodation to differences.

79. Jonathan Steinberg, *Why Switzerland?* (Cambridge: Cambridge University Press, 1976), p. 72.

80. Cross-cutting: when the divisions, "fissures," or "cleavages" of a society, such as sectionalism, ethnic, cultural, class, linguistic, or religious, differences do not neatly overlap for most of the population, so that any two individuals may be members of some of the same, and of several different, subdivisions of the society.

81. I am indebted to my colleague Barisa Krekic for discussions of the Yugoslav nationalities problem.

12

CRISIS MANAGEMENT:
FROM THERAPY TO GOVERNMENT
AND FROM THE OVAL OFFICE
TO THE COUCH

A consequence of the sudden end of the Cold War, is that we realize, with a shock of recognition, what a masterful mutual exercise of crisis management it was. Both the U.S. and Soviet leadership deserve credit for sagacity motivated by fear and realism that substantially preserved world peace for half a century. From 1946 to 1989 the two superpowers succeeded in avoiding the meeting in combat of U.S. and Soviet armed forces, thus preventing the preconditions of a nuclear conflagration.

Mental health professionals have skills in crisis intervention and crisis management that are structurally related to large-group and international crisis-management processes. The clinical enterprise may also learn from the realm of international diplomacy. To compare, contrast, and syncre-tize various paradigms of crisis prevention, intervention, and management offers the possibility of mutual insight and enrichment to political psy-chology in both directions: political to psychodynamic, and clinical to sociocultural. My clinical work, particularly with couples but also in indi-vidual psychotherapy, has benefited from a knowledge of the dynamics of political and international conflict and conciliation. Conversely, working with intense conflictual emotions closely, at different levels of experience and consciousness and over a long period of time, offers insight to the complexity and multiple valences of fighting and peacemaking.

I will relate and compare strategies of crisis management from the international, large-group, interpersonal, and intrapsychic systems, seek-ing structural dimensions that are common to all four systemic levels. I approach this problem from the four systemic levels or perspectives of diplomatic history, social-group process, interpersonal relations, and intrapsychic psychodynamics. The eight structural principles I will explore at these levels are control, time, violence, focus, consistency, asymmetry, face saving, and delinkage.[1]

Control

A principal must maintain control over its agent. In international diplomacy the political authority must govern military moves. Notable cases where this did not happen are in the buildup to World War One when the German strategic plan (the Schlieffen Plan) brushed aside diplomatic considerations of the consequences of the invasion of Belgium. This was the *casus belli* of the British entry into the war. In the last days before the German offensive in 1914, the kaiser asked whether an invasion of Belgium was necessary. By then it was too late: the rail lines had been laid, the logistics were in place, the mobilization plans were set, the troops were on the move. The government had lost control of events to the military.

In 1916 the German military-naval decision for unrestricted submarine warfare obviated the political-economic consequences of drawing the United States into the war, which German diplomats and strategists had warned would be decisive against the Central Powers. But Grand Admiral von Tirpitz and the high command prevailed over the civil government, and German U-boats began sinking neutral, including American, merchant ships, giving President Woodrow Wilson a *casus belli* to enter the war in April 1917.

During the Korean War General Douglas MacArthur campaigned to bomb the Yalu River bridges and the People's Republic of China for tactical reasons, overlooking the strategic consequences of expanding the war in Asia. President Harry Truman affirmed civilian political supremacy by relieving MacArthur of command.

In groups, the organizational leadership must exercise control over the periphery to prevent preemptory action. The Austrian civil war of 1934 was ignited when the local Social Democratic leadership in Linz took the initiative against the central party executive and called a *Schutzbund* rising under dangerous conditions, which resulted in defeat for the movement.[2]

For organized labor, a major problem is wildcat strikes that are unplanned and unauthorized by the union. This means that local leadership has taken the initiative, weakening and contesting the control of the central bargaining agent.

In interpersonal business relationships, the client must maintain control over his or her attorney or other agents. Mastery of the situation may be lost in complex medical, legal, engineering, or business negotiations.

Time

In the inner intrapsychic world, the rational, reality-oriented portions of the person need to keep the impulsive, aggressive, and immediate pleasure-seeking forces in check with the calculation that the higher pleasures will be more rewarding and longer lasting. A classic example is education, which involves the sacrifice of immediate pleasure, aggression, and income in return for more permanent, "higher," and more sophisticated pleasures and conquests.

The pace of the moves in a transaction must be slowed down to provide time for consideration of options and consequences. An ultimatum or a deadline immediately create a crisis. Negotiations require time to work. Each side must weigh possibilities and have time to prepare counterproposals, and to consider responses. But deliberately to provide time can also weaken the coercive bargaining pressure one might wish to exert upon the opponent as, for example, by issuing an ultimatum that sets a time limit for compliance with given demands. Time pressure increases stress, impairs decision making, and encourages recklessness.

The Austro-Hungarian ultimatum to Serbia of 25 July 1914 carried a forty-eight-hour time limit for Serbia to yield, without qualification, on every point. Serbian refusal to acquiesce completely on one point provided the "trigger" to World War One.

U.S. labor relations law calls for built-in "cooling-off" periods, including a thirty-day delay between a strike vote and the work stoppage, to give mediation a chance. American family law provides for substantial waiting periods in the dissolution of marriage (varying from six weeks to one year) to offer the parties a chance to think about options and consequences. Impulses and archaic fears must be kept under the governance of rational reality testing, of ego defenses, and coping devices for constructive, adaptive solutions to be developed.

Violence

The dimension of *violence* instantly alters and aggravates the emotional field of conflict. Deliberate or inadvertent violence in a transaction must be avoided, and threats should be employed cautiously because violence quickly dissolves all restraints and acquires a dynamic of its own. When there has been violence, the terms of the conflict immediately and unalterably change.

A cardinal principle of both Soviet and U.S. policy in the half century of Cold War was scrupulously to avoid permitting Soviet and U.S. troops to meet in combat. Shooting was not permitted because of the realization of how quickly it could get out of hand. The model case of a calculated tactic of confrontation that avoided overt violence was the Berlin airlift of 1948–1949, which was a carefully calibrated solution to avoid the unacceptable choice between an armored breaking of the blockade and withdrawal.

The sinking of the Argentine battle cruiser *General Bellgrano* outside the exclusion zone established by the British government for the conduct of operations in the Falklands-Malvinas War of 1982 may well have been ordered in response to legitimate military concerns. But the scale of the violence and cost in lives lost in the sinking sabotaged the continuing crisis-management efforts of the Peruvian president Fernando Belaunde Terry.

As soon as violence occurs in a labor dispute and police or national guard units are called in, the entire picture of the conflict changes. The coercive power of the state is enlisted to effect the outcome.

When interpersonal violence takes place, the terms of the transaction are irrevocably altered. New legal ramifications such as charges of assault and battery, potential future danger to the victims, injunctions against the perpetrator, and loss of custody rights must be dealt with. The party who has resorted to violence will be in a moral and legal "one-down" or disadvantaged position.

Within the individual superego and ego are in conflict with id forces when impulses toward violence are felt. The primitive, childish, rash, excited drives to strike out are in conflict with the socialized part of the person that cautions: "Don't hit; that is fraught with unforeseeable consequences: it will get you nowhere; it will lead to retaliation; you will be in the wrong. Don't let yourself be provoked! Find another way to achieve your goal."

Focus

Objectives and demands must be limited and placed into focus as narrowly as possible on each party's most important and legitimate objectives. In the Berlin Crisis of 1948 the United States made it clear that its aim was only to supply Berlin, not to "roll back" the Iron Curtain. The 1962 Cuban Missile Crisis was limited to the demand that Soviet missiles be removed from Cuba; the U.S. purpose was not to overthrow the Castro regime.

The road to success in any negotiation is in limiting the issues in dispute. In labor-management bargaining, for instance, to specific items of wages, hours, and working conditions. When the issue becomes or is perceived to be the destruction of the company and/or the destruction of the labor union, crisis management is rendered impossible.

Parties in an interpersonal dispute who enter conjoint psychotherapy are encouraged to address specific behaviors in the other person rather than expressing universal generalities about the person's being moral or immoral, "good" or "bad" or "decent," to establish one's own honor or rightness or some other attribute.

The individual in a conflict must constantly monitor his or her level of inner rage, keeping in mind that the opponent is striving for a definite cherished goal and wishes to impose defeat to achieve that purpose, not to bring about personal destruction or loss of self-worth and self-respect. By realizing this, the rational self may keep paranoid, persecutory feelings and reactive aggressive impulses within bounds.

Consistency

Communications must be coordinated and *consistent*. Discordances or mixed "signals" that confuse the opponent, create "noise" in the communication, or lead him or her to suspect a surprise attack is imminent. Military, political, and diplomatic moves must be integrated to send a consistent message.

The 1973 Mideast Crisis was a demonstration of diplomatic initiatives undertaken by the United States that were carefully coordinated with a strategic alert to send to the Soviet Union a message cautioning against intervention. The grounding of all Soviet military air traffic after President Kennedy's assassination in 1963 constituted a substantial unmistakable signal of reassurance to the United States. The Soviets disclaimed responsibility for the assassination and reassured Washington that the Soviet Union would not exploit the decapitation crisis. Conversely the withdrawal of the Royal Navy's South Atlantic squadron prior to the Falklands-Malvinas crisis of 1982 was misread by the Argentine government as a signal of strategic withdrawal and disinterest in the South Atlantic and interpreted as a green light for a forward military policy.

During the Vietnam War three diplomatic initiatives in the winter of 1966–1967 were frustrated because bombing was escalated, in one case with twice the intensity of the earlier raids. Robert McNamara writes: "We failed miserably to integrate and coordinate our diplomatic and military actions as we searched for an end to the war."[3]

Divisions or ambivalences in organized groups will often be expressed by a disjuncture between theory and tactics. This was classically demonstrated in the socialist movement of the Second International, 1870–1914, which was uncompromisingly Marxist revolutionary in theory but increasingly meliorist and parliamentary in practice. As the crisis of 1914 approached, the respective national parties of Social Democracy gave ambivalent signals: Marxist class war and antimilitarist rhetoric coupled with reformist nationalism and participation in the war efforts of their respective countries.[4]

Mixed messages are common among friends, married couples, parents and children. Ambivalence is communicated by a discordance between words spoken, which may be controlled sweet reasonableness, and feelings of anger and hostility as betrayed by body language: posture, clenched fists, muscular tension, voice, and so on. The converse also occurs: stalwart and aggressive language content conveyed with tones of fear and appeasement.

The double message from parents to child has been defined by Adelaide Johnson as the "super-ego lacunae," setting up the conditions for juvenile delinquency by communicating to the child an underlying admiration for the ruthless lawbreaker.[5] The "double-bind" theory of schizophrenia is based on the pervasive sending of conflicting double messages in a family.[6] In legal negotiations, messages between attorneys must be coordinated with filing and litigation to be persuasive. Threats or tough talk unsynchronized with action discredit the negotiator.

Signals of conflict within the individual include the parapraxes: slips of the tongue, pen, hearing; errors in ordinary daily routines; accidents. These are all clues of intrapsychic discordance that may be listened to and responded to. They are indicators of pending trouble. The aim of being aware of these signals is to achieve concord between thought, actions, language, and feeling, leading to integrated, comfortable, and open intrapsychic communication. The alternative is encapsulated, walled-off areas of feeling of which the person is unaware but that therefore have great potential eruptive power.

Asymmetry

Singularity in the demands of each side must be recognized as an opening of *asymmetry* for negotiation and should be utilized in order to grant each party as much as possible close to its fundamental interests. The Cuban Missile Crisis of 1962 removed strategic missiles proximate to the United States in return for a U.S. guarantee not to invade Cuba and the removal of U.S. missiles from Turkey. Israel could return the Sinai Peninsula to Egypt, and settlements there could be abandoned in return for a peace treaty and recognition. Each side received what it wanted most.

The different "coinages" of bargaining make up the components of a labor or a business negotiation: wages in return for productivity; working conditions in return for fringe benefits. Trade-offs of what one party cares about least in exchange for what it cares about most, for example, money for land; future rights in turn for current cash; honor for material goods.

The relative pressures of social and personal responsibility, aggression and sexuality, and reality demands must be worked out in each case. The person must decide which pleasures, immediate and long-term, should be sacrificed for which other values, such as stability, security, respectability.

Face Saving

Proposals and bargaining moves that give the opponent a *face saving*, self-respecting, "honorable" course of action should be drafted. When the counterplayer is forced into a passive position and made to feel humiliated, lust for revenge is to be expected. Face-saving invokes the empathic function of the negotiator.

In 1914, the classic case of the failure of crisis management, the Russians felt they had been humiliated in the Balkan Crisis of 1908 and that they could not allow this to happen again. President Jimmy Carter's Camp David peace initiative was predicated on the Egyptian self-esteem derived from the 1973 Yom Kippur War.

Negotiations between conflicting groups must be discreet and non-public. In labor negotiations if the union membership or the stockholders can view the entire bargaining process openly, positions become intractable. Therefore, negotiations are best conducted in a neutral space, such as a hotel or a legal office, rather than at the work site or company offices.

A third party's surveillance of a dispute may make the principals intransigent because compromise is perceived as "backing down" and losing face. Conversely, an audience may be a social influence for reasonableness, leading to compliance because of the surveillance by a neutral party. Awareness of the narcissistic balance and sources of self-esteem in the counterplayer is necessary for successful work on settlement options. This sensibility comes from being conversant with depreciated parts of the self.

Delinkage

When mediating, try to *delink* elements of the dispute. Not every issue is a matter of life or death. On issues that they regard as the vital core, disputants will be obstinate; however, they will flex on issues that appear to be tangential. Begin not at the point of greatest conflict between the parties but at the periphery, where you can obtain agreement.

The Antarctica Treaty of 1959 (ratified in 1961) saw the nuclear powers successfully agree to a nuclear-weapons-free zone, aerial inspection, and unilateral on-site inspection. None of these would have been possible in the metropolitan homelands at the time. But it was possible because the Antarctic was considered by the United States and the Soviet Union to be at the end of the earth.

The sovereignty of Jerusalem will probably be the last issue settled between Israelis and Arabs. Whereas the Sinai could be returned to Egypt and settlements there could be abandoned in return for a peace treaty, the height of religious feeling of three faiths about Jerusalem means that the usual bargaining of trade-offs of essential interests for marginal ones will not work.

Talleyrand once said: "You can do anything with bayonets except sit on them." The fits and tantrums of the nursery years, the impulsive, primitive reactions and the loss of temper of adults, are indications of helplessness and weakness rather than strength. Violence, the use of uncontrolled force, will produce consequences, but they are seldom the intended ones. I am not saying an individual or a polity should never resort to force. But I do affirm, as a psychoanalyst and a historian, that the impulse to resort to force as a first response instead of the last is a sign of inner weakness and low self-esteem, and it will not be effective in conferring security.

NOTES

1. I am influenced in my understanding of international crisis management by the seminal work of Alexander L. George, *inter alia*: "Crisis Management: Lessons from Past U.S.-Soviet Crises" (paper presented to the AAAS, 24 May 1984); with Gordon A. Craig, *Force and Statecraft: Diplomatic Problems of Our Time* (New York: Oxford University Press, 1983); ed., *Managing U.S.-Soviet Rivalry:*

Problems of Crisis Prevention (Boulder, Colo.: Westview Press, 1983); ed., with Philip J. Farley and Alexander Dallin, *U.S.-Soviet Security Cooperation: Achievements, Failures, Lessons* (New York: Oxford University Press, 1988); ed., *Avoiding War: Problems of Crisis Management* (Boulder, Colo.: Westview Press, 1991); *Forceful Persuasion: Coercive Diplomacy as an Alternative to War* (Washington, D.C.: U.S. Institute of Peace Press, 1991); *Bridging the Gap: Theory and Practice in Foreign Policy* (Washington, D.C.: U.S. Institute of Peace Press, 1993).

2. Peter Loewenberg, *Decoding the Past: The Psychological Approach* (Berkeley: University of California Press, 1985; New Brunswick: Transaction Publishers, 1995), pp. 186–87.

3. Robert S. McNamara, *In Retrospect: The Tragedy and Lessons of Vietnam* (New York: Times Books/Random House, 1995), pp. 247–52. The quotation is on p. 252.

4. Georges Haupt, *Socialism and the Great War: The Collapse of the Second International* (CITY?: Oxford University Press, 1972); James Joll, *The Second International, 1889–1914* (New York: Harper & Row, 1966); Carl E. Schorske, *German Social Democracy, 1905–1917: The Development of the Great Schism* (Cambridge: Harvard University Press, 1955).

5. Adelaide M. Johnson, "Sanctions for Superego Lacunae of Adolescents," in *Searchlights on Delinquency*, ed. Kurt R. Eissler (New York: International Universities Press, 1949, 1963), pp. 225–45.

6. G. Bateson, D. D. Jackson, J. Haley, and J. H. Weakland, "Toward a Theory of Schizophrenia," *Behavioral Science* 1 (1956): 251–64; and by the same authors, "A Note on the Double Bind—1962," *Family Process* 2 (1963): 154–61.

INDEX